SEVEN YEARS IN THE LIVES OF BRITISH FAMILIES

Evidence on the dynamics of social change from the British Household Panel Survey

Edited by Richard Berthoud and Jonathan Gershuny

D0714635

The POLICY PRESS

iiSER

INSTITUTE FOR SOCIAL & ECONOMIC RESEARCH

First published in Great Britain in November 2000 by

The Policy Press
34 Tyndall's Park Road
Bristol BS8 1PY
UK

Tel +44 (0)117 954 6800
Fax +44 (0)117 973 7308
e-mail tpp@bristol.ac.uk
www.policypress.org.uk

British Library Cataloguing in Publication Data

A catalogue record for this book is available from the British Library

ISBN 1 86134 200 4 paperback

A hardcover version of this book is available.

Richard Berthoud is Research Professor and **Jonathan Gershuny** is Director of the Institute for Social and Economic Research, University of Essex.

Cover design by Qube Design Associates, Bristol.

Photograph on front cover supplied by kind permission of Mark Simmons Photography, Bristol.

Printed and bound in Great Britain by Hobbs the Printers Ltd, Southampton.

Contents

List of tables and figures   iv

Acknowledgements   ix

The Institute for Social and Economic Research   x

List of acronyms   xii

one   Introduction: the dynamics of social change   1
Richard Berthoud

two   Patterns of household and family formation   21
John Ermisch and Marco Francesconi

three   Couples, work and money   45
Heather Laurie and Jonathan Gershuny

four   Work, non-work, jobs and job mobility   73
Mark Taylor

five   Dynamics of household incomes   107
Stephen P. Jenkins

six   Housing, location and residential mobility   133
Nick Buck

seven   A measure of changing health   161
Richard Berthoud

eight   Political values: a family matter?   193
Malcolm Brynin

nine   Seven years in the lives of British families   215
Richard Berthoud and Jonathan Gershuny

Index   239

List of tables and figures

Tables

1.1 Family structure of women aged 25 to 29 (1973 and 1996) 6

1.2 Household structure of adults aged 20 to 29 (1973 and 1996) 6

1.3 Employment rate of women, by family structure (1973 and 1996) 7

1.4 Employment position of family units, by type of family (1973 and 1996) 9

1.5 Growth in the number of social security claims by non-working families (1976 to 1996) 11

1.6 Car ownership, by family's employment position (1973 and 1996) 12

1.7 Housing tenure, by family's employment position (1973 and 1996) 13

2.1 Destinations 'next' year of young people who lived with their parents 'this' year 22

2.2 Simulated pattern of first destinations of young people up to the age of 30 23

2.3 Proportions of men and women who ever had a partnership by a certain age, analysed by birth cohort and partnership type 25

2.4 Survival of first cohabiting unions 29

2.5 Interval between first and second cohabiting unions 29

2.6 Determinants of the outcome of cohabiting unions 37

3.1 Wife's proportion of domestic work time, by couple's joint employment status 47

3.2 Two indices of the division of domestic labour 51

3.3 Correlations between three BHPS estimates of the division of labour (1997) 51

3.4 Correlation of estimates of the division of labour over successive years 52

3.5 Reported female shares of domestic labour, by wife's change in employment: continuing couples (1991 and 1997) 53

3.6 Calculated female shares of domestic labour, by wife's change in employment: continuing couples (1991 and 1997) 54

3.7 Couples' employment change and change in females' calculated share of domestic labour 56

3.8   Couples' money management: cross-sectional distributions   59
(1987 to 1995)

3.9   Who has the final say on big financial decisions (1991 to 1995)   59

3.10   Money management transitions (1991 to 1995)   60

3.11   Transitions in who has the final say on financial decisions   61
(1991 to 1995)

3.12   Money management and control, by women's education and   62
employment characteristics (1991)

3.13   Proportion of men and women taking a 'progressive' attitude   64
towards women's employment and family life, by education and
occupation: couples where woman was of working age (16 to 64)

3.14   Women's hours of work and financial involvement, by couples'   65
attitudes to women's employment and family life

3.15   Regression of shared money management and equal say in   66
financial decisions, by men's and women's employment changes:
continuing couples (1991 to 1995)

3.16   Regression results for egalitarian money management and control   68
(1995): continuing couples where the woman was aged 16 to 64

4.1   Labour market transition probabilities, by gender   88

4.2   Probability of working part-time or being self-employed, by age and   89
number of children (1991 to 1996)

4.3   Work status transition probabilities for single-adult families   95

4.4   Work status transition probabilities for couples   95

4.5   Labour market transition probabilities: men and women aged 55   98
to 60 at wave 1

5.1   Proportion of individuals in households below half average income   113
in 1979 and 1996/97, by family type

5.2   Trends in mean income, inequality and low income (1991 to 1996)   114

5.3   Outflow rates from this year's income group origins to next year's   114
income group destinations

5.4   Prevalence of low income   116

5.5   Income mobility as reduction in inequality when the income   117
accounting period is extended

5.6   Proportion remaining poor, and exit rates from poverty, by duration,   118
for all persons beginning a poverty spell

5.7   Proportion remaining non-poor, and poverty re-entry rates, by   120
duration, for all persons ending a poverty spell

5.8   Annual transition rates into and out of poverty, for individuals   122
      who remained in the same family type

5.9   Annual transition rates into and out of poverty, by family type   124

5.10 Movements out of and into low income, broken down by type   127
      of event

6.1   Housing tenure, by life stage (1973)   137

6.2   Housing tenure, by life stage (1991)   139

6.3   Housing tenure, by income decile group (1991)   140

6.4   Housing tenure at wave 2, by tenure at wave 1   141

6.5   Tenure change, by mobility status   142

6.6   Area deprivation, by housing tenure (1991)   145

6.7   Preferences for mobility and reasons for wanting to move, by   146
      housing tenure

6.8   Single-year mover status, by life stage at earlier wave   148

6.9   Distance moved, by reason for move   149

6.10 Distance moved, by household composition change   150

6.11 Chances of moving within a six-year period, taking into account   151
      initial life-stage

6.12 Housing tenure at wave 7, by tenure at wave 1   154

6.13 Wave 7 tenure for wave 1 owner-occupiers, by experience of   155
      social and economic 'shocks'

6.14 Whether moved to less deprived areas by wave 1 tenure: wave 1   156
      residents of most deprived 20% of areas

6.15 Tenure change for young people leaving the parental home   157

6.16 Household incomes of first-time purchasers compared with other   158
      young households

7.1   Answers to three BHPS health questions, by age group (wave 4)   166

7.2   Multiple regression equation between specific health problems and   167
      the other health questions (wave 4)

7.3   Cross-comparison between the three health questions (wave 4)   168

7.4   Year-on-year changes in the incidence of health problems   176

7.5   Changes in the three components of the index between t and $t+1$ 177

7.6   Correlations between changes in each of the health questions, t 177
      to $t+1$

7.7   Changes between $t+1$ and $t+2$, analysed by changes between t 178
      and $t+1$

7.8   Distribution of changes in full ill-health index, over one year and   179
       over two years

7.9   Movements in and out of 'illness' between wave I and later waves   181

7.10   Logistic regression equations predicting *falling* ill (longitudinal) and   184
       being ill (cross-sectional): 'medical' factors

7.11   Logistic regression equations predicting *falling* ill (longitudinal) and   188
       being ill (cross-sectional): 'socio-economic' factors

8.1   Logistic regression of the odds of voting Conservative and of   202
       switching from the Conservatives

8.2   Change in couples' party ID   205

8.3   An aggregate index of the impact of one partner's party preference   206
       on the preference of the other partner

8.4   Conservative partners over time   207

8.5   Conservative defection by men between 1992 and 1997 elections   209

8.6   Logistic regression of 1992 Conservative vote, analysed by own   210
       and partner's party ID in 1991

8.7   Children's votes, by parental votes (1992)   211

8.8   Children's votes, by parental votes (1997)   212

9.1   Definition of life-stages   231

9.2   Life-stages (1973 and 1996)   232

9.3   Rises and falls in income, by life-stages   235

Figures

1.1   Four aspects of family formation for women aged 18 to 40 (1973   4
       and 1996)

1.2   Percentage of men with a job, by age (1973 and 1996)   8

2.1   Actual proportion of women who ever married: two groups   31
       of cohorts

2.2   Simulated proportion of women who ever married: two groups   31
       of cohorts if their cohabitation and marriage rates were reversed

4.1   First labour market status, by year first left full-time education   77

4.2   Estimated probability of labour market status on first leaving   78
       full-time education, by age on leaving

4.3   Risk of leaving first job through quit, layoff and other exit, by   81
       labour market entry cohort: men

4.4   Risk of leaving first job through quit, layoff and other exit, by   82
      labour market entry cohort: women

4.5   Risk of leaving fifth job through quit, layoff and other exit, by   83
      labour market entry cohort: men

4.6   Risk of leaving fifth job through quit, layoff and other exit, by   83
      labour market entry cohort: women

4.7   Promotion rates by age   84

4.8   Career status in year following a promotion   85

4.9   Probability of promotion, by overtime hours   86

4.10 Probability of being unemployed, by highest qualification and labour   92
      market status one year ago: men

4.11 Distribution of work across families   94

4.12 Probability of entering retirement, by age   97

5.1   Average (median) income for the poorest tenth through to the   110
      richest tenth of the population for 1996/97

5.2   Classification of 'income events' and 'demographic events' associated   126
      with a low-income transition between 'last' year and 'this' year

7.1   Distribution of scores on the full index of ill-health (wave 4)   169

7.2   Average score on the full index of ill-health, by age and sex (wave 4)   170

7.3   Average number of visits to the GP and average number of other   171
      health and welfare services used in the past year, by score on full
      index of ill-health (wave 4)

7.4   Proportion of men who were unable to work because of long-   172
      term sickness, and of individuals who received care from a
      household member, by score on full index of ill-health (wave 4)

7.5   Estimated risk of death in the next year, by age and score on the   173
      index of ill-health (waves 1 to 6)

7.6   'Medical' precursors of falling ill and recovering   182

7.7   'Socio-economic' precursors of falling ill and recovering   186

8.1   Identification with the Conservatives and competing choices   200

Acknowledgements

This book is largely based on findings from the British Household Panel Survey (BHPS), the first large-scale enquiry in this country to follow the members of a sample of adults over a long sequence of years.

Perhaps the authors' largest single debt is to David Rose of the Institute for Social and Economic Research (ISER). He, more than anyone, pushed for the establishment of a household panel survey at the University of Essex. He was there during the early years of the project, insisting that nothing but the best would do. Without his contribution, none of this book could have been written.

The UK Economic and Social Research Council (ESRC) has supported this work since 1989, in two ways: by paying for the design, fieldwork and data preparation of the survey since its inception; and by supporting substantive research based on analysis of the BHPS data through core funding of the Research Centre on Micro-social Change. Most of the analysis and interpretation reported here was located within the ESRC core programme. The book itself contributes to the current phase of ESRC-funded work on the longitudinal analysis of social policy.

As the authors of each chapter acknowledge, much of the material summarised here draws on the analysis and scholarship of other ISER colleagues, past and present. The book has been a team effort based on the work of every member of ISER's research group, listed overleaf.

We also want to thank the other current and recent members of the Institute's survey staff who manage the huge annual BHPS operation, the computing staff who handle the data and support the analysis, the library staff who provide a two-way link between the BHPS and the rest of the academic world, and the administrators and secretaries who keep the organisation running.

Thanks, too, to Nick Moon and his colleagues at NOP Social and Political, and to their dedicated team of interviewers, who visit members of the panel sample each year and achieve such astonishingly high year-on-year response rates.

And thanks, of course, to the 10,000 men and women who patiently tell us about the latest steps in their lives. This book is based on the first seven years of their participation: by the time it reaches readers, they will be recording their tenth annual interviews.

The Institute for Social and Economic Research

Jonathan Gershuny is the Director of ISER and the other contributors to this book are members of the research team at the Institute for Social and Economic Research.

The Institute was set up at the University of Essex in 1989 to identify, explain, model and forecast social change in Britain at the individual and household level. It was one of the first of the ESRC's interdisciplinary research centres.

A central element of ISER's work has been the design, implementation and dissemination of the British Household Panel Survey. The BHPS involves repeated annual interviews with about 10,000 individuals drawn from a nationally representative sample of more than 5,500 households. The data is made available to the British and international research community through the ESRC Data Archive, also based at the University of Essex.

Since 1999, the UK National Longitudinal Resource Centre, established within the Institute, has been assigned overall responsibility for developing all ESRC longitudinal data, including the major birth cohort studies and possible new enquiries, as well as the continuing BHPS.

Meanwhile, the Institute continues its programme of research and publications through the Research Centre on Micro-social Change. Concentrating again on longitudinal data, the research includes projects on: labour market behaviour; income and wealth; residential mobility; household dynamics; time-budgeting; and aspects of panel methodology.

The Institute has strong links with research colleagues in Europe, North America and Australasia. The European Centre for the Analysis in the Social Sciences encourages study visits by researchers who wish to make use of our facilities and expertise. The European Panel Analysis Group, coordinated by ISER, is a consortium of experts in longitudinal analysis working in six countries.

Current members of staff, and past colleagues who have worked for the Institute for at least two years, are listed overleaf.

Administration

Gilly Burrell
Eileen Clucas
Helen FitzGerald
Penny Martin
Elizabeth Mirams
Lindsay Moses
Marcia Taylor
Jenifer Tucker
Kate Tucker
Tracey Varnava
Barry Villars
Janice Webb
Jane Worton

Information Technology

Randy Banks
Adrian Birch
Tom Butler
John Lane
Elaine Prentice-Lane
Paul Siddall
Frances Williams

Research Resources Unit

Hilary Doughty
Judith Egerton
Mary Gentile
Cathy Groslin
Barbara Harris
Lesley Lingard
Jane Rooney
Terry Tostevin

Survey

Catherine Askew
Anitra Baxter
Jill Brunning
Jonathan Burton
John Brice
Karen Clissold
Pam Campanelli
Ann Farncombe
Sandra Jones
Heather Laurie
Iain Noble
Holly O'Toole
Sara Panizza
Donna Pringle
Lynne Scott
Charanjit Singh
Alison Smith
Jillian Smith
Rachel Smith
Sarah Wicks

Research

Elena Bardasi
Richard Berthoud
Martin Biewen
René Böheim
Alison Booth
Malcolm Brynin
Nick Buck
Ken Burdett
Tim Butcher
Andrew Clark
Opeoluwa Coker
Louise Corti
Anthony Coxon
Francesco Devicienti

Shirley Dex
Muriel Egerton
John Ermisch
Kimberly Fisher
Marco Francesconi
Jonathan Gershuny
Brendan Halpin
Carmel Hannan
Andrew Hildreth
Maria Iacovou
Sarah Jarvis
Stephen Jenkins
Andrew McCulloch
Karen O'Reilly

Ray Pahl
David Pevalin
John Rigg
Karen Robson
David Rose
Jonathan Scales
Jacqueline Scott
Anthony Shorrocks
Laura Smethurst
Liz Spencer
Alan Taylor
Mark Taylor
John Treble
Vijay Verma

List of acronyms

BHPS — British Household Panel Survey

DSS — Department of Social Security

ECHP — European Community Household Panel

ESRC — Economic and Social Research Council

EU — European Union

GHS — General Household Survey

ISER — Institute for Social and Economic Research

LA — local authority

NCDS — National Child Development Study

ONS — Office for National Statistics

PSID — Panel Survey of Income Dynamics

SCELI — Social Change and Economic Life Initiative

ONE

Introduction: the dynamics of social change

Richard Berthoud

The album tells us stories. Perhaps the studious child, curled up with a book in the corner of the frame of an old black and white photo at the start of the album, reappears in a graduation photo towards the end. Perhaps the mother-to-be is found again, as we turn the pages, with two toddlers and a less convincing smile. The walk-up flat in the background becomes a three-bedroom semi, and later acquires a roof-light and a downstairs extension, or the semi is exchanged for a studio apartment with a care assistant down the hall. Some faces recur throughout the book, older but still recognisable; we see others for a few pages, and then no more.

Each snap tells us something, but we learn more from the sequence of photographs, and more still from the connections we make between the people shown in them.... The whole album provides a picture that is more than the sum of the individual pictures, more than we would get from, say, a random collection of photos from different families in successive decades of the century. The family album tells about the complex pattern of continuity and change that make up the lives of individuals and households. (Buck and others, 1994, p 10)

'The family' is a subject of enormous academic, political and popular interest. It is a central feature of most people's lives, the framework within which other relationships, activities and events take place. Families have changed hugely during the past generation: not only in the formal demographics of marriage, cohabitation and childbearing, but also in the social and economic relationships between men and women, and between adults and children. Journalists and politicians have been eager to comment on these changes, and to propose policies that would speed them up or slow them down.

The family is a fertile subject of enquiry among demographers, sociologists, economists and analysts of public policy. However, much of the research has been hindered by the use of surveys and censuses that measure an individual or a family's position only at the time that they were interviewed. Information about what happens to people over a period of years has been much more limited. We could gain a fuller understanding of the processes involved if we were able to follow the important *events* in people's lives: leaving home, getting a job, starting a family, winning promotion, becoming ill, giving up work, falling into poverty, experiencing deprivation. Being able to follow the rises and falls of people's fortunes in this way – the opportunities they see, the decisions they take, the risks they face – would give a much greater understanding of the processes driving change, and of the complex inter-relationships that exist between employment, family structure, income and living standards.

The British Household Panel Survey (BHPS) has been set up to achieve this. A sample of more than 5,000 households was identified in 1991. Each of the adults interviewed then has been followed up every year since. The annual surveys are linked together to provide a continuous sequence of the events in the lives of each individual, and of the households of which they are members. We now have data running from 1991 to 1997. The survey has been analysed by teams of specialists to build up our understanding of the dynamics of the family in such fields as household formation, employment, income and so on. Most of this work has been based on sophisticated analytical techniques, and published as articles in scholarly journals. However, the material has now grown to the point at which the various lines of enquiry can be combined to provide a synoptic picture of 'seven years in the lives of British families'.

The 'changing family'

In the concluding chapter of this book we distinguish between two very different concepts of 'change': the events experienced by individuals, and the trends observed throughout society as a whole. Most of the research summarised in this book is concerned with transitions reported by individuals and families from one year to the next during the 1990s – events in their own lives that altered their situation, such as getting married or losing a job. There are many transitions of this sort overall every year, but this might lead to little change from year to year in the sense that patterns of marriage or employment were no different at the end of a period than they had been at the beginning. If as many children are born every year as old people die, the population will not change over time.

However, there have also been huge changes over the years in patterns of partnership, parenting and employment. The nature of the family has been transformed in the course of a generation. These long-term trends have not been the subject of much direct analysis in this book (the next chapter, on family formation, is an exception). However, an understanding of the remarkable changes that have occurred in family life during the past 25 years or so is an essential background to the detailed analysis of the current pattern. It is worth focusing on these longer-term changes before moving on to describe the BHPS itself.

A generation ago the burgeoning development of empirical social research was symbolised by the launch in the early 1970s of the General Household Survey (GHS). Since it covered a new sample every year, it could not provide evidence about transitions in the same way as a panel survey. However, the repeat surveys have tracked the trends in British socio-economic life almost every year since then, and provide a convenient set of benchmark measures on which to compare the late 1990s with the early 1970s, roughly representing one generation difference (ONS, 1998). Much of the following review is based on a direct comparison between the GHS of 1973 and the latest edition, 1996[1].

Changing families

Some of the key changes are shown in Figure 1.1, which plots the current family position of women between the ages of 18 and 40 at the two GHS dates.

Official statistics (ONS, 1999) show that about 347,000 women married for the first time in 1971, but only 188,000 did in 1997 – little more than one half the number of weddings celebrated just 26 years earlier[2]. The signs are that the overwhelming majority of people still get married eventually, but tend to do so later. The average age on first marriage was 22.6 in 1971 and 27.5 in 1997. The 1973 GHS showed that 63% of women in their early 20s were already married; by 1997, the proportion had fallen to just 17%.

Figure 1.1: Four aspects of family formation for women aged 18 to 40 (1973 and 1996)

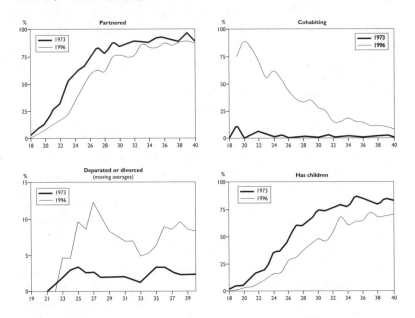

The postponement of marriage means that more men and women remain unattached. However, an increasing proportion of them has formed partnerships without marrying. In 1973, cohabiting was so rare (and considered so embarrassing) that the GHS did not ask a question about it; a rough-and-ready estimate based on household composition suggests that about 1% of all partnerships may have been non-marital, peaking at perhaps 2% of cases where the woman was in her early 20s[3]. By 1996, cohabiting was clearly identified in the survey and represented 11% of partnerships, the majority (62%) of those being where the woman was aged 20-24. As John Ermisch and Marco Francesconi show in Chapter Two, most of these live-in informal relationships are not lifelong. Within five years, most of the couples either marry each other, or split up.

Married couples split up too, and the rate at which they do so has climbed. In 1971, the divorce rate was 5.9 per thousand marriages; it has been around 13 per thousand throughout the 1990s (ONS, 1999). In the 1996 GHS, 13% of women in their mid-20s who had ever been married were already living apart from their former husbands, and that does not include those who had since married again; the equivalent figure for 1973 was only 2%.

These major changes in the pattern of partnership have had important knock-on effects on childbirth and parenting. The total number of babies being born has remained rather stable during the 1980s and 1990s, although it had fluctuated up and down during the 1970s. Women have been having children later – the average age at first birth increased by about two years between the mid-1970s and mid-1990s. However, the proportion of all births outside marriage rose from just 8% in 1971 to 37% in 1997 (ONS, 1999). More than half of these extra-marital births are registered by both parents, giving the same address, who are probably in stable cohabiting relationships. As will be seen in Chapter Two, many of the parents marry after their child is born. However, many others separate while the child is still young, and go on to form a one-parent family. The growth in the number of children being brought up by one parent is well known (Haskey, 1998). The GHS records 5% in 1973 and 12% in 1996.

These trends in partnering and fertility have had a huge effect on the structure of families. A generation or two ago, there was a standard trajectory whereby young people completed their education, got married and had children – and stayed that way until their own children left home. This was never an obligatory or universal path, but it was recognisably the standard thing to do. The massive increase in the diversity of family formation is encapsulated in Table 1.1, which homes in on women in their late 20s. In 1973, two thirds of all young women between 25 and 29 were already married with children. Almost all the remainder were in the stages that would be expected to precede that condition: they were single, or married without children. By 1996, the number of women in that 'standard' family situation had more than halved: less than one third were married with children. There were big increases in almost all the other options. Many more remained unattached. Many now had a partner and/or a child without having married.

Another remarkable change has been in the number of people who do not live with any member of their nuclear family: neither their parents, nor their spouse, nor their children. This trend is important at both ends of the adult life-course. The rapid increase in the number of elderly widows (combined with the long-run reduction in the proportion of elderly people who live with their adult children) signifies an increase in the number of old people living entirely alone. The more striking change of behaviour, though, has been among younger adults. The proportion

Table 1.1: Family structure of women aged 25 to 29 (1973 and 1996), in column percentages

		1973	1996
Single	without children	11	22
	with children	1	8
Cohabiting	without children	1	10
	with children	*	7
Married	without children	16	15
	with children	68	31
Ex-married	without children	1	1
	with children	3	6

Source: GHS, author's analysis. * = less than 1%

Table 1.2: Household structure of adults aged 20 to 29 (1973 and 1996), in column percentages

	1973	1996
Lives with parents	30	30
Lives entirely alone	3	9
Lone parent with children but no other adults	1	6
Lives with non-relatives	4	9
Cohabits with partner	1	19
Lives with husband or wife	62	27

Source: GHS, author's analysis. A small number of people who lived with other relatives have been included in the 'Lives with parents' category

still living with their parents has remained stable, but there is an increasing tendency for young people to leave home and then return again. The reduction in the rate of marriage, or the delay in getting married, has resulted in the rise of a range of intermediate household arrangements. Table 1.2 shows that the proportion of men and women in their 20s who lived with neither their parents nor a (married) spouse rose from a mere 9% in 1973 to 43% in 1996. In that context, living with a partner outside marriage can be seen as a state of semi-independence, not very distant from the full independence available to those living alone or with friends.

This increasing diversity of family form for men and women in their 20s and 30s suggests a much wider range of options than were available and socially acceptable in the past. For many, this will have involved a greater degree of flexibility and perhaps choice, although not everyone would necessarily have chosen the positions they found themselves in.

Table 1.3: Employment rate of women, by family structure (1973 and 1996), in cell percentages

	With partner		Without partner	
	1973	1996	1973	1996
Child aged less than 5	16	39	27	20
Child aged 5 to 10	46	52	46	34
Child aged 11 plus	53	60	55	43
No dependent child	56	63	78	64

Source: GHS, author's analysis. Table confined to women aged 18-59 who were not students. 'Employment rate' counts work of less than 24 hours per week as half a job

Have these changes in the formal bonds between men and women in families been associated with adjustments to the nature of relationships? There is a mountain of literature, both directly feminist and more broadly sociological, arguing about the existence or otherwise of new men and new women. Heather Laurie and Jonathan Gershuny in Chapter Three use data for the 1990s to discuss some of the patterns of activity and responsibility among married and cohabiting couples, and this shows that we are still a long way from the ideal of perfectly balanced partnerships. On the other hand, many of today's relationships are also far-removed from the old stereotype in which men took the decisions and women took the orders. Unfortunately, very little hard evidence is available (in the form of identical questions asked over a period of time) to show the extent of change.

Changing employment

However, there is good empirical evidence about trends in the options available in the labour market. Mark Taylor's review of BHPS findings about employment transitions in the 1990s (in Chapter Four) shows that inequalities remain between men and women, although the gap has narrowed. But, as Table 1.3 demonstrates, the common view that women (as a group) are much more likely to work than they used to is far too simple a summary of the position. It is true that women with partners have higher employment rates than they used to, and this is especially true of women with school-age children. Counting part-time jobs as 'half' a job, the proportion of women with a partner and young child who also had a paid job more than doubled, from 16% to 39%, between

Figure 1.2: Percentage of men with a job, by age (1973 and 1996)

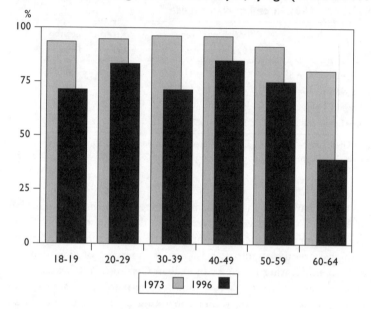

1973 and 1996. Much smaller increases were logged by women with partners who either had no children, or whose children were of school age. On the other hand, there was a substantial reduction in the rate of employment among women who had no partner, and especially women heading one-parent families. Some trends, such as the increase in the number of unattached women, and the rising rate of employment among married mothers, have tended to increase the economic status of women relative to that of men. But others, such as the growth of lone parenthood and the reducing employment rate for lone mothers, have operated in the opposite direction.

The number of men in work has also been falling (see Figure 1.2). In 1973, 95% of (non-student) males had a job, right through from 18 to 59; among 60-64 year olds, the proportion was still 80%. By 1996, the number in work had fallen across all age ranges. The drop was especially marked among younger men (where unemployment is largely to blame) and among older men (where the trend is based on a more complex mix of unemployment, disability and voluntary retirement). This means that the increase in the number of women who are combining work with marriage and motherhood has occurred during a period when the overall level of employment has been falling.

Table 1.4: Employment position of family units, by type of family (1973 and 1996), in column percentages

		Lone parents	Single adults	Couples with children	Couples without children
1973	No job	46	20	5	4
	One job	54	80	52	35
	Two jobs	na	na	43	61
1996	No job	57	32	9	9
	One job	43	68	31	23
	Two jobs	na	na	60	68

Source: GHS, author's analysis. Table confined to families whose 'head' was aged 18-59 and was not a student. Part-time jobs have been counted on the same basis as full-time. na = not applicable

Most of the trend in male labour market activity has affected men at the beginning and end of their potential careers, rather than those in their 20s, 30s and 40s who would be in the 'family' period of their life-cycle. Men with partners are more likely to be in work than those without, and have experienced less of a reduction in employment during the 24-year period. Much has been made of the polarisation of employment during the 1980s (Gregg and Wadsworth, 1996). According to this hypothesis, roughly the same number of jobs has been more unequally divided between families. An increasing number have become work rich, with two jobs; while other families have become work poor, with no job at all.

Table 1.4 illustrates the pattern of change (using the 1973 and 1996 General Household Surveys). As expected from the analysis of women's employment in Table 1.3, there has been a small increase in the number of dual-earner couples without children, but a much more substantial increase in two-job families with children. Double work is now the majority option for both categories of couple (although many of the second jobs held by parents are part-time). Meanwhile, the proportion of couples with no job at all has doubled over the period, to reach 9%. However, the polarisation is much more striking when couples are compared with men and women without partners. The earlier analysis of family structures showed an increase in the number of single-people and one-parent families. Both groups of non-partnered individuals had lower employment rates than couples in 1973, and both groups were substantially worse off in that respect by 1996. Only two thirds of unattached adults and less than half of lone parents had any employment in the 1990s.

A point of detail, not shown in Table 1.4, is that the number of formally married couples with children who had no job at all hardly changed between 1973 and 1996. The increase in the number of non-earning couples with children was entirely accounted for by cohabiting couples with children, among whom one in five had no job at the end of the period. Much more detailed analysis is needed to explain this potentially important difference, but this is one of a number of signs that cohabiting couples should not always be seen simply as married couples without an official license.

These changes in family employment have major implications for economic relationships within families, and between families and other institutions. Changing norms have been associated with some of the most striking social and economic transitions of the past generation. Men used to be expected to work between the ages of, say, 20 and 65; women (at least, married women and mothers) were expected not to. This implied a very heavy level of dependence by women on family support. These assumptions have changed radically. It is increasingly acceptable for men to retire at the age of 60 or, on health grounds, even earlier. Meanwhile, married women and mothers increasingly expect, and are expected, to take paid employment. This change in the social division of employment has led to a polarisation of jobs and incomes and a transformation of lines of dependence. Reduced dependence of women on men coincides with increased dependence of whole families on the state.

Changing incomes

Not surprisingly, the trend has been of interest to governments, anxious on the one hand to reduce the number of people in poverty, and on the other to control the increase in public spending. For many years, concern about the 'burden' of the welfare state focused on the natural increase in the number of elderly people as life expectancy has extended. However, as Table 1.5 shows, the number of claims by non-pensioners has increased more during the past two decades – not only as a proportionate increase, but also in absolute terms. There are nearly two million more disabled people out of work and claiming benefit, a million more unemployed and nearly a million more one-parent families: these trends are at least as important for the analysis of dependence and poverty as they are for the level of public expenditure. Perhaps the most disturbing single statistic is

Table 1.5: Growth in the number of social security claims by non-working families (1976 to 1996), in millions

	1976	1996	Increase Number	%
Pensioners	8.1	10.3	2.2	27
Unemployed	1.1	2.2	1.1	100
Disabled	0.6	2.5	1.9	317
Lone parents	0.3	1.1	0.8	267
Children on Income Support	1.2	3.1	1.9	168

Source: Social Security Statistics (DSS, 1997a). The first four rows count the number of claims on each of four grounds, excluding dependent spouses and children. The last row counts the number of dependent children whose parent(s) claim Income Support

the number of children living in families (with either one or two parents) who claim Income Support – the social assistance benefit offering a minimal weekly allowance for those who would otherwise have next to nothing. For 1996, the figure of 3.1 million represented just less than a quarter of all children being in officially sanctioned poverty.

There have also been substantial changes in the incomes of those in work (DfEE, 1999). Most of the groups who already had high earnings in the 1970s now receive much higher salaries and pay much less tax; but the incomes of those in poorly paid jobs (or with no job at all) have hardly changed in real terms. The well-off have been getting better off, while the poor have been getting relatively poorer. In 1977, only 6% of the population was living in households whose income was below half the national average; by 1992, the proportion was 20% DSS, 1997b). Stephen Jenkins' analysis of the dynamics of household incomes in the 1990s (in Chapter Five) takes place in the context of a dramatic increase in the level of poverty.

It would be interesting to be able to demonstrate the effect of the changing distribution of income on families' experiences of prosperity and poverty. There is plenty of evidence about the extent of hardship suffered by those at the bottom of the income scale, but there is a serious scarcity of consistent questions being asked over the years which would have revealed how households have reacted to changes in the absolute or relative levels of their income. The questions that are asked tend to change over time. In the GHS, for example, the list of 'consumer durables' has been altered in response to changing expectations and developing technology. In 1973, they asked whether households had such things as

Table 1.6: Car ownership, by family's employment position (1973 and 1996), in column percentages

		No job	One job	Two jobs
1973	No car	70	39	26
	One car	25	45	58
	Two or more	6	16	16
1996	No car	50	17	5
	One car	40	49	43
	Two or more	10	35	52

Source: GHS, author's analysis

a fridge or a vacuum cleaner, a radio or a (black and white) television. In 1997, it was pointless to ask about those near-universal items of equipment, and the questions focused on a freezer, a tumble-dryer, a hi-fi system and video. Nevertheless a few questions do provide a direct comparison. A combination of increased prosperity, relative reductions in prices and scarcity of public transport means that far more people have the use of a car now than could afford one in the 1970s (see Table 1.6). The trend has occurred across economic divisions, so that the proportion even of non-working families with a car increased from 30% to 50% during the period. However, the proportion of two-worker families with two or more cars increased even more rapidly – from 16% in 1973 to 52% in 1996.

Changing housing

Nick Buck's analysis of housing and migration (in Chapter Six) also covers a policy area that has changed significantly – not so much in the quality and quantity of the accommodation occupied as in the ownership of the asset, and in the distribution of the cost of housing over the life-cycle. At the beginning of the century, 90% of households rented their home from a private landlord. During most of the subsequent period, the two main tenures of owner-occupation and council housing expanded roughly in parallel, as the private-rented sector declined. Until the early 1970s, council house rents were kept low by a general subsidy. As the figures for 1973 in Table 1.7 show, this meant that the distribution of tenure was very similar for both workers and non-workers: roughly half owners, one third social tenants and one sixth private tenants.

Since the 1970s, the subsidy has been transferred from the bricks and

Table 1.7: Housing tenure, by family's employment position (1973 and 1996), in column percentages

		No job	One job	Two jobs
1973	Owner	42	45	51
	Social tenant	39	38	34
	Other tenant	19	17	14
1996	Owner	52	71	87
	Social tenant	37	17	7
	Other tenant	10	12	6

Source: GHS, author's analysis

mortar to the individual tenant though a means-tested rent rebate. Millions of council houses and flats have been sold to their tenants at knock-down prices. This was good news for the new owners with modest incomes. But it will have been less welcome to the poor tenants who depended increasingly on housing benefit, could not obtain even a small mortgage and remained, increasingly isolated and stigmatised, in property owned by their council or housing association. The figures for 1996 in Table 1.7 show a steep inequality in tenure. By this time, only one third of the families in social housing had any employment. Not surprisingly, public housing is increasingly seen as one of the marks of poverty – trapping families in disadvantage rather than helping them to escape from it.

Changing health

It is tempting to argue that all of the social and economic factors studied in the chapters that follow have been the subject of radical change during the period 1973-96. But there are exceptions. In the field of health (analysed in Chapter Seven) the trends have been far too mixed for any simple overall conclusion to be drawn. Cures have been found for some diseases, but new ones have taken their place. Mortality rates continue to fall, but that sometimes means that morbidity rates have increased. The GHS question that has been used as the standard benchmark for measuring long-term trends in health suggest a slow rise in the proportion of people in all age groups below 65 who report limiting long-standing illness (ONS, 1999). However, the trend has not been steady, and is not visible at all in the older age groups who have reported high levels of limiting illness all along.

From a different perspective, though, there have been trends in ill-health that have important potential links with many of the family-level trends considered in this book. In 1971, there were 2.6 million men and women in the UK aged 75 or more; by 1996, the number had risen to 4.3 million. The rate of increase of those older than 85 was even faster – doubling from 0.5 million to 1.1 million. The proportion of these very old people who suffer ill-health or infirmity may have remained fairly steady, but the number of them requiring medical services and personal support has increased simply as a result of their prolonged life-expectancy. Questions about who should provide or pay for such support have not yet been settled – whether it should be the old people themselves (through insurance schemes), their children or the state. The important point is that any resolution of that question is unlikely to remain stable from generation to generation. In 50 years time, very old people are likely to have more money than they have now, but their families will be both smaller and more complex.

Changing politics?

At the end of the book (Chapter Eight), Malcolm Brynin offers some new insights into political preferences and behaviour in the 1990s. The period since the 1970s has witnessed massive change in this arena too, but we seem to have returned almost to the original position. The Heath government in 1970 to 1974 was one of the last representatives of the post-war 'Butskellite' consensus combining full employment and a welfare state. By the general election of 1983, the nation had to choose between a Conservative Party that had moved sharply to the right, and a Labour Party that had lurched equally far to the left. Yet the newly right-inclined Labour government that came in at the 1997 election seems remarkably similar to the old left-inclined Conservative government that was defeated in 1974. One of the turning points in the history of social security policy was the integration of tax allowances and social security benefits for children, and the introduction of a means-tested benefit to provide incentives for families in low-paid work. That happened in 1971. Plus ça change!

The British Household Panel Survey

Some of the astonishing changes over the years in family structures and labour market positions have not been analysed in as much detail as they should have been, given their importance to our understanding of social and economic relationships, and to the development of public policy. The overall trends are an essential component of the patterns of activity documented in this book, but they are not the direct object of the BHPS analysis. The primary focus is on changes that families and their members experience from one year to the next. We are not so much interested in whether there were more or less unemployed people in 1997 compared with 1991; what we do want to know (and this unique data source is able to tell us) is how many people lost their job during that period, which of them experienced unemployment as a result, and what their chances were of returning to work. The number of people unemployed at any one time (the 'stock') is an outcome of the processes of losing and finding jobs (the 'flow'). It is processes such as these that are the central focus of the research on which the following chapters are based.

Another central issue is stability. How long do marriages last? Is it the same people who contribute to the unemployment statistics every year? Is poverty a permanent or a temporary condition? How many of those who fall sick then recover their health?

The majority of empirical data available to social scientists is based on 'cross-sectional' enquiries – surveys in which a random sample of people were all interviewed once, at about the same time. This produces a 'snapshot' of the situation at that time – the level of unemployment, the proportion of mothers in work, the extent of poverty, and so on. Surveys repeated at intervals can show net changes in these measures, such as fluctuating unemployment, or widening inequality. Valuable though these data sources have been, they lack the picture of changes in individuals' experiences that would contribute to an understanding of the processes at work. A cross-sectional survey tells us, for example, how many people are unemployed, and what sort of people they are. Longitudinal data would offer a 'movie' rather than a 'snapshot'. It would allow us to show which workers were at risk of becoming unemployed, what unemployed people's chances were of returning to work, and whether someone's experience of unemployment in the past was directly or indirectly associated with his or her prospects for the future.

There are several types of longitudinal data:

- retrospective recall of events that have already taken place;
- repeat surveys following up the same sample on two or three occasions;
- cohort surveys in which a group of people who all experienced an event in a certain period are interviewed again and again at intervals.

Each of these methods is highly appropriate for a number of specific analytical purposes, but the longitudinal method with the widest general applications is the household panel survey. A sample representative of all households is identified at the start. Every adult member of the household is interviewed. The panel members are then re-interviewed every year, using largely the same set of questions on each occasion. The children of the original panel members are recruited to the survey as they reach the age of 16, so data remains representative of the population over the years, and even across generations.

The pioneering Panel Survey of Income Dynamics (PSID) was set up in the United States in 1968; now that it has traversed a generation it is of unparalleled value to American social scientists seeking to understand the processes of social change and the impact of policies during the past decades. In Europe, substantial panels have been launched in several countries, starting with Germany in 1983. Some early comparative analyses have been based on harmonised data from surveys undertaken separately in different countries. However, a major development was the introduction in 1994 of the European Community Household Panel survey (ECHP, also known as the Europanel). This covered initially the 12 nations of the pre-expansion European Union (EU), and is being extended to other member states as they join.

This book is based almost entirely on the British Household Panel Survey. A random sample of households, representative of all households in Great Britain, was identified in 1991. Interviews were undertaken in 5,500 households, containing 9,900 adults (aged above 16). Each of the adults then became a 'panel member', and has been interviewed every year since. Each of the panel members' children has been enrolled in the panel as soon as they were 16[4], and has been interviewed every year after that. Some will die during a year, so the panel remains representative of the population as a whole from year to year.

Every adult member of the original sample of households was interviewed. This provides rich information about the households as a whole, and about the links between household members – husbands and wives, parents and (adult) children, and so on. To retain this household perspective on sample members' lives, the survey includes every adult who lives in the same household as a panel member, in every subsequent year. So if a new person joins the household, or if a panel member leaves his or her original household and forms a new one, the new relations or friends are interviewed. However, they are included only as long as they continue to live with one of the members of the true panel – either one of the original 9,900, or a child of an original member.

The validity with which a sample survey represents the population as a whole is heavily dependent on the success of the interviewers in reaching and maintaining contact with a high proportion of those originally selected. It is estimated that 69% of all the adults living in the original households were interviewed in the first wave (1991). The particular problem for panel surveys is to maintain the response rate over time, and much effort has been taken to maintain contact with the panel members from year to year. A total of 88% of the original sample was re-interviewed again the following year (excluding from the base those who are known to have died or left the country). Many of those who are missed one year are nevertheless contacted again the next year, but inevitably the number declines slightly at each wave. In 1997 (wave 7), 76% of the original sample was still included (excluding ineligibles). Of the continuing sample, 9 out of 10 members were interviewed on all seven occasions, providing the most valuable information of all. The decline in numbers from the core continuing panel has almost stopped: 98% of those who were interviewed in all of the first six waves contributed again to the seventh. Their loyalty has contributed hugely to our knowledge of the processes of social and economic change in Britain. These response rates compare very favourably with those of other panel surveys[5].

Although the BHPS is primarily a panel survey, directly measuring change from year to year, it also obtains information by asking respondents to remember what had happened in the past. Each year, for example, they tell us not only about their current position, but also about changes that have occurred during the past 12 months in such key areas of their lives as family structure and employment. In 1992 and 1993, they provided life histories, recording every change of job and period of unemployment since they left school, and dates of marriages, cohabitations and divorces, and the birth of children. These life histories are especially useful for analysing changes between cohorts – as illustrated in the discussion of changing patterns of family formation in the next chapter.

Most of the analysis reported in this book is based on successive waves of the true panel data. Any one wave offers a cross-section of the British adult population, directly equivalent to that derived from a normal survey. Comparing the results of wave 2 with wave 1 provides a measure of changes or 'transitions' from one year to the next. All the pairs of waves (1 to 2, 2 to 3, 3 to 4 and so on) are pooled to provide a sample of all the year-on-year transitions that occurred during the survey period. A common way to present these pooled transitions is to analyse the number of events that occurred between 'this year' and 'next year' – often referred to as year *t* and year *t+1* respectively. Analysis of the correlates of an event is based on the characteristics at *t* of people who do or do not experience a transition between *t* and *t+1*.

As its name makes clear, the BHPS is a 'household' survey, and much of the data being analysed is concerned with *household* characteristics: family structure, housing tenure, total income and so on. Household level information can be assembled unequivocally in each wave, and can be analysed either in its own right, or as an associated characteristic of individuals. However, it is not possible to look at year-to-year transitions affecting whole households, because the household itself may change from one year to the next. People marry and separate, their children leave home, their mother comes to live with them. Because of this, we always focus on transitions affecting *individual adults*. This person lived in a poor household in wave *t* and did not in wave *t+1*. Such a transition might have occurred either because all the members of the household moved out of poverty together, or because this person moved out of a poor household and into a non-poor one.

Much of the analysis in the following chapters is based on the first seven waves of the BHPS – the 'seven years' of the title. Some of the text summarises earlier analysis based on only six waves. In principle, this should make no difference to the generalisability of the findings, although results are always more reliable the more waves that can be included in the database.

About this book

Like good wine, a panel survey improves as it ages. The first wave is no different from a normal cross-sectional survey. At the other extreme, a survey as old as the American PSID provides data about a whole generation of US families and can provide direct comparisons between the life-cycle trajectories of parents and their children. In general, the longer the series of waves, the greater the analytical value that can be obtained from the data.

The second BHPS wave, undertaken in the autumn of 1992, provided the first year-on-year data ever available from a household panel survey in Britain. The Essex research team immediately assembled a book – *Changing households* (Buck and others, 1994) – which demonstrated the value of year-on-year comparisons to social and economic research across a whole range of domains. The book established a base for the longitudinal analysis of social and economic structures which was to follow.

Now that we have a sequence of seven years' data, it can be said that the BHPS has come of age. Not only do we have six sets of transition matrices, with six times as many 'events' as were recorded in the first pair of waves, it is now possible to look at sequences of events across a period, so that we can say what had happened before one change or after another. The survey is maturing in another way, too: analysts at Essex and at other research centres in Britain and abroad have been using the data, developing analytical approaches, and building a picture of family dynamics. Much of this work has been published in academic papers and in reports sponsored by government departments, research foundations and commercial organisations.

Seven years in the lives of British families is intended to bring the findings of the BHPS to the attention of as wide an audience as possible. Some of the chapters that follow review and summarise existing findings already reported by a variety of researchers – the chapter on employment transitions, for example. Others, such as the chapter on the dynamics of health, contain entirely new material, analysing sectors of the BHPS data that have been under-used in the past. Most of the chapters contain a mixture of old and new findings.

One of the book's aims is simply to set out our stall: showing what the BHPS can do; summarising some of the main conclusions that have already been drawn; encouraging other analysts to make use of our data or, perhaps, to replicate our analysis in other countries. At the same time, it is intended that the whole should exceed the sum of the parts – that by assembling so much material we can contribute to a synoptic view of the interactions between family, employment, income and other elements of the development of the family in modern Britain.

Notes

[1] Most of the following findings are based on direct analysis of the 1973 and 1996/97 GHS data sets, rather than on published results. 1973 is the first year in which the original data is available in a readily accessible format. The 1996/97 survey was the latest available when the analysis was undertaken. The latter took place between April 1996 and March 1997 and is referred to as 1996 for short. Thanks to Kimberly Fisher for her contribution to the analysis.

[2]These figures are for England and Wales, but the trend was similar in Scotland.

[3]The estimate is based on: households where the 'head' was recorded as having a 'spouse' even though the latter's marital status was not 'married'; households where the only adults were a non-married man and a non-married woman who were not related to each other and whose ages were less than 10 years apart.

[4]Since 1994, questions have also been asked of children aged 11 to 15, but they are not seen as full panel members. No material from the sample of young people is included in this book.

[5]See Taylor (1994) for an assessment of the accuracy of the BHPS in relation to the 1991 Census.

References

Buck, N., Gershuny, J., Rose, D. and Scott, J. (1994) *Changing households: The British Household Panel Survey 1990-1992*, Colchester: ESRC Research Centre on Micro-social Change, University of Essex.

DfEE (Department for Education and Employment) (1997) *New Earnings Survey 1999*, London: The Stationery Office.

DSS (Department of Social Security) (1997a) *Social Security Statistics 1996*, London: The Stationery Office.

DSS (1997b) *Households below average income 1979-1995/96*, London: The Stationery Office.

Gregg, P. and Wadsworth, J. (1996) 'More work in fewer households', in J. Hills (ed) *New inequalities*, Cambridge: Cambridge University Press.

Haskey, J. (1998) 'One parent families and their dependent children in Great Britain', in R. Ford and J. Millar (eds) *Private lives and public responses*, London: Policy Studies Institute.

ONS (Office for National Statistics) (1998) *Living in Britain: Results from the 1996 General Household Survey*, London: The Stationery Office.

ONS (1999) *Population trends*, London: The Stationery Office.

Taylor, A. (1994) 'Appendix: sample characteristics, attrition and weighting', in N. Buck and others, *Changing households: The British Household Panel Survey 1990-1992*, Colchester: ESRC Research Centre on Micro-social Change, University of Essex.

TWO

Patterns of household and family formation

John Ermisch and Marco Francesconi

During the past 25 years, two major changes have occurred in the patterns of household and family formation (as identified in the Introduction). Marriage and childbearing are occurring increasingly later in people's lives, and there has been a dramatic increase in childbearing outside marriage. These two changes are likely to affect family life dramatically. The way in which men and women form and dissolve their families has direct consequences on the way in which they allocate their time inside the household (see Chapter Three on the role of partners within families) and in the labour market (see Chapter Four on employment). The allocation of time within and outside families is also likely to shape the situations that men and women face when forming and dissolving their families. This chapter will argue that the two major changes in the patterns of family life can be primarily accounted for by the large increase in the tendency to cohabit in first partnerships (rather than marry immediately). In doing so, it will analyse when and in what way young people leave their parental home, when they enter their first partnership and whether it is a cohabitation or marriage, the stability of cohabiting unions, repartnering after cohabitation dissolution and the timing of motherhood. In the light of the importance of cohabiting unions in the emergence of these major changes in family formation patterns, the chapter also analyses who is likely to cohabit in their first partnership, and it investigates the factors associated with the dissolution of cohabiting unions and their conversion into marriage. While this is likely to provide a direct framework for the subsequent analyses of household incomes (Chapter Five) and housing tenure (Chapter Six), it may be useful to place other aspects of life (such as health and political affiliation analysed in Chapters Seven and Eight) into a context characterised by increasing complexity and uncertainty.

Leaving the parental home and returning to it

On average, 12.7% of men and 17.5% of women aged 16-30 leave their parental home each year. Estimating age-specific rates allows the patterns of these departures to be examined in more detail[1]. The annual rate of departure from the parental home increases with age for each sex. If these age-specific rates were constant for all the women under analysis who were born between 1961 and 1981 (the 1961-81 'birth cohort') and primarily represented first departure from the parental home, then just over half of them would have left home by the age of 22. The age at which half of men would have departed from their parents' home (the median leaving age) is about 23. Comparison with estimates made by Ermisch and Di Salvo (1997) for those born in 1958, who were leaving home between about 1976 and 1985, suggests that while men's median leaving age was about the same during 1991-97 as during 1976-85, women's median leaving age increased by about one year[2].

Who young people go to live with when they leave their parents is also of interest, and it appears to have changed more during the 1990s relative to the 1958 birth cohort. Three mutually exclusive destinations (also defined as 'competing risks') are distinguished:

• a student in full-time education not living with a partner
• living with a partner
• living alone or with others (but not a student, nor in a partnership).

Table 2.1 shows the destination-specific annual departure rates. Women have higher rates to every destination, but particularly to leave to live with a partner (in marriage or cohabitation).

Table 2.1: Destinations 'next' year of young people who lived with their parents 'this' year, in column percentages

	Men	Women
Student	3	4
Partnership	6	9
Other	4	5
Stay with parents	87	83

Note: Obtained for the 1961-81 birth cohort

Table 2.2: Simulated pattern of first destinations of young people up to the age of 30, in column percentages

	Men	Women
Student	23	23
Partnership	38	46
Other	28	28
Still with parents at age 30	11	3

Note: Obtained for the 1961-81 birth cohort

The observed departures from home represent *first* departure in the vast majority of cases. A detailed analysis of housing mobility and tenure can be found in Chapter Six. If we assume that estimates of age and destination-specific departure rates represent first departure rates and they uniformly apply to our cohorts of men and women, we can calculate the destination distribution of first departures from the parental home by the age of 30. This is shown in Table 2.2. These estimates suggest major changes relative to the 1958 cohort in young people's destinations when they leave their parents. In the 1958 cohort, living with a partner was the destination for 60% of the women and about 55% of the men, but the proportion leaving for this destination is now only about two fifths (46% of women and 38% of men).

Table 2.2 also suggests a large increase in the proportion of young people leaving the parental home to study relative to the experience of the 1958 cohort. This is consistent with the fact that the proportion of a cohort in full-time education at age 18 more than doubled between the 1958 and 1974 cohorts.

Among persons aged less than 30 not living with any parents, 3.3% return to live with at least one parent each year. Not surprisingly, the annual return rate declines with age; it is 7.5% for those below the age of 25. For those in this latter group who were neither cohabiting nor married in the previous year it is higher (11.1%), and among these the rate is higher for men (14.8%) than women (8.2%).

If the estimated age-specific return rates are assumed to apply to a cohort, then the proportion who are expected to return to their parents' home at least once can be calculated. If a person leaves home at the age of 21, these return rates suggest that 28% of men and 21% of women would return some time before the age of 30. This suggests an increase in returns to the parental home relative to the members of the 1958 cohort, one fifth of whom returned to the parental home at least once (Ermisch and Di Salvo, 1997). The increase during the 1980s in the percentage of young people living in their parental home (see Murphy and Berrington, 1993) appears primarily to reflect this increased tendency to return to their parental home.

This pattern is intimately related to the changing labour market opportunities (see Chapter Four on employment) and may have relevant consequences for income inequality and poverty distribution (see Chapter Five on household incomes). An unemployment spell provides a strong encouragement to return to the parental home: the return rate is 7.6% for unpartnered persons aged less than 25 not experiencing unemployment during the year compared with 18.3% among those having an unemployment spell. The cross-section association showing that unemployed young people are more likely to live with their parents comes about because of *returns* to the parental household among unemployed, unpartnered young people; those experiencing unemployment are *more* likely than others to *leave* their parents' household (Ermisch, 1999).

Formation and dissolution of cohabiting unions

Changing patterns of people's entry into their first partnership and the timing of their first marriage are closely linked to changes in the formation and dissolution of cohabiting unions. This section considers, in turn, the timing of first partnership and whether it is a marriage or a cohabiting union, the duration and outcomes of cohabiting unions and repartnering after union dissolutions.

First partnership: cohabitation or marriage?

The previous section has indicated that while a large minority of young people in the 1990s move directly from their parental home into their first partnership, the majority will enter a partnership while living independently from parents. In the following analysis, we ignore whether or not people are living with their parents and focus on when a first partnership is formed and the type of partnership. After reaching the age of 16, each person faces three options in each month: he/she can marry, cohabit outside of marriage, or remain single (without a partner). To examine change over time, the analysis is carried out for three sets of birth cohorts (1930-49, 1950-62 and 1963-76), all of whom were making partnership decisions in the post-war period. Table 2.3 shows the estimated proportions of people who entered their first partnership by type of partnership, age, sex and birth cohort[3].

Table 2.3: Proportions of men and women who ever had a partnership by a certain age, analysed by birth cohort and partnership type, given as cumulative rates per 1,000

Partnership type and birth cohort	20	24	At age 28	32	36
Men					
Marriage[a]					
1930-49	47	473	721	809	840
1950-62	62	327	467	523	536
1963-76*	18	110			
All	43	336	536	624	656
Cohabitation[b]					
1930-49	8	29	49	67	79
1950-62	42	163	278	342	371
1963-76*	107	387			
All	45	144	209	245	257
Any union[c]					
1930-49	55	502	770	876	919
1950-62	104	490	754	865	907
1963-76*	125	497			
All	88	480	745	869	913
Women					
Marriage[a]					
1930-49	231	700	837	875	887
1950-62	228	544	625	642	649
1963-76*	66	210			
All	179	518	641	697	709
Cohabitation[b]					
1930-49	8	33	44	53	58
1950-62	87	207	270	294	307
1963-76*	204	448			
All	88	183	213	234	240
Any union[c]					
1930-49	239	733	881	928	945
1950-62	315	751	895	936	956
1963-76*	270	658			
All	267	701	854	931	949

Note: Figures are obtained from maximum likelihood estimates of transition rates to marriage and cohabitation by single year of age. Partnership type refers to the way in which partnerships started

Key: * Estimates at age 24 are based on people born during 1963-68; and estimates at age 20 are based on people born during 1963-72
a Excludes marriage after cohabitation
b Whether married first partner or not
c Includes 'marriage' and 'cohabitation'

Cohabitation has become a much more important route into first partnership. By their 24th birthday, more than two fifths of the women in the most recent cohort, who reached their 20th birthday between 1983 and 1996 (and, thus, were born between 1963 and 1976), had entered cohabitation, compared with one fifth of the women in the previous birth cohort (those born between 1950 and 1962). There was a corresponding fall in the proportion of women who went directly into marriage, from 54% to 21%. Among those who reached their 20th birthday between 1970 and 1982, almost one third of women and two fifths of men who ever had a partner (by age 36) cohabited in their first partnership[4]. Although we do not know yet what would happen to some of the younger members of the 1963-76 cohort, the estimates suggest that the proportion cohabiting in their first partnership has risen to 68% (448/658) for women and 78% (387/497) for men. The relative proportions marrying directly and cohabiting are reversed between the two cohorts, and cohabitation has become the more common mode of first partnership.

Partnerships are also being postponed. The proportion of women who have ever had a partnership has declined between the latest two cohorts: 75% of women in the 1950-62 cohort had entered a first partnership by the age of 24, but this had declined to 66% for the 1963-76 cohort ('Any union' in Table 2.3). This translates into a rise in women's median age at first partnership of one year between the two cohorts, from 21 years, 3 months to 22 years, 3 months. Postponement among men is not evident up to the age of 24, which is approximately the median age for first partnership in both the 1950-62 and 1963-76 cohorts. However, men are also postponing first partnerships: 60% of men in the 1950-62 cohort had partnered by age 26, and this had fallen to 52% for the 1963-76 cohort.

Evidence from the BHPS panel data during the 1990s suggests further delay in first partnerships among more recent cohorts. If we take 1991–97 partnership rates for never-married people as being *first* partnership rates, these suggest a median age at first partnership of 23 for women and 25 for men. The proportions cohabiting in their first partnership also appear to have risen, to 75% for women and 82% for men[5]. While these estimates may seem high, they are not inconsistent with the evidence from the General Household Survey (GHS), which shows that 7 out of 10 first marriages in the early 1990s were preceded by the spouses' cohabitation (Haskey, 1995).

The type of first partnership (cohabitation versus marriage) varies depending on whether or not the young person lives with his/her parents before it. Restricting our attention to never-married people aged 17-35 between 1991 and 1997, about 25% of men and 35% of women do not live with their parents (that is, they live on their own). Of all women who move into a cohabitation every year, 7% were living with their parents and 12% were living independently prior to that. For men, the difference in the family situation before their first partnership is even more marked, with only 5% living with their parents and 12% living on their own. When we look at the movement into first marriage, the preceding living arrangements do not play any role in the case of women. Of those who marry every year, 2.5% were living with their parents and 2.4% were living independently. In the case of men, instead, we detect a significant difference in living arrangements before marriage: 1.1% of them were living with their parents and 2.8% were living on their own. Although the people who do not live with their parents tend to be older, we find similar patterns when we control for age.

Duration of cohabiting unions

How long do people live together in cohabiting unions before either marrying their partner or dissolving their union? Using the BHPS life history data, Table 2.4 indicates that cohabitations are rarely long term. Less than one fifth continues for five years or more, and less than one tenth survives 10 years or more. Among those unions beginning after 1980, the median duration is just less than two years. About three fifths of British first cohabitations turn into marriage and about 30% dissolve within 10 years[6] (Ermisch and Francesconi, 2000a).

Similar patterns emerge from the 1990s panel data. Each year, 29% of cohabiting unions involving never-married women end. If the estimated transition rates were constant over time, they suggest a median duration of two years and less than 4% of unions lasting 10 years or more[7]. Again, about three fifths of the cohabitations turn into marriages, while the remaining two fifths end in separation.

The small increase in median duration compared with the estimates from the retrospective data suggests longer durations of cohabitations in the 1990s than earlier. This is consistent with the trends across union cohorts in Table 2.4 and with data on the median duration of cohabitations in progress. Haskey and Kiernan (1989) and Kiernan and Estaugh (1993, Table 2.5) estimate median elapsed durations of cohabitation of 20 and 21 months respectively from samples from the 'stock' of never-married cohabiting women in 1986/87 and 1989 (obtained from the GHS). Haskey

(1995) estimates that this median elapsed duration increased to 29 months in 1990-93. However, the distribution of elapsed durations among people cohabiting at a point in time usually differs from the distribution of completed durations among people beginning cohabitations at the same time (see Lancaster, 1990, pp 91-7), and it is the latter that is estimated in the current analysis.

Repartnering

If a person's first partnership was a cohabitation that dissolved, almost all of those who repartnered cohabited in their second partnership. The estimates in Table 2.5 indicate that after a cohabiting first partnership has dissolved, the median period before the next partnership was five years, which is somewhat higher than we expected. However, estimates from the panel data indicate faster rates of repartnering after cohabitation dissolution. They suggest a median time of three years until the next union.

After marriages dissolve, it is more common for those that repartner to cohabit. In our life history data combining the information on all people, 70% of second partnerships following dissolution of a first marriage started as cohabiting unions, and during the panel years (1991-97), two thirds of divorced and separated people who then repartnered cohabited (at least to start with). Our ability to identify trends across people who dissolved their unions in specific time periods is limited by small sample sizes, but it is feasible to divide the group who dissolved first marriages into those doing so before and after 1981 (producing roughly equal sample sizes). There was an increase in the proportion of cohabitations among second partnerships between these two disruption cohorts for this group (for example, an increase from 63% to 75% for women repartnering). This trend is broadly consistent with evidence from the GHS, which shows an increase in the percentage of women cohabiting before their second marriage from around 30% in the late 1960s to about 90% for second marriages in the early 1990s (Haskey, 1995).

Cohabitation and the decline in first marriage rates

Thirty years ago, 9 out of 10 women had married by their 30th birthday; today this proportion is two thirds. The corresponding proportions for men are four out of five and one half. For all ages, the proportion of women who have ever married is lower for each succeeding cohort from

Table 2.4: Survival of first cohabiting unions, given by percentage still intact

Men

Union cohort	Years since beginning of union					
	1	2	3	4	5	10
1961-70	66	36	28	21	15	
1971-80	66	38	24	19	18	11
1981-92	69	45	29	21	17	5
All	68	42	27	21	17	8

Women

Union cohort	Years since beginning of union					
	1	2	3	4	5	10
1961-70	58	40	21	13	12	
1971-80	71	45	27	20	15	7
1981-92	73	48	35	25	19	4
All	71	47	32	23	17	6

Note: Obtained from maximum likelihood estimates of transition rates from first cohabitation. Total includes some unions started before 1961

Table 2.5: Interval between first and second cohabiting unions, given by percentage that have repartnered

	Years since end of previous union					
	1	2	3	4	5	10
Men	16	27	36	44	51	65
Women	14	28	35	42	50	62

Note: Obtained from maximum likelihood estimates of transition rates to second cohabitation conditional on the dissolution of the first cohabitation

the 1961 birth cohort onwards (and the same is true for men). If we look at a group of people who became 30 in one of the panel years, for example the 1966 cohort, the median age at marriage is 26 for women and more than 29 for men. On the other hand, although more recent cohabitations appear to be lasting longer before dissolving or being turned into marriage, only a small percentage (about 5%) survive 10 years or more (see Table 2.4).

Thus, there appears to be a puzzle: long-term cohabitations are rare, but recent generations of young people are not marrying. The answer appears to lie in the combination of four factors, highlighted already: the large proportion of persons who cohabit before any marriage; the time spent cohabiting; the relatively high risk that cohabitations dissolve; and the time it takes to cohabit again. All of these contribute to a longer time before any marriage takes place and increase the chances that a person never marries. The shift to cohabitation as the more common mode of first partnership is the main engine for the trends in marriage patterns. Although this conclusion is drawn from analysing data on women, similar conclusions are obtained for men.

A simulation of the marital outcome of partnership formation and dissolution behaviour up to a woman's 45th birthday based on recent partnership formation and dissolution rates is shown by the dashed line in Figure 2.1[8]. The median age at marriage (26) and the proportion ever married at age 30 (65%) are close to those observed from registration statistics for the 1965 birth cohort (who were 30 in 1995). The figure suggests that nearly 90% of women in the cohorts born in the mid-1960s may eventually marry. It is just taking a much longer time because of intervening cohabitations.

The solid line in Figure 2.1 shows the results of a simulation of the series of partnership formation and dissolution decisions using the same rates for the outcomes of cohabitations and for repartnering as those used to generate the dashed line, but using rates for first partnership based on the experience of women born during 1950-62, rather than those born during 1963-76. The median age at marriage (22) and the proportion ever married at age 30 (83%) are close to those observed from registration statistics for the 1956 birth cohort. The difference between the two curves indicates the postponement of marriage, which would arise simply because of changes in the patterns of first partnership, both its delay and the substitution of cohabitation for direct marriage. The proportion ever marrying (by age 45) is about 6 percentage points lower for the later generation, as a consequence of the change in first partnership rates at ages below 28.

As discussed above, the major change in first partnership patterns is the approximate reversal of the proportions cohabiting and marrying directly in their first partnership between the two groups of birth cohorts. However, there was also a tendency for first partnerships to be later. To remove this latter aspect of change, a simulation, which uses the first partnership rates for the 1950-62 cohorts but reverses the cohabitation

Figure 2.1: Actual proportion of women who ever married: two groups of cohorts (in numbers per 1,000)

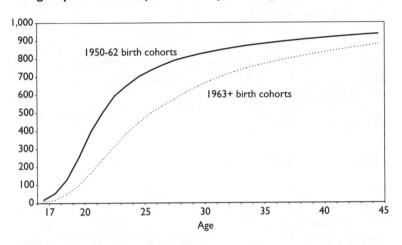

Figure 2.2: Simulated proportion of women who ever married: two groups of cohorts if their cohabitation and marriage rates were reversed (in numbers per 1,000)

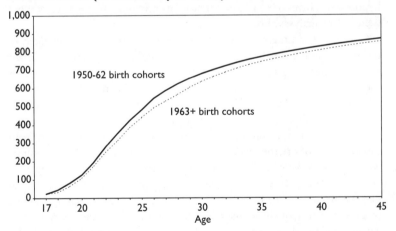

and marriage components of these rates (at ages below 28), is shown as the solid line in Figure 2.2, and the dashed line represents the same as the dashed line in Figure 2.1. Comparison of these two curves suggests that the large increase in the proportion of women who cohabit in their first partnership may explain most of the delay in marriage between these two simulated (or 'synthetic') cohorts. As indicated by the difference between these two curves, a later age at first partnership only accounts for a small proportion of the delay in marriage.

However, a later age at first partnership has played a larger role in the trend towards later marriage among cohorts born since the mid-1960s. If we take 1991-97 partnership rates for never-married people as being the relevant *first* partnership rates for these more recent cohorts (with the same cohabitation dissolution and repartnering rates as before), the median age at marriage rises to 28 for women; only 57% are married by age 30 and only about 82% marry by age 45.

Cohabitation and the delay of motherhood

One half of women born in 1964 had become mothers by their 27th birthday (the median age at first birth for this cohort was 27), which is two years later than for the 1956 birth cohort[9]. The postponement of marriage discussed in the previous section and the fact that at least three fifths of first births are still within marriage immediately suggest that the shift to cohabitation as the dominant form of first partnership was also strongly associated with the postponement of motherhood. This hypothesis is investigated more formally using the same methods as those used in the analyses above.

Consider again the two synthetic cohorts of women: one subjected to the partnership formation and dissolution and fertility rates of women born during 1950-62 from their 16th birthday onward and another subjected to the transition rates of women born during 1963-76. In the 1950-62 cohort, the median age at motherhood is 26.4, and this rises to 27.5 for the cohort of women born during 1963-76[10]. If the rates of first entry to a cohabiting union and marriage had remained the same as in the 1950-62 cohort, the median age at motherhood in the 1963-76 cohort would have *decreased* to 25.2. In other words, changes in childbearing behaviour and partnership formation and dissolution rates other than first partnership entry rates would have reduced the median age at first birth, while it actually increased. This indicates that the delay in first partnership and the move toward cohabitation away from direct marriage are jointly responsible for the delay in motherhood between the two synthetic cohorts[11].

When we remove the delay in first partnership while allowing the shift towards cohabitation in women's first partnership (a simulation that uses the first partnership rates for the 1950-62 cohort, but reverses the cohabitation and marriage components of these rates at ages below 28), the median age at motherhood increases between the two cohorts from 26.4 to 26.8. It appears that the delay in first partnership and the substitution of cohabitation for direct marriage contribute comparable amounts to the delay in motherhood. The further delay in first partnership for cohorts born since the mid-1960s acted to continue the increase in the median age at motherhood for more recent cohorts.

Cohabitation and childbearing outside marriage

There has been a dramatic rise in the percentage of births in England and Wales that occur outside marriage, from 9% in 1975 to 36% in 1996, with the upward trend steepening after 1980. Ermisch (1999) shows that while in 1969 the majority of babies conceived outside marriage among women aged below 25 were born within marriage (63% of those to women aged below 20 and 55% of those to women aged 20-24), it was very rare to have a premaritally conceived birth within marriage by 1995 (for these two age groups, only 5% and 10% respectively). A large majority of births conceived outside marriage are now also born outside marriage *and jointly registered by both parents*, and about three quarters of all jointly registered births outside marriage in 1996 were to parents living at the same address[12]. These can be plausibly interpreted as births to a couple in a cohabiting union. It appears that about three fifths of all recent out-of-wedlock births occur within cohabiting partnerships[13].

A simple decomposition of the change in the ratio of births outside marriage to births inside marriage indicates that the increase in the prevalence of childbearing outside marriage is primarily attributable to the increase in the proportion of women who are not married. Ermisch (1999) shows that less than one fifth of the increase can be attributed to the increase in the fertility rate of unmarried women relative to the fertility rate of married women. Along with the conclusions reached before, this strongly suggests that it has been the steep increase in the proportion of women who cohabit in their first partnership that lies behind the increase in childbearing outside marriage.

However, there has also been a large increase in the proportion of cohabiting unions that produce children. Estimates from the BHPS life history data indicate that, among women born during 1963-76, 18% of women whose first union was cohabiting had a baby before the cohabitation ended, an increase from 9% for those born during 1950-62 (Ermisch, 1997).

Simulation methods are used to identify the extent to which increasing cohabitation, increasing childbearing within cohabitation and births outside a live-in partnership each contribute to the increase in the proportion of births outside marriage. Analogous to the previous two sections, two synthetic cohorts of women are considered: one subjected to the transition rates of women born during 1950-62 from their 16th birthday onward and the other subjected to the transition rates of women born during 1963-76 (for details see Ermisch, 1999). In the 1950-62 cohort, 10% of first births (by age 33) are outside marriage, with one third being in a cohabiting union. The out-of-wedlock first birth ratio increases to 29.2% for the cohort of women born during 1963-76, three fifths of these occurring within a cohabiting union[14]. If the rates of first entry to a cohabiting union and marriage had remained the same as in the 1950-62 cohort, the out-of-wedlock first birth ratio would only have increased to 15.6%. This means that more than two thirds of the 19.2 percentage point increase in the out-of-wedlock first birth ratio between the two cohorts can be accounted for by the large increase in the propensity of women to cohabit in their first partnership and the delay in first partnership, the former being the dominant of these two reasons. A simulation that uses the first partnership rates for the 1950-62 cohort, but reverses the cohabitation and marriage components of these rates at ages below 28 ('removes' the delay in first partnership) produces an out-of-wedlock first birth ratio of 28.2%. This shows that it is the substitution of cohabitation for direct marriage in women's first partnership that accounts for most of the increase in the proportion of first births born outside marriage.

If, in addition to first partnership rates, we also hold the first birth rate within cohabiting unions to its value for the 1950-62 cohort, the out-of-wedlock first birth ratio would only have increased to 12.6%. Thus 86% (29.2-12.6)/(29.2-10) of the increase in the out-of-wedlock first birth ratio can be accounted for by the combined increase in the tendency to cohabit in first partnerships and in the first birth rate within cohabiting unions[15].

Who cohabits in their first partnership?

It is clear from the previous sections that whether or not individuals start their first partnership as a cohabitation is important in explaining their age at first marriage, age at motherhood and whether or not a first birth is outside marriage. Differences in first marriage and motherhood patterns are intimately related to associations between people's socio-economic background and values and their chances of cohabiting or going directly into marriage. There are few variables in the BHPS that could legitimately be called independent of partnership decisions. For instance, education attainment is likely to be mutually dependent with these decisions, and influenced by similar underlying factors. Because of this, the analysis focuses on the social background of the person, as measured by the following characteristics: his/her father's occupation when he/she was aged 14, and religious activity. We also allow for trends across birth cohorts within each of two broad cohorts: 1950-62 and 1963-76.

The father's occupation is classified into three groups, indicating whether he was in a professional job, a managerial job or other jobs (the reference group). This classification was chosen after testing for differential first partnership behaviour among other occupational groups. Religious activity is defined as follows: 'active Catholic' means that a respondent reports being Roman Catholic *and* attends religious services at least once a month; 'active Anglican' is defined in an analogous way. The reference group includes those who report a religion but do not attend services at least once a month ('non-active'), those who report no religion and those active in religions other than Catholic or Anglican ('other active')[16]. Over time, an increasing majority of the sample is not active in any religion, and most of the reference group is not religiously active. The details of this analysis can be found in Ermisch and Francesconi (2000a); the main findings are discussed in the remainder of this section.

The odds of cohabiting relative to marrying when in your first partnership continue to increase among more recent cohorts. As expected from Table 2.3, there is an increasing cohabitation trend and a falling marriage trend within the 1950-62 cohort. The declining marriage trend is even more evident in the 1963-76 cohort, and there continues to be an upward trend in the cohabitation rate. The large negative trend in the marriage rate relative to the upward trend in the cohabitation rate for the more recent cohort means that young people are also spending an increasing proportion of their young adult years single and unpartnered. This is likely to be related to the dramatic rise in the proportion of young people pursuing higher education: one third of 18 year olds was in full-time education in 1992, compared with 15% in 1979.

There was a social class gradient in the odds of cohabitation relative to marriage in the 1950-62 cohort, rising with the father's job status. However, this has diminished as cohabitation in the first partnership has become more common. For the 1950-62 cohort of women, compared to all other occupations, the odds of cohabiting relative to marrying are 2.8 times higher for women having a father in a professional job and are 30% higher for women whose father was in a managerial job, but these differentials disappear for the later cohort. Similar findings were recorded for men. These results suggest that while the upper-middle class were pioneers in cohabitation, the social class difference has virtually disappeared in more recent cohorts.

The differentials in the time spent single by occupational status of the father are larger in the later cohort of women. Among the 1963-76 birth cohort, young people with a father in a professional occupation have both the lowest marriage and cohabitation rates, which implies that they remain single longer than those whose fathers were in lower status jobs. Women who had a father in a managerial job have lower marriage and cohabitation rates than those in the reference group of occupations. These differentials partly reflect class differences in participation in higher education.

In both cohorts, young people who are active Catholics are much less likely to cohabit in their first partnership than those not religiously active or active in religions other than Anglican or Catholic (the reference group). Catholics also tend to partner later. While active female Anglicans are more likely to marry and less likely to cohabit than the reference group in the 1950-62 cohort, the 'discouraging effect' on cohabitation disappears in the later cohort. Active Anglican men are more likely to marry and less likely to cohabit in both cohorts.

Whose cohabitation dissolves?

The analysis in previous sections indicates that another important determinant of the timing of first marriage and of motherhood is whether and when young people convert their cohabitation into marriage. For instance, in the simulation illustrated in Figure 2.1, 73% of recent cohorts of young women either marry directly (29%) or marry their partner in their first cohabiting union (44%). Analysis of whose cohabitation dissolves and whose is converted into marriage is easier than the analysis of first partnership for at least two reasons:

- these young people have, for the most part, completed their education, and so the competition between further education and partnering is almost absent;
- there is information on both potential marriage partners.

Table 2.6: Determinants of the outcome of cohabiting unions, given as logistic regression coefficients

	Impact on log odds of union dissolution	Impact on log odds of marriage
Log (duration of union)[a]	−0.160	−0.131
Age at start of union	−0.092*	−0.013
(Partner in job) (Earnings)/100[a]	−0.032	0.020
Student[a]	1.386*	−1.455
Couple has children[a]	−0.201	−0.921*
Constant	0.382	−1.054

Note: Coefficients are obtained from the discrete-time competing risk transition rate model.

Key: [a] Variable is measured in preceding period. * Significant at 5% level.

To capitalise on the second advantage, the BHPS panel data for 1991-95 is used. The panel data also offers a richer set of observable explanatory factors, which can also vary over time in the union.

A distinct advantage of the BHPS is that the panel data can be used in combination with the life history data. The latter is used to calculate the person's age at the start of the cohabiting union and the union duration for unions in progress at the start of the panel in 1991. These two demographic characteristics have often proved to be valuable in accounting for variation among persons in partnership dissolution patterns (for some recent studies see Berrington and Diamond, 2000; Weiss and Willis, 1997). It is also important to know the union duration in the multivariate analysis that follows. The focus will be on cohabiting unions containing never-married women aged 50 and below[17]. In our sample of 694 woman-year observations, 28.7% end their cohabitation in each year, 17.7% of these converting it into marriage and the remaining 11% dissolving their union.

Estimates of the impacts on the odds of dissolving the union and marrying the partner (relative to remaining in the cohabiting union) are shown in Table 2.6 (for details see Ermisch and Francesconi, 2000a). They show that there are few significant predictors of the outcomes of cohabiting unions. Those that show some predictive power are not known for certain at the start of the union, but rather evolve during the union. The annual rates of union dissolution and marriage fall with the duration of the union. This association may reflect a tendency for the population of cohabiting couples to be increasingly (with duration) made up of couples with unobserved traits that produce a lower risk of union dissolution and a lower propensity to marry.

The estimates also show that higher earnings for a woman's partner decrease the chances that the union is dissolved and increase the chances that it is converted into marriage. Information about the partner's earnings prospects may be limited at the time the union was formed, and so the experience of high (low) partner's earnings during the union tends to strengthen (weaken) it. This finding suggests that besides the role played by preferences and expectations at the beginning of the union, new information is important for the outcome of cohabitations.

People who form a cohabiting union earlier in their life are likely to have searched for a shorter time and therefore are more likely to be less informed about themselves, their current mates and the pool of potential partners. As a result, they may be more likely to dissolve the union in the future[18]. In fact, the younger women were when the union started, the more likely it was to dissolve. Unions in which the woman is a full-time student are four times more likely to dissolve, but these are very rare (2.3% of the person-year observations).

Finally, the estimates show that being a mother has virtually no impact on the odds of union dissolution, and it actually *reduces* the odds of converting the union into marriage by 60%[19]. If the effects of motherhood on the two competing risks are taken into account together, it becomes clear that cohabitations with children are more likely to dissolve eventually, because they are subject to the high dissolution risk of cohabitations for longer. However, mothers also tend to stay in cohabiting unions longer than non-mothers do.

These women may not have become mothers within the current union – the panel data do not tell us the exact timing of births relative to union formation. However, the data do suggest that about one quarter of mothers in cohabiting unions had their youngest child before the start of the union. If these mothers are distinguished in the multivariate analysis, they are as likely to marry (or dissolve) as childless women. The odds of marriage (relative to continuing to cohabit) for women who have their youngest child *within* the union are 67% *lower* than for childless women, and the odds of dissolution are also lower, but not significantly so[20].

It appears that births within cohabiting unions substantially reduce the odds of marriage, which ultimately leads to more of these unions dissolving than for childless cohabitations, because these unions are subjected to the high dissolution rate of cohabiting unions for longer. As measured by conversion of the union into marriage, childbearing within cohabiting unions does not signal longer-term commitments, but it does signal longer cohabitations. This may in fact be a selection mechanism in which couples who are not favourable towards marriage but anticipate a longer-term commitment are more likely to have a child. However, they are still subject to a high risk of union dissolution, and so many of these fertile unions end up dissolving.

Conclusions

The dramatic shift to cohabitation as the mode of first live-in partnership (more than 70% of first partnerships) is primarily responsible for the major changes in family formation patterns: the delay in marriage and motherhood and the increase in the proportion of births outside marriage. Our analysis suggests that while the upper-middle classes were pioneers in cohabitation, social class differences in the odds of cohabiting relative to marrying no longer exist. The cohabitation odds continue to increase among more recent cohorts, and these young people are also delaying first partnership. Nevertheless, it appears that this only adds up to a postponement of marriage, not a large-scale rejection of it. Long-term cohabitations are rare.

Cohabiting unions last only a short time before being converted into marriage or dissolving: their median length is about two years. About three in five cohabitations turn into marriage and 35% dissolve within 10 years. After a first cohabitation has dissolved, the median duration to the next cohabitation is five years.

The results of the analysis of cohabiting union dissolution and conversion into marriage are consistent with the importance of *new information* – particularly information on a woman's partner's earnings, acquired subsequent to union formation – to the outcome of cohabiting unions. Higher partner's earnings increase the chances of marriage and reduce the risk of union dissolution. Along with the relatively short time spent living together in cohabiting unions before the partners either marry or break up, these results suggest that cohabitation is used while waiting to resolve uncertainties, to signal economic success and as a learning experience before stronger commitments are made – a way of coping with uncertainty.

The sharp rise in cohabitation in first partnerships has important implications for the types of families in which children grow up. Childbearing within cohabiting unions has become more common, with 22% of children being born into such unions in 1997, compared with 2% 20 years ago. These fertile unions are much less likely to be converted into marriage and more likely to dissolve eventually than childless unions, which themselves have high dissolution rates. A simple simulation of the potential sequences of partnership formation and dissolution, based on transition rates estimated from the BHPS, indicates that 70% of children born within marriage will live their entire childhood (to their 16th birthday) with both natural parents, but only 36% of children born into a cohabiting union will live with both parents throughout their childhood.

The higher risk of experiencing their parents' partnership break-up that children born in cohabiting unions face is likely to be a cause for policy concern because of the difficulties faced when partnerships dissolve, particularly those that arise when the child is living with only one parent figure in the household (Ermisch and Francesconi, 2000b; see also Chapter Five on household incomes). Policy concerns may also arise in relation to the housing market, because of the potentially increasing pressure on housing demand (see Chapter Four). Simulating subsequent partnership formation and dissolution makes it possible to calculate the average number of years that a child will spend with two parents or a parent and a step-parent according to the partnership context of the birth. Children born outside a live-in partnership will spend, on average, 6.6 years with just one parent, while children born into a cohabiting union average 4.3 years with just one parent, compared with 1.7 years for children born within marriages[21]. Given that the incidence of childbearing within cohabiting unions is rising, these substantial differences in expected years in a one-parent family depending on the partnership context of a child's birth indicate that more British children will spend significant parts of their childhood in families with only one parent.

Notes

[1] The data for the analysis of departure from the parental home is obtained from pooling wave-on-wave data on departure from the parental home from the first seven waves of the BHPS. This produces 5,818 person-year observations for those 'at risk' of leaving home in the following year (ie they reside with at least one parent in the preceding year).

[2] The median ages calculated from both the 1958 birth cohort (National Child Development Study) and the BHPS are comparable to the 'crossover age of those living away from the parental home' calculated from the Labour Force Survey by Berrington and Murphy (1994); the 'crossover age' is the age at which the proportion living outside the parental home first exceeds those living inside.

[3] This analysis uses the partnership history data collected retrospectively in the second wave (1992) of the BHPS. For further details of this analysis and comparison with other countries, see Ermisch and Francesconi (2000a).

[4] By way of comparison, 35% of women and 40% of men in the 1958 birth cohort, surveyed in the NCDS, had cohabited in their first partnership by the time of their 33rd birthday (Berrington and Diamond, 2000), compared with 30% of women and 35% of men for the 1950-62 BHPS cohort. The proportions of those who had ever had a partner by age 33 in the NCDS were very similar to those in the 1950-62 BHPS cohort.

[5] These may be underestimates of the importance of cohabitation, because the panel data would miss cohabitations that started and ended between two annual waves of the panel. However, the median age of first partnership may be overestimated for this same reason.

[6] We have not been able to compute exact counterparts for the 1958 birth cohort, but Berrington and Diamond (2000) find that, by age 33, 28% of first cohabiting unions had dissolved, 64% were converted into marriage and 8% were intact.

[7] With constant transition rates, the median duration of cohabitation is given by $ln(0.5)/ln(1-q_m -q_d)$, where q_m and q_d are the annual marriage and dissolution transition rates, respectively.

[8] These are the rates that lie behind the partnership estimates discussed earlier, with first partnership rates at ages below 28 being based on women born during 1963-76. First partnership rates at ages above 27 are based on the experience of the 1950-62 cohorts, but the results are not very sensitive to different assumptions for ages 28-44 (for example, rates 50% higher or lower). For details, see Ermisch and Francesconi (2000a).

[9] For the 1967-69 cohorts, only 48% of women had become mothers by their 27th birthday (ONS, 1997, Table 10.3).

[10] Direct estimates of the median ages of motherhood from the BHPS life history data indicate a rise between these cohorts from 26 to 27.5; thus, the simulation estimates, which are based on a number of simplifying assumptions, are quite close.

[11] If we also hold the first birth rate within cohabiting unions to its value for the 1950-62 cohort, the median age at motherhood would have declined by slightly less (to 25.4). This indicates that the increase in the birth rate in cohabiting unions worked to bring motherhood forward in women's lives.

[12] The proportion of births conceived outside marriage registered by the mother alone has either declined (for the 20-34 age group) or remained about the same (for those aged below 20).

[13] Ermisch (1997) estimates, on the basis of estimates using partnership and childbearing histories from the BHPS, that a similar proportion of extra-marital *first* births is born within cohabiting unions.

[14] The percentage of first births outside marriage is larger than the percentage of all extra-marital births, because a disproportionate number of births outside marriage are first births (see Cooper, 1991, Table 6). On the basis of Cooper's estimates (from the GHS) of the proportions of births that are first births inside and outside marriage, we estimate that of the first births outside marriage the figure is 14% for 1970-82 and 30% for 1983-92, making the simulated proportions of the right order of magnitude.

[15] Using far from ideal data from the 1989 GHS, Lelièvre (1993) concludes that "seventy nine per cent of the increase across the two younger birth cohorts [born 1945-54 and born 1955-64] in the proportions having a birth [by age 25] while single is due to births occurring during spells of cohabitation" (p 117). This is in line with the argument here.

[16] This classification was chosen after having tested several specifications. Among the religiously active people, the Anglicans are the largest group, while the Catholics have a strong position on opposing cohabitation. Other religiously active groups are too small to be separately identified in our BHPS sample.

[17] While we focus on women, cohabiting men in the panel would be in unions with the women in our sample, and we include some characteristics of the male partners as explanatory variables in the analysis along with attributes of the couple. In this way, it is close to an analysis of unions. The results are similar for all women in cohabiting unions; this is not surprising since 70% of the woman-year observations come from never-married women in cohabiting unions.

[18] For example, the negative relationship between age at first marriage and the probability of marital dissolution found in most studies is consistent with this argument. See Becker and others (1977) and Weiss and Willis (1997).

[19] This finding is consistent with Leliévre's (1993) results in her Figure 7.7 (p 120), based on data from the 1989 GHS.

[20] The coefficient for a birth within a union in the marriage odds equation is -1.128, with a standard error of 0.344, while the corresponding coefficient in the dissolution odds equation is -0.502, with a standard error of 0.409.

[21] For simplicity, this simulation is for first-born children. Multistate life-table estimates for the US by Bumpass and Lu (2000) are broadly similar to these, with expected years in a one-parent family of 7.7, 4.2 and 2.1 respectively. The simulation here uses duration-specific rates for entering a cohabiting union and marriage after a first birth outside a live-in partnership, and constant (Markov) transition rates for all subsequent partnership formation and dissolution rates.

References

Becker, G.S., Landes, E. and Michael, R. (1977) 'An economic analysis of marital instability', *Journal of Political Economy*, vol 85, no 6, pp 1141-87.

Berrington, A. and Diamond, I. (2000) 'Marriage or cohabitation?: a competing risks analysis of first partnership formation among the 1958 British birth cohort', *Journal of the Royal Statistical Society*, Series A, vol 163, no 2, pp 127-51.

Berrington, A. and Murphy, M. (1994) 'Changes in the living arrangements of young adults in Britain during the 1980s', *European Sociological Review*, vol 10, no 3, pp 235-58.

Bumpass, L. and Lu, H.H. (2000) 'Trends in cohabitation and implications for children's family contexts in the United States', *Population Studies*, vol 54, pp 29-41.

Cooper, J. (1991) 'Births outside marriage: recent trends and associated demographic and social changes,' *Population Trends*, no 63, pp 8-18.

Ermisch, J. (1997) 'Pre-marital cohabitation, childbearing and the creation of one-parent families', in C. Jonung and I. Persson (eds) *Economics of the family*, London: Routledge.

Ermisch, J. (1999) 'Cohabitation and childbearing outside marriage in Britain', Institute for Research on Poverty Conference on Non-marital Fertility, University of Wisconsin-Madison, 29-30 April.

Ermisch, J. and Di Salvo, P. (1997) 'The economic determinants of young people's household formation', *Economica*, vol 64, no 256, pp 627-44.

Ermisch, J. and Francesconi, M. (2000a) 'Cohabitation in Great Britain: not for long, but here to stay', *Journal of the Royal Statistical Society*, Series A, vol 163, no 2, pp 153-71.

Ermisch, J. and Francesconi, M. (2000b) 'Family structure and children's achievements', *Journal of Population Economics*, forthcoming.

Haskey, J. (1995) 'Trends in marriage and cohabitation: the decline in marriage and the changing pattern of living in partnerships', *Population Trends*, vol 80, Summer, pp 5-15.

Haskey, J. and Kiernan, K. (1989) 'Cohabitation in Great Britain: characteristics and estimated numbers of cohabiting partners', *Population Trends*, vol 58, Winter, pp 23-32.

Kiernan, K. and Estaugh, V. (1993) *Cohabitation: Extra-marital childbearing and social policy*, Family Policy Studies Centre Occasional Papers, no 17, London: Family Policy Studies Centre.

Lancaster, T. (1990) *The econometric analysis of transition data*, Cambridge: Cambridge University Press.

Lelièvre, E. (1993) 'Extra-marital births occurring in cohabiting unions', in M. Ní Bhrolcháin (ed) *New perspectives on fertility in Britain*, London: The Stationery Office.

Murphy, M. and Berrington, A. (1993) 'Household change in the 1980s', *Population Trends*, no 73, pp 18-26.

ONS (Office for National Statistics) (1997) *Birth Statistics*, London: The Stationery Office.

Weiss, Y. and Willis, R.J. (1997) 'Match quality, new information, and marital dissolution', *Journal of Labor Economics*, vol 15, no 1, pp S293-S329.

THREE

Couples, work and money

Heather Laurie and Jonathan Gershuny

Within-marriage consequences of change in employment structure

Changes in patterns of family formation in Britain in recent decades have been documented in the previous chapter. In tandem with this, there have been changes in the labour market. As Chapter Four will show, male employment has become less secure while women are entering the workforce in increasing numbers, albeit often in part-time rather than full-time jobs.

The contrast with marriage and family life in the 1950s is stark, where the economic roles of spouses were symmetrical but markedly different. Men had jobs, and in an era of full employment, this meant that virtually *all* men worked between the end of full-time schooling and the statutory retirement age. There is a debate as to how to characterise women's longer-term employment histories, but with some specific exceptions, women left the paid labour force at marriage, or at the birth of their first child, or they may never even have entered it. A minority of those who left during the early part of marriage returned later. These patterns gave a characteristic lop-sided M-shape to the graph of women's employment by age (Dale, 1987). Instead of paid work in the labour force, during the early stage of family formation women took virtually sole responsibility for unpaid work within the household, and maintained this irrespective of any subsequent re-attachment to the labour market. The evidence suggests that the total amounts of paid work done by men roughly balanced the total time spent on unpaid work by women (Young and Willmott, 1974). However, the work itself was strongly segregated by gender.

The segregation of male and female roles between paid employment and unpaid domestic work had a major consequence in terms of power within the marital relationship. The traditionally male role of 'breadwinner' conferred both economic power and status on men within the household, while confirming the economic dependence of women. The woman's role was managing and transforming goods and services purchased through the man's labour power. The husband, as the determinant of the family's economic wellbeing in the crucial sense of access to purchased goods and services, necessarily maintained a position of power relative to the wife. The formal legal position of the 'partners' might be approximately equal, but the economic relation still corresponded to the medieval notion in which the husband was the master of the 'domus'. This was particularly clear in relation to families' patterns of financial management. Generally, the husband had *his* wage, out of which he paid his wife an allowance, in effect *her* wage that was to be spent on the household's needs.

Since the 1960s there has been a major change in the family's external economic relations. We have seen a remarkable growth in women's paid employment, and particularly a growth in levels of employment of married women with children (see the Introduction). As Chapter Four shows, women with domestic responsibilities are more likely to be in part-time employment and form a stable element of the labour market. In broad terms, women now make up half the paid workforce in Britain (although, since they are working shorter hours, they account for rather less than half of the total volume of paid work in the society). During the same period there has been a reduction in men's paid work, reflecting both more time spent on schooling and the tendency to take earlier retirement, as well as a growth in unemployment.

This emergence of women from the family into the labour economy is a remarkable phenomenon of the second half of the century. It goes along with, partly as a cause and partly as a consequence, the extraordinary diversification and longitudinal destabilisation of family structures (revealed in Chapter Two). However, the question for this chapter concerns things that are going on *within the marital relationship.*

Dividing unpaid domestic work

The employment change, in the second half of the 20th century, amounts almost to a transformation, yet change within the domestic sphere lags behind. When women enter the labour force they do not lose their differential unpaid work responsibilities. Responsibilities that were separate but equal become joint and unequal – hence what sociologists refer to as

Table 3.1: Wife's proportion of domestic work time, by couple's joint employment status, in cell percentages

	1974/75	1997
Both work full-time	68	62
Husband works full-time, wife part-time	78	64
Husband works full-time, wife not employed	81	72

Note: Based on UK couples, controlling for age of youngest child

the 'dual burden'. Women in the workforce retain their *other* job (Meissner and others, 1977).

This is not to say that there is no change. Wherever we find proper measurement, there is evidence of a long-term decline in women's unpaid work, and of a small increase in men's. However, the change in housework patterns has not been on the same scale as the transformation in paid work. Table 3.1 compares two family-based UK time-use studies from 1974/75 and 1997 (Gershuny, 1999). It shows that families in each of the three main spouse-employment categories have shown some shift in the direction of gender-equality. In the case where both are in full-time employment, the wife's proportion of the domestic work has been reduced from 68% to 62% over the period. However, this still means that overall, in couples where both have full-time jobs, the husband is doing hardly more than one third of the housework, whereas the wife is doing nearly two thirds. The question is: given the extent of change outside marriage and the family, why is change inside the marital relationship so slow?

The explanation in the sociological literature is that these within-couple patterns reflect 'gender ideologies' formed in childhood. They consist of pictures of how men and women relate to each other within the home, and they are, in a rather deeply established way, *constitutive of personality*. They provide the detailed pictures of masculinity and femininity, out of which we construct our own understanding of what it is to be a man or woman. Images of gender distributions of work outside the home may also be to a degree constitutive of personality. The segregated nature of male and female occupations within the labour market serves to reinforce the cultural construction of gender stereotypes (Crompton, 1989). While some have argued that being in a job does not necessarily imply that the work is a central element of your own identity (Hochschild, 1990), it is also clear that paid employment provides an opportunity to form an independent identity.

Women's employment participation is a key influence on the changes that have occurred within partnerships and marriage. As Dex (1985) has argued, women's work is now taken seriously and the notion that careers are for men and jobs for women is being challenged. In a qualitative study of dual-career couples, Hardhill and others (1997) have suggested that within the decision-making processes of these couples " ... it seems that attitudes and preferences are becoming more equitable, especially among couples aged under 40 years, providing some evidence of a gradual change in domestic practices, but the examples of role reversal were very rare". The perception that women are primarily *responsible* for domestic labour has remained remarkably resilient (Warde and Hetherington, 1993). Bittman (1991) suggests that, for many working women, being in paid employment entails 'juggling' time to ensure that familial and domestic responsibilities can be met. This is in part a pragmatic response to the difficulties of combining family and paid employment that does not necessarily signal fundamental changes in attitudes to gender roles within the marital relationship. On the other hand, for men who may wish to have greater involvement with raising their children, for example, the perception that the man's proper role is to work and provide an income for the family can be a disadvantage.

The distribution of household roles within partnerships and marriage is slow to change. There is a recursive process. Change in the private sphere requires that men and women both learn and unlearn their modes of participation in various forms of domestic production and consumption. Men must learn to do the housework and women must learn to expect them to do so. Slow change within the domestic sphere means that the women whose husbands have not yet learned to do the household work must themselves do it in addition to their jobs. This means that they in turn have less time and energy to devote to their jobs, so that women's penetration into the paid labour market is incomplete.

If the change is too slow, some of the most put-upon women may simply leave their partners, with consequent effects on their income levels. As will be seen in Chapter Five, changes in household composition, and divorce in particular, are associated with moves into poverty, shifts that affect women more severely than men. Seeing these processes in action, some women may choose not to take on a partner in the first place. There is likely to be an interaction between the within-partnership processes of change in domestic practices and the processes of family formation and dissolution, although this is beyond the scope of this chapter.

Couples and money management

There has been a wealth of research, both qualitative and quantitative, on how couples manage their money and the impact of differing forms of access to money on the relative wellbeing of individuals within families (see, for example, Pahl, 1980; Vogler, 1989). Much research has been concerned with the extent to which there is equality within the marital relationship and whether there is any evidence of a shift in gender relations from a traditional male 'breadwinner' role to one where men and women see themselves as equal partners.

Couples' money management along with the type of access each person has to money entering the household has been used as an indicator of power relations within the household (Pahl, 1989; Morris, 1989). It has been argued that the couple is more egalitarian in terms of gender roles and practices where the management and control of money are reported as equally shared between them (although the tendency for couples to present the relationship as 'shared' even if this is not entirely the case has also been noted). Others have suggested that a better measure of women's financial independence is not whether they have an equal say with their partner over money, but rather whether they manage and access their own finances independently of their partner (Treas, 1993). A recent qualitative study of money in remarriage (Burgoyne and Morison, 1997), found that remarried couples were more likely to maintain separate finances rather than opt for any form of shared pooling of their finances. This was usually a conscious choice in response to the experience of their previous marriage or relationship. Examining how money is distributed between married or cohabiting couple members can provide insights into whether there is a gradual shift in gender relations, in what circumstances these occur, and the extent to which traditional gender roles remain embedded within the domestic sphere.

One of the hypotheses implicit in much research to date is that as women enter the labour market in greater numbers, they will become less economically dependent on their male partners. This in turn will alter existing roles and gendered patterns of behaviour within the household, changes that will include greater equality in access to and control over money for women. As with the domestic division of labour, we would expect to see these processes change fairly slowly, as roles and responsibilities within the household are renegotiated over time.

In the remainder of this chapter, the BHPS is used to illustrate aspects of these slow processes of change in domestic practices. In the seven-year life of the panel study there is little net change. However, using the panel, there is evidence of much gross change, as men and women move in and out of the labour force. This makes it possible to consider the long-term process in which the internal workings of couple households and families adapt to change in the labour market – and conversely, how the workings of the household may promote or inhibit change in men's and women's wider economic roles.

Evidence on the distribution of work within the household

Who does the housework? The best way to measure individuals' contribution to household activities is to use a time diary, in which respondents keep sequential records of the timing of all their daily activities. The amount of time each person spends on unpaid work can then be calculated. This method is now well developed (Juster and Stafford, 1991); it was used to provide the estimates of the division of labour given in Table 3.1. However, diaries of the sort that are needed are quite onerous for respondents to complete, sometimes produce relatively low response rates, and hence are inappropriate for a general purpose panel survey such as the BHPS.

Instead, two simpler sets of questions that are in the BHPS will be used. These have been shown to produce results that are similar to the more precise estimates derived from time diaries. The first asks both the husband and the wife to say what share they take of each of five activities: family cleaning, cooking, shopping, laundry and childcare. From this it is possible to calculate a straightforward index of the division of domestic labour: we simply code the 'Who does the ...?' variables so that where the particular task is mostly done by the female partner the task is coded as 1, where it is mostly done by the male, it is coded as 0, where it is either shared or done by a paid worker it is coded as 0.5. Averaged over the five activities, this provides a direct, though crude, estimate of the proportion of domestic labour undertaken by the female partner.

Each BHPS respondent with a co-resident partner completes these 'Who does?' questions, giving two different views of how the domestic work is divided up within the family. As the top half of Table 3.2 shows, the female BHPS respondents take a slightly less rosy view of their partners' contribution than the men do of their own contribution to these unpaid family tasks. The male reports yield shares that are systematically slightly lower than are the female reports of the same families' practices which

Table 3.2: Two indices of the division of domestic labour

	1991	1992	1993	1994	1995	1996	1997
Percentage of female work reported by:							
Male partners	78			76	76	75	76
Female partners	82			81	81	80	80
Average female reported share	80			79	78	78	78
Hours of own domestic work reported by:							
Male partners		6.0	6.6	6.0	6.2	6.0	5.9
Female partners		21.5	21.6	20.2	19.8	18.9	18.4
Calculated female share (%)		78	77	77	76	76	76

Note: Hours of own domestic work were not collected in 1991. The questions on
'Who Does' various tasks were not collected in 1992 and 1993

suggests men see these tasks as being shared rather than 'female' responsibilities. However, overall the reports are reasonably similar. Most importantly, they both show just the same historical trend: a slow move away from the female specialised pattern.

There is an alternative basis for making estimates of the division of unpaid work. This stems from the questions from wave 2 (1992) onwards, asking each adult for an estimate of their own weekly hours of unpaid domestic work. As the second half of Table 3.2 shows, male partners' accounts of their own unpaid work hours have remained roughly constant over the six-year period (with a blip in 1993). Female partners appear, even over this short period, to have reduced their unpaid work time quite substantially. So the average proportion of work done by women declined slightly. Reassuringly, the overall estimate of the division of labour is very similar, whichever of the two methods of calculation is used: the 'calculated' share is just a couple of percentage points lower than the 'reported' share. Table 3.3 shows that the three estimates of the between-partner division of labour are all quite highly correlated.

Table 3.3: Correlations between three BHPS estimates of the division of labour (1997), given as correlation coefficients

	Male reported share	Female reported share
Male reported share		
Female reported share	0.77	
Calculated share	0.65	0.69

Table 3.4: Correlation of estimates of the division of labour over successive years, given as correlation coefficients

	1993	1994	1995	1996	1997
Calculated share in 1992	0.70	0.61	0.59	0.54	0.52

Table 3.4 shows that there is some stability in these indices over time. Where the couples remained together (and were interviewed) in successive years, the calculated share in 1992 has a correlation of 0.70 with that of 1993. (The same statistics for each successive pair of adjacent years, not shown in the table, all lie in the range 0.69 to 0.73.) However, as years pass, the coefficient reduces gradually: the correlation between the share calculated in years 1992 and 1997 is 0.52. Very similar patterns of cross-time stability emerge for the male and female versions of the 'reported shares' questions.

Impacts of changing family work patterns on the division of domestic labour

The net changes (those averaged across all couples) during the 1990s in the division of domestic labour are small, but consistently in the same direction – towards (although still quite distant from) gender equality (this is the case for both methods of estimation described above). However, the net estimates disguise the extent of gross change; the cross-time correlations in Table 3.4 do suggest some change of view by the same couple. Not all couples move in the same direction; some couples move substantially towards equality in domestic work allocation, while others move substantially away from it. One major causal factor in these substantial movements is a change in the wife's employment status, as indicated by Table 3.5.

Table 3.5 shows the reported divisions of labour in 1991 and 1997, for those 'consistent couples' with the same partners in both years, broken down by the change in the wife's employment status between those two years. There is a clear, regular and explicable pattern of association between the employment changes, and the differences in each group's behaviour at home. For example, when the wife moves from non-employment into full-time paid employment, there is a substantial downward shift in the proportion of the housework she is reported to do – according to her own account, from 83% to 73%. By contrast, when she moves from full-

Table 3.5: Reported female shares of domestic labour, by wife's change in employment: continuing couples (1991 and 1997)

	Man's account			Woman's account		
	1991 (%)	Change (% points)	1997 (%)	1991 (%)	Change (% points)	1997 (%)
All couples	79	−2	77	82	−2	80
Stays non-employed	80	−6	74	82	−4	78
Moves from non-employed to part-time work	84	−1	83	88	−3	85
Moves from non-employed to full-time work	82	−6	76	83	−10	73
Moves from part-time work to non-employed	84	−2	81	85	−1	84
Stays in part-time work	83	0	84	90	−3	87
Moves from part-time to full-time work	82	−5	77	87	−7	80
Moves from full-time work to non-employed	77	5	82	80	2	83
Moves from full-time to part-time work	75	5	80	75	10	84
Stays in full-time work	72	−2	70	77	−2	74

time employment to non-employment, the balance of domestic work shifts in the opposite direction.

Note that these male and female versions are reasonably consistent despite the fact that they come from separate sources. The wife's account shows a slightly firmer shift as a consequence of her change from non-worker to full-time employment. The 'reported share' reflects a subjective impression of an underlying reality; in the case of the wife's account, the lived experience is, according to this evidence, an increase in her dual burden.

However, the starting point for wives who move *into* employment during the period (83%) is suspiciously similar to the end points of those who move *out of* employment (even though we might have expected the divisions of domestic labour for those moving out of employment to be slightly more egalitarian). This may suggest that the accounts of domestic divisions that these indices are based on may be influenced by convention rather than by the actual practices.

Table 3.6 gives the equivalent picture, but using the indices calculated on the basis of each spouse's estimates of their own contribution; in this

Table 3.6: Calculated female shares of domestic labour, by wife's change in employment: continuing couples (1991 and 1997)

	1991 (%)	Change (% points)	1997 (%)
All couples	78	−2	76
Stays non-employed	81	−4	77
Moves from non-employed to part-time work	84	−4	80
Moves from non-employed to full-time work	82	−16	65
Moves from part-time work to non-employed	80	1	81
Stays in part-time work	83	−2	82
Moves from part-time to full-time work	80	−10	70
Moves from full-time work to non-employed	71	7	78
Moves from full-time to part-time work	69	6	75
Stays in full-time work	69	−1	68

case communicated descriptions of 'who ought to do what' in particular circumstances cannot account for the changes. The effect seems more substantial, at least in the case where the wife moves into full-time employment: the husband's proportion of the domestic work just about doubles, from 18% to 35% (although most of this change comes from the wife's reduction in housework rather than the husband's increases [Gershuny and others, 1997]).

The change in the division of labour as she moves *out* of the labour force is smaller (although in the expected direction of reducing gender equality) than the contrary change as she moves *into* it. We might interpret this as a sort of ratchet process, in which husbands and wives are gradually trained to adjust their domestic work practices. The effect of the experience of the husband's contribution during the wife's period in employment changes the couple's background expectations of the domestic division of labour in a permanent way.

Overall, Table 3.6 provides a quite coherent picture: moves (albeit small ones) in the expected direction as the wife increases or decreases her degree of engagement in the labour force, and with a general drift, small but consistent across the different groups, in the direction of greater gender equality in housework for those with an unchanged employment status.

Unfortunately, the story is not quite this neat. There are other sources of variation that need to be controlled for. During this period people have themselves aged, and some people who once had younger children now have older children. Different birth cohorts are more likely to find themselves in some of the Table 3.6 employment categories than in others. Most importantly, the wives have husbands, and in some cases their employment changes may be systematically associated with their husband's employment change. Suppose, for example, that a husband's employment instability or unemployment is what motivates the wife to take a job: what might be the implication for the division of domestic labour?

Table 3.7 attempts to deal with these possibilities by including them all in a pair of regression models that predict the 'calculated share' of domestic labour in successive years. The regression output is presented in 'multiple classification analysis' format. This is to be read simply, as follows: the 'grand mean' gives the overall average share for the sample as a whole, then each of the following rows of 'effect parameters' represents the effects of belonging to one of the particular categories on the mean value (controlling for the effects of all the other factors). Immediately it becomes clear that the age of the couple's youngest child has relatively little regular effect (other than that those with adolescent children seem to be a little less egalitarian than others). However, the (husband's) birth cohort has a systematic effect, those born after 1950 having relatively gender-egalitarian patterns (controlling for the other influences).

Again it can be seen that the employment change effects are the substantial drivers of change in the share of labour. The wife moving from non-employment to full-time employment shifts the index from 79 to 70. There is also a gradual process of change while the wife remains in employment – the relevant row shows, for the pairs of years covered in this table, a small movement in the direction of equality. Where the wife moves from full-time employment into non-employment there is a shift from 65 to 76. So the ratchet process appears again: the wife reduces the proportion of domestic work as she enters employment, reduces it further while she remains in employment, and when she leaves employment returns as a housewife to a slightly less inegalitarian division of domestic work. Husbands moving out of employment show a large shift towards an egalitarian distribution, while those moving from non-employment into paid work show a smaller shift in the inegalitarian direction.

As part of the long-term and very slow drift towards greater gender equality in the allocation of domestic work, there appears to be process of 'ratcheting up' through which growth in wives' employment outside the home does (slowly) lead to a (small) reduction in gender inequality within the home.

Table 3.7: Couples' employment change and change in females' calculated share of domestic labour, given as regression coefficients

	'This' year	Change	'Next' year
Grand mean	0.76	0.00	0.76
Wife's employment change			
Stays non-employed	0.07	0.00	0.07
Moves from non-employed to part-time work	0.06	−0.02	0.04
Moves from non-employed to full-time work	0.03	−0.08	−0.06
Moves from part-time work to non-employed	0.04	0.05	0.09
Stays in part-time work	0.03	0.00	0.02
Moves from part-time to full-time work	−0.06	−0.01	−0.07
Moves from full-time work to non-employed	−0.11	0.11	0.00
Moves from full-time to part-time work	−0.06	0.01	−0.05
Stays in full-time work	−0.11	0.00	−0.12
Husband's employment change			
Stays non-employed	−0.11	0.00	−0.11
Moves from non-employed to part-time work	−0.08	0.01	−0.07
Moves from non-employed to full-time work	−0.06	0.09	0.03
Moves from part-time work to non-employed	−0.04	−0.02	−0.06
Stays in part-time work	−0.05	0.00	−0.05
Moves from part-time to full-time work	0.02	0.00	0.02
Moves from full-time work to non-employed	0.03	−0.13	−0.10
Moves from full-time to part-time work	0.02	−0.03	0.00
Stays in full-time work	0.06	0.00	0.06
Birth decade			
born 1900-1909	0.06	0.01	0.07
born 1910-1919	0.02	−0.01	0.01
born 1920-1929	0.02	0.00	0.02
born 1930-1939	0.03	0.00	0.03
born 1940-1949	0.02	0.00	0.02
born 1950-1959	−0.02	0.00	−0.02
born 1960-1969	−0.04	0.00	−0.04
born 1970-1979	−0.03	0.00	−0.03
Age of youngest child			
0-4	0.01	−0.01	0.01
5-9	0.01	0.00	0.01
10-15	0.03	0.00	0.03
No children	−0.01	0.00	−0.01
Multiple R squared	17.9%		17.5%

Evidence on financial management

Research on money management and control was developed by Jan Pahl in the 1980s. She categorised couples into what she termed 'household allocative systems' to indicate what type of financial arrangements existed between partners. Pahl's work addresses the issue of inequities within the marital or cohabiting relationship, in which differentials of power are traced through the allocation and control of financial resources. Her focus is on the extent to which patterns of allocating money reflect inequalities in power between husband and wife. Tracing flows of money within families and the mechanisms by which money is distributed to different family members is, she suggests, an empirical indicator of power within the couple relationship. Pahl's 'household allocative systems' are:

- *Whole-wage system:* one person, usually the woman, is responsible for managing all household expenditure.
- *Allowance system:* partners have defined spheres of responsibility for expenditure with, usually, the woman being given 'housekeeping' money.
- *Shared management:*
  › *common pool:* both partners have access to all income and share responsibilities for all expenditure decisions;
  › *partial pool:* both partners put some proportion of their earnings into the common pool and use retentions for personal spending money.
- *Independent management:* partners keep their incomes separate and each is responsible for different items of expenditure.

These 'allocative systems' identify which member of the couple manages the distribution of income within the family, as well as who is responsible for different items of household expenditure. The model draws a distinction between the management and control of household funds; this is because being the day-to-day manager of money does not necessarily confer greater control over money entering the household or over financial decisions. The whole-wage system, for example, is commonly found in low-income families where the task of stretching inadequate financial resources can be a stressful chore for women rather than a source of greater equity within the relationship. For Pahl, the decision-making process is a crucial indicator of power within marriage, with the dominant decision maker being the partner most likely to control household funds.

The strongest association, therefore, was that between power in decision-making and the control of finances. One can conclude that the link between money and power holds within the household as well as outside it; however, power in decision-making is more strongly associated with controlling money than with managing it. (Pahl, 1989, p 176)

The BHPS interview asked two questions from 1991 to 1995 (Taylor and others, 1992) on how couples organise their money (these questions were dropped after 1995, giving a slightly shorter period to observe changes in financial management than was available for the domestic division of labour):

People organise their household finances in different ways. Which of the following methods comes closest to the way you organise yours? It doesn't have to fit exactly – just choose the nearest one.

1. I look after all the household money except my partner's personal spending money.
2. My partner looks after all the household's money except my personal spending money.
3. I am given a housekeeping allowance. My partner looks after the rest of the money.
4. My partner is given a housekeeping allowance. I look after the rest of the money.
5. We share and manage our household finances jointly.
6. We keep our finances completely separate.
7. Some other arrangement (specify).

In your household, who has the final say in big financial decisions?

1. Respondent has the final say.
2. Spouse/partner has the final say.
3. Both have an equal say.
4. Other (specify).

The first of these questions was also carried in the Social Change and Economic Life Initiative (SCELI) survey in 1987 (Vogler, 1989), the only other large-scale British survey data to have collected this information. When the data from these sources is compared, the similarity of distributions and apparent level of stability across time from the different

Table 3.8: Couples' money management: cross-sectional distributions (1987 to 1995), in column percentages

	SCELI			BHPS		
	1987	1991	1992	1993	1994	1995
Whole-wage	36	36	36	35	36	36
Housekeeping allowance	12	11	11	10	9	10
Shared management	50	50	50	51	52	51
Independent/other	2	3	3	4	3	3

surveys is striking (see Table 3.8). There has been little change at the aggregate level and these arrangements change very slowly over time, if at all.

The 'financial decisions' question was carried in the BHPS only (Table 3.9). The cross-sectional distributions are once again quite similar across the five-year period, although there is some slight indication of a trend away from the man having the final say towards reporting having an equal say in financial decisions.

The distributions for men and women are very similar on both the management and control questions. However, despite similarities at the aggregate level between men's and women's responses, partners do not necessarily perceive their financial arrangements in the same way as each other, with a significant proportion giving differing reports of how they manage their money. In 1991, 30% of couples did not agree about how money was managed, while 26% disagreed about who held the final say on financial decisions.

What types of changes are reported and which allocative systems are fairly stable over time can also be examined. From 1991 to 1995, the most stable of the money management arrangements were the female whole-wage and shared-management categories, with more than two

Table 3.9: Who has the final say on big financial decisions (1991 to 1995), in column percentages

	1991	1992	1993	1994	1995
Male partner	25	22	21	20	20
Female partner	9	10	10	11	10
Equal say	65	68	68	69	70
Other	1	0	1	0	0

Table 3.10: Money management transitions (1991 to 1995), in column percentages

1995 response	1991 response				
	Female whole-wage	Shared management	Male whole-wage	House-keeping allowance	Inde-pendent*
Female whole-wage	68	18	4	10	13
Shared management	26	69	35	26	49
Male whole-wage	1	6	41	14	8
Housekeeping allowance	3	5	17	47	11
Independent/other	1	2	2	2	19

* The cell sizes are small and should be interpreted with caution

thirds of respondents placing themselves in those same categories at both interview points (Table 3.10). At the other end of the spectrum, the independent managers in 1991 were the least likely to report being in the same category in 1995, with only 19% doing so. What is noticeable, for all 1991 categories, is the tendency to have moved to the shared-management category by 1995. One quarter of respondents who were in the female whole-wage category in 1991, and almost half of those who considered themselves to be independent managers in 1991, had moved to the shared-management category by 1995. On the other hand, many of those who started in the shared-management category redistributed themselves among the other answers, to maintain the stable overall distribution shown in Table 3.8.

On who has the final say on financial decisions (Table 3.11), the responses during the five-year period tend to show a shift towards the equal-say category and away from control by one or other couple member. The stability of responses suggests that respondents have a clearer idea of who controls the money in the relationship, at least where they profess to having an equal say. Of those who said they shared financial decisions with their partner in 1991, 82% gave the same response in 1995. This compares with 52% of those who said the man had the final say in 1991 and 1995 and 42% of those cases where the woman had the final say in 1991 and 1995. It may be that the relative stability of the equal-say category is partly due to the desire to present the partnership in an egalitarian light, where saying that one or other partner has the final say would be deemed socially unacceptable by the couple members (Pahl,

Table 3.11: Transitions in who has the final say on financial decisions (1991 to 1995), in column percentages

| | 1991 response | | |
1995 response	Male partner	Female partner	Equal say
Male partner	52	8	10
Female partner	6	42	7
Equal say	42	48	82

1989; Laurie, 1992). Nonetheless, where a pattern of shared financial decision making has been established, this would seem to hold over time.

Women's employment and money within the family

A number of transitions in the way people report their family's financial arrangements have become apparent during the five-year period. But is there any evidence of a systematic move towards greater equality for women in the management and control of household money as a result of their participation in paid employment? The main hypothesis is that as women enter jobs in greater numbers and gain a more permanent attachment to the labour market, the balance of power within the marital relationship will shift. Women will become less economically dependent on their male partners, which in turn will alter existing roles and gendered patterns of behaviour within the family. As well as having an impact on the distribution of unpaid work within the home, women in particular may benefit from greater equality in access to and control over money within the family as the couple moves to more egalitarian arrangements.

As Table 3.12 shows, there is a clear association between how money is organised and women's level of qualifications and current employment status. Women with higher qualifications, those who are in managerial or professional positions, and those who work full-time are more likely to share in the management of household money and to have an equal say in financial decision making.

The attitudes partners hold towards women's employment and family life would also be expected to influence women's employment participation. Attitudes held about family life and marriage would also be expected to affect how money is organised between partners. Earlier qualitative work has highlighted how couples see the sharing of money and financial decisions as tangible evidence of a healthy relationship (Laurie

Table 3.12: Money management and control, by women's education and employment characteristics (1991), in row percentages

	Shared or independent management	Woman has say in decisions
Qualifications		
Degree or better	74	85
Teaching/nursing	63	82
A/O levels	53	80
Commercial/CSE	54	70
Other	33	75
None	47	72
Occupation		
Managerial/professional	67	83
Clerical/craft	58	80
Service/sales	52	76
Other	48	77
Not employed	48	73
Usual weekly hours		
30 and above	64	84
16-29	53	74
1-16	50	75
Not employed	48	73

Note: 'Woman has say' includes women who were reported as the main decision maker, as well as those with an equal say

and Sullivan, 1991; Laurie, 1992). Couples also describe the process of organising their finances as 'evolving' over time as the relationship develops. For many couples the financial arrangements they reach are not the outcome of a conscious and concrete decision-making process but are the result of ideologies about the meaning of partnership and marriage combined with habits and patterns of behaviour that form over time (Laurie, 1992).

The BHPS carries a set of nine attitudinal questions on women's employment and family life, which can be coded to create a scale from 'traditional' to 'progressive' attitudes. Respondents are asked whether they agree or disagree with each of the following statements, using a five-point scale from strongly agree to strongly disagree (Taylor and others, 1992):

- a pre-school child is likely to suffer if his or her mother works;
- all in all, family life suffers when the woman has a full-time job;
- a woman and her family would all be happier if she goes out to work;
- both the husband and wife should contribute to the household income;
- having a full-time job is the best way for a woman to be an independent person;
- a husband's job is to earn money; a wife's job is to look after the home and family;
- children need a father to be as closely involved in their upbringing as the mother;
- employers should make special arrangements to help mothers combine jobs and childcare;
- a single parent can bring up children as well as a couple.

Each partner's answers to the attitude questions were combined to give a score that indicated whether his or her views tended to the more 'traditional' or the more 'progressive' end of the scale. One point was awarded for agreeing with each 'progressive' statement or disagreeing with a 'traditional' statement; two points were awarded if the respondent agreed or disagreed strongly. Where the answers tended to the 'traditional' view, one or two points were subtracted. Each individual scoring six or more on this scale was labelled 'progressive'; those scoring minus six or less were labelled 'traditional'. This is a fairly arbitrary device, but it is nevertheless of potential value for comparing the ideologies of partners in different circumstance. Overall:

- 29% of women in couples gave 'progressive' answers
- 6% of women in couples gave 'traditional' answers
- 19% of men in couples gave 'progressive' answers
- 10% of men in couples gave 'traditional' answers.

So both sexes tended to the 'progressive' view, although women more strongly so than men. As Table 3.13 shows, graduates (both men and women) were more 'progressively' minded than people with other qualifications, but there were not large variations among non-graduates. Women who had managerial or professional jobs were more 'progressive' than those in other occupations; among men, occupation did not seem to make any systematic difference. These variations in attitude are in the direction that might have been expected, but education and occupation do not seem to provide a very strong explanation for variations in family ideology.

Table 3.13: Proportion of men and women taking a 'progressive' attitude towards women's employment and family life, by education and occupation: couples where woman was of working age (16 to 64), in cell percentages

	Women	Men
Qualifications		
Degree or higher	49	31
Teaching/nursing	32	19
A/O levels	29	17
Commercial/CSE	20	18
Other	28	22
None	25	18
Occupation (if in work)		
Managerial/professional	41	20
Clerical/craft	35	22
Service/sales	28	21
Other	34	19

It is not clear whether a woman's decision about taking a paid job is influenced by her attitude to the principle of combining work and parenthood, or whether those who have taken a job tend to the more 'progressive' view as a result of their working experience. Either way, the association between attitude and behaviour in the first panel of Table 3.14 is very strong. More than half of women who took a traditional view, and more than half of women whose *partner* took a traditional view, were not employed at all. However, where either the woman's or the man's views tended to the 'progressive' position, more than half of the women had full-time jobs. It is interesting that the relationship was just as strong, whether it was the woman's or the man's opinion which is used as the measure of the couple's theoretical position.

There was also a clear association between couples' generally expressed views about the rights and wrongs of family life, and their reports of the financial relationships that are the central focus of this analysis (Table 3.14). Only 38% of 'traditional' women said that they used the shared management system, compared with 64% of 'progressive' women. The analysis based on the opinions of men gives similar results, although the association is not so strong. Surprisingly, though, having an equal say on big financial decisions was much less strongly associated with the measure of ideology; and it was among men, rather than women, that the link seemed more clear-cut.

Table 3.14: Women's hours of work and financial involvement, by couples' attitudes to women's employment and family life, in column percentages

	Women's attitudes			Men's attitudes		
	'Trad- itional'	Med- ium	'Pro- gressive'	'Trad- itional'	Med- ium	'Pro- gressive'
Usual weekly hours worked by wife						
30 and above	14	29	61	13	34	60
16-29	10	19	15	17	18	17
1-16	16	16	8	17	16	6
Not employed	60	36	16	53	33	16
Shared management	38	51	64	47	54	60
Equal say on financial decisions	71	74	84	67	75	85

Dynamics of money management

While the cross-sectional associations between women's work and financial involvement are clear, the question remains as to whether *changes* in women's employment, when taken together with their partner's employment circumstances, have any immediate effect on how money is organised between them. Using the panel data we can examine these issues directly. Table 3.15 gives regression results for 1991 and 1995 as predicted by the range of possible employment shifts during the five-year period. While certain shifts in women's employment during the five years appear to support the hypothesis that women who move into paid employment will be more likely to move to an egalitarian form of money management, the effect of some other moves contradicts that idea. For example, a woman moving from no paid employment into part-time employment has a positive effect on whether she shares the management of money and has a say in financial decisions in 1995. Similarly, women who move from either full-time or part-time employment to no paid employment are less likely to have egalitarian arrangements in 1995 than in 1991. On the other hand, a move for women from non-employment to full-time employment appears to have a negative effect on whether women have an equal say in financial decisions as does a shift from part-time to full-time employment, when in both cases the reverse might have

Table 3.15: Regression of shared money management and equal say in financial decisions by men's and women's employment changes: continuing couples (1991 to 1995), given as regression coefficients

	Shared money management			Equal say financial decisions		
	1991	Change	1995	1991	Change	1995
Woman's employment change						
Stays non-employed	−0.12	0.09	−0.03	−0.07	−0.03	−0.10
Moves from non-employed to part-time work	−0.13	0.19	0.06	-0.08	0.07	−0.01
Moves from non-employed to full-time work	0.04	−0.02	0.02	0.04	−0.02	0.02
Moves from part-time work to non-employed	0.12	−0.14	−0.02	−0.06	−0.04	−0.10
Stays in part-time work	−0.13	0.14	0.01	−0.05		−0.05
Moves from part-time to full-time work	−0.09	0.10	0.01	0.07	−0.02	0.05
Moves from full-time work to non-employed	0.09	−0.07	0.02	0.01	−0.02	−0.01
Moves from full-time to part-time work	0.06	0.04	0.10	0.02	−0.04	−0.02
Stays in full-time work	0.07	0.06	0.13	0.09	−0.01	0.08
Man's employment change						
Stays non-employed	0.05	−0.06	−0.01	0.00	0.08	0.08
Moves from non-employed to part-time work	−0.21	0.03	−0.18	0.04	0.01	0.05
Moves from non-employed to full-time work	0.11	−0.11	0.00	0.01	0.01	0.02
Moves from part-time work to non-employed	−0.02	−0.14	−0.16	0.05	0.02	0.07
Stays in part-time work	−0.16	0.09	−0.07	0.01	−0.06	−0.05
Moves from part-time to full-time work	−0.10	0.04	−0.06	−0.01	0.04	0.03
Moves from full-time work to non-employed	0.07	−0.05	0.02	0.02	0.00	0.02
Moves from full-time to part-time work	−0.01	−0.01	−0.02	−0.07	0.05	−0.02
Stays in full-time work	0.12	0.03	0.15	−0.16	−0.03	0.13

been expected. So the movement, in response to these relatively short-term employment changes during a five-year period, is not consistent.

The fact that the data reveals only limited responses consistent with what might be expected following a change in women's employment may be partly explained by other factors that influence whether women choose to take a job. Women with qualifications are more likely to be in paid employment and to work full-time, and it is these women who are more likely to report egalitarian arrangements in relation to money. If we accept that couples' money management may not fluctuate as a pragmatic response to immediate current circumstances, then it is likely that the process of change occurs in a more subtle way over a longer period of time.

To test these ideas, we ran two sets of regression analyses to identify the factors associated with egalitarian financial arrangements at the end of the panel period (1995). The first set ignored the answers given to the same questions four years earlier (in 1991) and can be taken as a straight analysis of current patterns. The second analysis took account of the 1991 position, and can be interpreted as painting a picture of continuity or change over the period.

These analyses are based on the woman's account of what the financial arrangements were, and included as variables the:

* woman's qualifications
* presence of dependent children
* the man's *and* the woman's attitudes to the family
* woman's employment situation across the period 1991-95 (the nine combinations used in Table 3.15).

A 'stepwise' procedure was used to identify the key variables that were most significantly associated with egalitarian management practices – that is, all the variables just listed were offered to the analysis, which selected those that provided the best fit, after allowing for the influence of each of the other variables.

The first set of calculations took no account of what the respondent had said about financial arrangements at the start of the period, and can be said to offer a general statement of the influences on couples' arrangements. The results are shown in the left-hand column of Table 3.16. The strongest effects for the management of money are, in descending order, the woman's qualifications, whether she remained in full-time employment over the relevant period, her own attitudes to family life

Table 3.16: Regression results for egalitarian money management and control (1995): continuing couples where the woman was aged 16 to 64, given as logistic regression coefficients

	Model 1	Model 2
	Ignoring 1991 answer	Taking account of 1991 answer
Shared or independent management, 1995		
Woman in full-time employment both years	0.08**	0.07**
Woman has a degree	0.20***	0.14***
Woman has 'progressive' attitudes to family life (per point)	0.01*	ns
Woman's age (per year)	–0.01*	ns
Shared management in 1991		0.41***
Equal say in financial decisions, 1995		
Woman in full-time employment 1991 and 1995	0.06*	ns
Woman non-employed 1991 and 1995	–0.06*	–0.05*
Husband has 'progressive' attitudes to family life (per point)	0.01***	0.01**
Equal say in 1991		0.42***

*	= significant at 95% confidence level
**	= significant at 99% confidence level
***	= significant at 99.9% confidence level
ns	= not significant

and her age, with older women being less likely to share the management of money. On whether the woman has a say in financial decisions, remaining in full-time employment had a positive effect while remaining out of paid employment had a negative effect. This time, it was the husband's attitudes to family life that were most closely associated with financial equity.

Model 2 controls for the reported arrangements at 1991. The contribution of the 1991 answer to a prediction of the 1995 answer indicates the extent to which couples retained the same system across the years; the (remaining) contribution of *other* predictor variables indicates the influences on change during the period. The right-hand column of Table 3.16 shows a strong effect of the established patterns for both the management of money and whether the woman has a say: couples tended to stick to the same arrangements as before. On the management of money, women in full-time employment in both years, and graduates, were more likely to move towards an egalitarian position (or less likely to move in the opposite direction). However, the woman's attitudes and age dropped out as predictors – their influence had been entirely accounted for by the starting position recorded in 1991. On the control of money, the effect of women remaining in full-time employment drops out. The continued non-employment of women has a negative effect once again while women were more likely to increase their say if their husband had 'progressive' attitudes to family life.

The implication of this analysis is that couple's allocations of responsibility for money are fairly stable (unlike the division of domestic labour discussed in the first part of this chapter). They are influenced mainly by fixed characteristics such as education, and long-term decisions on whether to work or not to work during a period of years; they do not fluctuate from year to year as women find jobs or lose them. So, while women's employment and level of qualifications are clearly a factor in determining how couples manage and control their money, changes in money management and control as a result of changes in women's employment will need to be examined over the longer term as data become available. The process of negotiation that takes place as the relationship develops, to produce either explicit or implicit agreements about how money will be handled, clearly has an enduring effect within the relationship over time. As more women develop a secure attachment to the labour market in full-time employment, we may see gradual shifts over the longer term as new patterns of money management become established. The combination of women delaying childbearing while establishing their careers with the changing patterns of partnership formation described in Chapter Two can also be expected to effect how couples organise their money. However, that will remain a question for future research.

Conclusions

In the two areas of domestic practices discussed in this chapter, it is clear that, despite the survival of more traditional patterns of behaviour, wives' movement into the workforce is associated with *some* redivision of husbands' and wives' responsibilities. Women moving into the workforce do, it appears, a somewhat lesser proportion of their households' unpaid work as a consequence, and when they move out of it the return movement is somewhat smaller. Men moving out of employment do seem to pick up some of the housework as a result. Left open, in the preceding analysis, is any discussion of the possible connections between these two processes. However, it does raise interesting issues for the study of household work strategies (Pahl, 1984).

Some aspects of women's employment patterns and status within the labour market play a significant role in predicting how money is managed and controlled within the marital relationship over time. Women who were in full-time employment during the five-year period were more likely than other women to report a shared system of management and equality in financial decisions in 1995. Women who were not employed throughout the five years were significantly less likely to report having a say in financial decisions in 1995. These findings suggest that women with a secure attachment to the labour market over time do report greater equality within their marital relationship as far as money is concerned. On the other hand, there is also evidence that where traditional gender roles exist, these continue to be a factor for women in determining their access to and control over family money. In this case, short-term changes in employment do not have immediate consequence for negotiated allocations of domestic roles.

The emergence of women into the labour force during the last third of the last century has not been without consequences for how families organise themselves internally. There are also clear traces of the impact of changing employment status on household organisation. However, we are still far from a position in which the balance between the sexes in the workplace, corresponds to the balance of work, and economic power, within the home.

References

Bittman, M. (1991) *Juggling time: How Australian families use time*, Canberra, Australia: Office of the Status of Women.

Burgoyne, C.B. and Morison, V. (1997) 'Money in remarriage: keeping things simple – and separate', *The Sociological Review*, vol 45 no 3, pp 363-95.

Crompton, R. (1989) *Occupational segregation*, SCELI Working Papers 2, Oxford: The Social Change and Economic Life Initiative, Nuffield College.

Dale, A. (1987) 'Occupational inequality, gender and life cycle', *Work, Employment and Society*, vol 1, no 3, pp 326-51.

Dex, S. (1985) *The sexual division of work*, Brighton: Wheatsheaf.

Gershuny, J. (1999) 'The work/leisure balance and the new political economy of time', Colchester: Institute for Social and Economic Research, University of Essex (mimeo).

Gershuny, J., Bittman, M. and Brice J. (1997) 'Exit, voice and suffering: do couples adapt to changing employment patterns?', *Working Papers of the ESRC Research Centre on Micro-Social Change*, 97-8, Colchester: University of Essex.

Hardhill, I., Green, A.E., Dudleston, A.C. and Owen, D.W. (1997) 'Who decides what?: decision making in dual-career households', *Work, Employment and Society*, vol 11, no 2, pp 313-26.

Hochschild, A.R. (1990) *The second shift: Working parents and the revolution at home*, London: Piatkus.

Juster, F. and Stafford, F. (1991) 'The allocation of time: empirical findings, behavioural models and problems of measurement', *Journal of Economic Literature*, vol 29, no 2, pp 411-522.

Laurie, H. (1992) 'Multiple methods in the study of household resource allocation', in J. Brannen (ed) *Mixing methods: Qualitative and quantitative research*, Aldershot: Avebury.

Laurie, H. and Sullivan, O. (1991) 'Combining qualitative and quantitative data in the longitudinal study of household allocations', *The Sociological Review*, vol 39, no 1, pp 113-30; reprinted (1992) as *Working Papers of the ESRC Research Centre on Micro-Social Change*, 92-7, Colchester: University of Essex.

Meissner, M., Humphreys, E., Meis, S. and Scheu, W. (1977) 'No exit for wives: sexual division of labour and the cummulation of household demands', *Canadian Review of Sociology and Anthropology*, vol 12, pp 424-39.

Morris, L. (1989) 'Household strategies: the individual, the collectivity and the labour market: the case of married couples', *Work, Employment and Society*, vol 3, no 4, pp 447-64.

Pahl, J. (1980) 'Patterns of money management within marriage', *Journal of Social Policy*, vol 9, no 3, pp 313-35.

Pahl, J. (1989) *Money and marriage*, Basingstoke: Macmillan Education.

Pahl, R.E. (1984) *Divisions of labour*, Oxford: Blackwell.

Taylor, M. with Brice, J., Buck, N. and Prentice, E. (1992) *British Household Panel Survey user manual, Volume B: Codebook*, Colchester: University of Essex.

Treas, J. (1993) 'Money in the bank: transaction costs and the economic organisation of marriage', *American Sociological Review*, vol 58, no 5, pp 723-34.

Vogler, C. (1989) *Labour market change and patterns of financial allocation within households*, SCELI Working Papers, 12, Oxford: The Social Change and Economic Life Initiative, Nuffield College.

Warde, A. and Hetherington, K. (1993) 'A changing domestic division of labour? Issues of measurement and interpretation', *Work, Employment and Society*, vol 7, no 1, pp 23-45.

Young, M. and Willmott, P. (1974) *The symmetrical family*, London: Routledge and Kegan Paul.

FOUR

Work, non-work, jobs and job mobility[1]

Mark Taylor

Introduction

During their working lives individuals can experience key labour market transitions, and it is these that are the focus of this chapter. Data from the first seven waves of the British Household Panel Survey and the lifetime employment and job histories are used to study changes in economic activity such as the transition from school to work, unemployment experiences and retirement. Career progression is also investigated by analysing the length of time people remain in the same job, career mobility, and transitions into and out of part-time and self-employment. By applying longitudinal data to these analyses, it is possible to identify those lifetime and job-related events that influence subsequent labour market changes – such as losing or gaining a job, or being promoted – and thus have direct policy relevance.

Although the labour market is complex, for the purpose of this study individuals' working lives are categorised into three broad stages that correspond to major life-cycle events: the transition from school to work; labour market experiences over working lives; and entering retirement. These stages do not work in isolation. However, this approach provides an analytical structure to a large and wide ranging set of issues, allowing broad patterns of labour market behaviour to be established. The first stage, concerning initial labour market experiences on leaving full-time education, for many coincides with leaving the parental home and moving away from their parents' region of residence (detailed later in Chapter Six). People leave education at different ages: some leave at 16 (at the earliest legal opportunity); others move into further education and enter the labour market at 18. It is becoming more common in Britain for individuals to remain in education longer and to attend further or higher education institutions, leaving education at the age of 21 (or perhaps older) with a degree, a diploma or other higher level qualification. Consequently, other events, such as partnership and family formation, occur on average at older ages (as detailed in Chapter Two). The first section of this chapter looks at how first labour market experiences differ by age on leaving education, and how these have changed over time.

The second stage of individuals' working lives concerns their job and career progression, including movements between labour market states and from job to job. Throughout their career individuals lose and gain jobs, move into and out of unemployment and between different types of employment (full-time, part-time or self-employment). At the same time, domestic partnerships are being formed (and possibly dissolved), families are being raised and financial responsibilities are changing. The second section of the chapter investigates job stability through examining changes in job tenure over time, and how these differ with experience. Following on from this is a section studying in detail career mobility in Britain in the 1990s by looking at promotions within a firm; it also considers the extent and determinants of such career moves. To gain a more complete picture of work experiences in Britain, it is necessary to consider movements between other labour market states. This is achieved in the next section of the chapter by studying movements between full- and part-time employment, self-employment, unemployment and non-work activities, and examining how the probability of entering these states varies across life-cycle stages.

A major concern of many Western governments in recent years has been persistently high rates of unemployment, resulting in a range of policies targeted at the unemployed in market economies worldwide. The penultimate section concentrates on unemployment experiences among men in 1990s Britain. Unemployment is strongly related to moves into poverty (see Chapter Five) and imposes a financial burden on the exchequer, so it is important for policy purposes to investigate the characteristics of those who enter unemployment and the relationship between past and current unemployment experiences. Unemployment experiences affect individuals and their families. An out-of-work adult puts additional pressures on other family members, especially if children are present. Recent research has shown an increase in both the proportion of families with no working members and where all working-age family members are employed. For example, in 1975, 4% of households were workless, compared to approaching 15% in the 1990s (see Gregg and Wadsworth, 1996). The final section investigates this in some detail by examining the work patterns of various family types and how these change year by year in the 1990s.

Having looked at the working lives of young and middle-aged people in Britain, the focus will move on to the labour market transitions of older individuals. In particular, the last major labour market transition, the entry into retirement, is considered. Retirement involves individuals withdrawing their labour from the market, by which time many financial and familial responsibilities may have eased. However, the loss of labour market earnings may also signal the entry into poverty. The retired constitute a significant and growing proportion of the population, while state retirement pensions account for some 40% of government expenditure on social security benefits (5% of GDP) (ONS, 1999, Table 10.21). The final section investigates the age at which this withdrawal occurs, and looks at transition rates into retirement from the other labour market states.

This analysis, and the life-cycle context within which it is set, provides a unique insight into the labour market experiences of men and women in Britain in the 1990s. It also provides comparisons, showing how these experiences differ from the past.

The data

Panel data

The BHPS annual questionnaire provides data on the employment status of individuals at the time of each interview. It includes information on current labour market status (full- or part-time employed, self-employed, unemployed and searching for work, retired, on maternity leave, under family care, in full-time education, on a government training scheme, or something else) and the date at which that status was entered. For those in some form of employment, data on a range of job characteristics are available. The questionnaire also includes an account of all labour market transitions occurring since the September of the previous year. This contains information on type of employment (or status if out of the labour force), spell start and end dates, occupation, industry and the reason for leaving any jobs. These rich sources of employment data, together with the household and demographic information collected at each date of interview, make the BHPS particularly important for labour market research.

Lifetime employment and job history data

At wave 2 (1992), individuals were asked to recall their lifetime employment history, detailing the start and end dates of each spell of employment (full- or part-time), self-employment, unemployment and economic inactivity experienced to date during their lifetime since first leaving full-time education. This provides rich data on individuals' employment and career trajectories. Although it is possible that these accounts suffer from problems of recall error, this problem was minimised in the BHPS by first asking respondents to reconstruct their marital and fertility histories (since these are events that are less likely to be forgotten). Developing a chronological ordering of personal histories helps individuals to recollect employment-related events.

At the wave 3 interview (conducted in 1993), individuals were asked to provide details of each employer and of each self-employment spell (employment type, industry, occupation, and why each spell was ended) providing details of each firm at which individuals have been employed. However, individuals may not be able to remember with any degree of precision details of spells experienced many years ago. Spells recorded in the early years of the work history for older members of the sample may underestimate the number of transitions and be a measure of the longer spells that are more likely to be remembered (see Elias, 1996; Paull, 1996).

Transition from full-time education to work

Until relatively recently, it has been assumed that on leaving education, young men enter full-time employment where they will spend most of their active life, while women fluctuate between periods of work and raising a family and domestic labour. However, the increasing youth unemployment of the 1970s and 1980s, the growth in non-standard forms of employment and the rise in female labour market participation have altered perceptions and expectations, and changed the employment patterns of young people. The lifetime employment histories collected at wave 2 allow analysis of individuals' first labour market experiences.

Figure 4.1 illustrates individuals' labour market status on first leaving full-time education, for different time periods. This highlights the decline in full-time employment as a first labour market destination from 90% of men and women in the 1950s and 1960s (a period of excess demand for youth labour) to one third in the 1990s. There has been a corresponding

Figure 4.1: First labour market status, by year first left full-time education

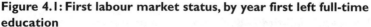

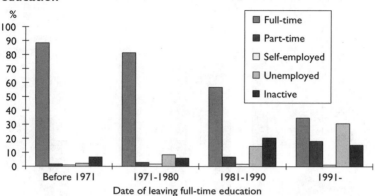

increase in the proportions exiting education to part-time employment, to being out of the labour force, and particularly to unemployment. Before 1970, less than 5% of men and women exited full-time education to unemployment. In the 1990s this has grown to almost 1 in 3[2]. Even when controlling for other observable differences between individuals, more recent cohorts have a higher probability of entering unemployment and inactivity on leaving full-time education. More recent cohorts also have a higher probability of entering part-time work and self-employment, all things being equal[3].

This increased prevalence of unemployment among new labour market entrants could have a serious impact on their future labour market career if a causal link exists between current unemployment and future labour market behaviour. For example, it is possible that previous unemployment experience increases the probability of future unemployment. Through a study of school leavers in Leeds, Banks and Jackson (1982) found evidence of a direct impact of unemployment on motivation. Those entering unemployment on leaving school tended to develop symptoms of psychological ill-health, while the psychological health of those entering work improved. Workers with a history of job mobility and unemployment incidence may be offered less secure jobs because they lose valuable work experience or human capital while unemployed, or because employers view their unemployment experience as a signal of their low productivity (Phelps, 1972; Lockwood, 1991; Pissarides, 1992; Blanchard and Diamond, 1994).

School to work transitions are important to individuals' subsequent

Figure 4.2: Estimated probability of labour market status on first leaving full-time education, by age on leaving

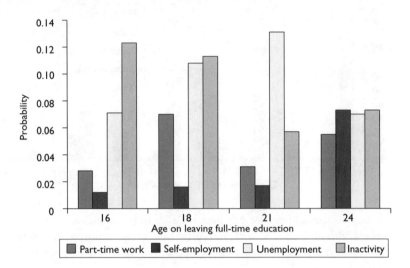

life opportunities. Decisions on whether or not to stay on at school at age 16 will have substantial effects on their accumulation of human capital and skills. Low education attainment is one mechanism through which childhood disadvantage is translated into poor social and economic opportunities (Gregg and Machin, 1997; Feinstein, 1998). Research suggests that education, both directly and through its impact on occupational status, has effects on economic wellbeing that last into retirement (Crystal and others, 1992).

To examine how subsequent labour market status varies with age on leaving full-time education, Figure 4.2 shows the predicted probabilities of men and women being observed in a particular state, controlling for other observable characteristics[4]. Predicted probabilities are given for the most common ages for leaving full-time education: age 16, 18, 21 and 24. The probability of entering self-employment on leaving education increases almost continuously with age of leaving education, with those leaving at age 24 being four times more likely to enter self-employment than those leaving at 16. Individuals leaving education at the age of 18 are three times more likely to enter part-time work than those leaving at age 16. However, entering tertiary education would appear to reduce this probability by about one half.

There is an equally noticeable increase in the probability of entering unemployment as the school leaving age increases, from 7% when leaving school at 16, to 13% among those leaving at 21. Although this relationship may appear counter-intuitive, it should be remembered that these plots do not explore the reasons for unemployment or unemployment duration. Individuals leaving the education system at a later age may be more selective in their job search, or may be unemployed for a relatively short time compared to those leaving at an earlier age. The proportion of young people remaining out of the labour force on leaving full-time education is highest for school leavers aged 16 or 18 years. Those remaining in tertiary education have relatively low rates of economic inactivity, as would be predicted by economic theory. Such individuals have an increased incentive to seek a return on their investment in education and to be active in the labour market on leaving education.

These figures have emphasised the recent growth in part-time work, self-employment, unemployment and economic inactivity relative to full-time employment among men and women leaving full-time education. The transition from education into employment is becoming increasingly uncertain, with more men and women experiencing unemployment before entering full-time work for the first time. This may have implications for their psychological wellbeing, their future careers and their life chances. The increasing prevalence of non-standard work forms, such as part-time and self-employment, is an illustration of the changing structure of the British labour market, with the decline in the availability of full-time permanent employment. It may also reflect the changes in labour supply, with the increase in female labour market participation associated with an increase in the availability of part-time work.

Having entered work, individuals experience different patterns of labour market mobility and success. These depend on factors such as their education, gender, personal ambition and motivation, family environment and macroeconomic conditions. The subsequent sections focus in detail on these issues, starting with how individuals' jobs and careers progress.

Job tenure in Britain

The previous section highlighted the increasingly uncertain and complex transition from school to work for more recent cohorts. Have jobs also become more unstable for recent labour market entrants? The decline in the average length of time people remain in the same job (typically known as job tenure) in Britain has been well documented from cross-sectional sources (Gregg and Wadsworth, 1995; Burgess and Rees, 1996). This section investigates changes in job tenure over time and how these changes differ across individuals' careers, using the lifetime job histories collected at wave 3 of the BHPS. These histories do not collect information on within-employer promotions, and so job tenure is compared for those who leave jobs because of quits, layoffs and/or other reasons. A rather narrow definition of 'quits' is used, referring to changes to better or different jobs, while 'layoffs' include both dismissals and redundancies. Leaving a job for 'other reasons' covers termination of contract, ill-health, retirement, pregnancy, family care, national service and full-time education. As previously, analysis is conducted separately for men and women[5].

Booth, Francesconi and Garcia-Serrano (1999) show that quitting is the main reason for terminating the first job for both men and women. This accords well with job-shopping theory (Stigler, 1962), with young workers more likely to sample a variety of jobs to acquire knowledge about the labour market and their own tastes, implying high quit rates in early jobs. Quitting remains the principal reason for all subsequent job terminations for men, but the main cause for women leaving subsequent jobs is other reasons (most of which are pregnancies and family care). Layoffs become increasingly important as a reason for job termination for men as the number of jobs grows. Gender differences exist in the propensities to quit a job and be laid off, with men more likely to quit from any job than women, and almost twice as likely to be laid off.

Examining the relative risks of leaving the first and fifth job for men and women, by reason for exit and date of entry into the labour market will help reveal whether more recent labour market entrants experience different job tenure patterns. Those in their first job are at the beginning of their careers, while those in their fifth job are more advanced, so focusing on these two groups will show job tenure at different stages of labour market experience. There are a number of reasons why more recent cohorts might be expected to have different job tenure profiles than earlier cohorts. For example, earlier cohorts of women may have been more likely to have left a job for family-related reasons, whereas improved childcare facilities at work and the increased availability of part-time work and jobsharing make combining a career and family responsibilities easier for recent cohorts. Increased labour market flexibility and deregulation are likely to have had an impact on job tenure. The weakening of employment protection has made it easier for firms to lay off workers (Booth, 1995). Recent years have also seen an acceleration in the rate of technological change, which may render obsolete certain skills held by

Figure 4.3: Risk of leaving first job through quit, layoff and other exit, by labour market entry cohort: men

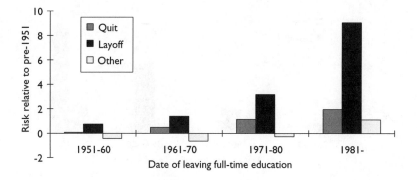

older members of the workforce. There has also been a rapid growth in the proportion of small firms in Britain, and jobs may last a shorter time in small firms.

Figures 4.3, 4.4, 4.5 and 4.6 quantify the effects of date of entry into the labour market on the likelihood of the job terminating due to quitting, being laid off, or for other reasons, in comparison to those who entered the labour market prior to 1951[6]. Figure 4.3 focuses on first job tenure for men, and shows that first jobs are less likely to terminate for other reasons for men entering the labour market between 1951 and 1980 than for those entering before 1951. However, first jobs started since 1950 are more likely to be terminated by quits and layoffs than those before 1951, and the size of these effects has increased for the most recent cohorts. Men entering the labour market since 1980 are twice as likely to quit and nine times more likely to be laid off from their first job than those entering the labour market before 1951. It is likely that these estimates suffer from recall error, with earlier cohorts perhaps omitting short spells experienced many years ago. However, the comparison between even the two most recent cohorts is striking.

Figure 4.4 looks at the effects of labour market entry cohort on first job duration for women. Women entering the labour market since 1950 are more likely to leave their first job for any reason than those entering before 1951. In particular, women leaving education since 1980 are five times more likely to be laid off from their first job than those leaving before 1951. The date of entry into the labour market is an important determinant of all forms of job termination for men and women. The

Figure 4.4: Risk of leaving first job through quit, layoff and other exit, by labour market entry cohort: women

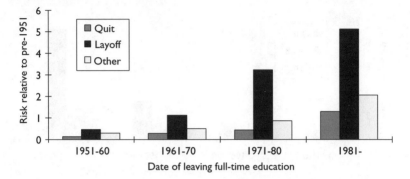

Date of leaving full-time education

more recent the entrant to the labour market, the more likely the first job is to end. It is noticeable that for the most recent cohort (those leaving education since 1980) the pattern for men is similar to that for women.

Figures 4.5 and 4.6 focus on the effect of the date of labour market entry on fifth job tenure by reason for exit for men and women, providing some comparisons among people further into their working lives. The patterns revealed in these pictures are similar to those in the first job, with the fifth jobs of more recent cohorts being more likely to end for any reason compared with those leaving education before 1951. If anything, the magnitude of the risks is larger by the time of the fifth job than for the first. However, job termination among men and women is much more comparable across all cohorts by the time of the fifth job, with men more likely to exit into non-market activities. These figures show that the probability of leaving a job for any reason has been increasing consistently across labour market entry cohorts, indicating a decline in the average length of jobs. The main cause of this is the large increase in the likelihood of being laid off. Being able to distinguish reasons for job termination is important, allowing comparison between worker-initiated and employer-initiated separations.

A number of important results have emerged from this analysis. The date of first leaving full-time education is an important determinant of all forms of job termination for men and women. The more recent the labour market entrant, the more likely the job is to end for any reason.

An important related issue is whether shorter jobs are associated with higher wages as compensation for greater flexibility, or whether such jobs tend to be concentrated at the lower end of the earnings distribution.

Figure 4.5: Risk of leaving fifth job through quit, layoff and other exit, by labour market entry cohort: men

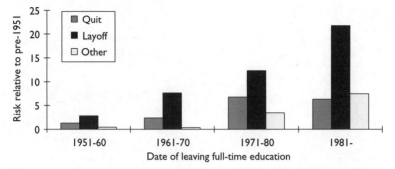

Date of leaving full-time education

Figure 4.6: Risk of leaving fifth job through quit, layoff and other exit, by labour market entry cohort: women

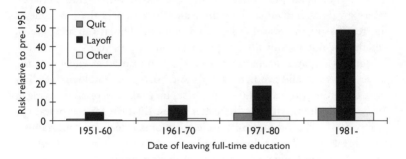

Date of leaving full-time education

This will clearly have an impact on the observed earnings inequality in Britain, and is an important avenue for future research. The analysis in this section has focussed only on inter-firm mobility, which accounts for just 60% of total labour turnover. To gain a complete picture of career progression in Britain, the next section uses panel data to examine promotions within the same employer.

Promotions in the 1990s

Little is known about patterns of career mobility in Britain, although Francesconi (1999) shows that promotions are an important source of wage growth and job satisfaction for both men and women. This section uses BHPS panel data to examine the extent of such career moves in the

Figure 4.7: Promotion rates by age

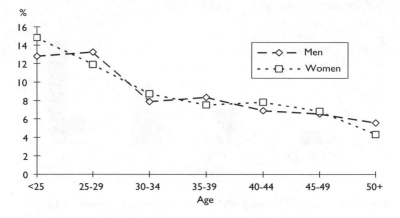

1990s[7]. For each job ended during the 12-month period between interview dates, individuals give the reason for stopping the job. One of the reasons on the available list is promotion. This is our measure of whether or not an individual is promoted in a given year.

Figure 4.7 graphs promotion rates by age measured at entry into the survey for men and women in full- and part-time employment. For men, the promotion rate initially increases up to the age of 30 (peaking at 14%) and declines with age thereafter to less than 6% for the oldest age group, 50+. The promotion profile for women declines continuously with age from 15% for those aged below 25, to 4% for the oldest age group. This figure suggests that promotion rates among men and women are very similar. This could in part reflect the sample selection criteria: individuals of working age and for whom the BHPS has at least two years of labour market data. This ensures that the individuals are at least fairly strongly attached to the labour market.

To investigate the frequency with which promotions occur, Figure 4.8 shows the distribution of the career status of men and women one year after experiencing a promotion. It shows, for example, that more than 60% of those promoted one year ago are in the same job with the same employer, one year later. This indicates a considerable amount of career stability. However, the figure also reveals that one in five men and women who have been promoted are again promoted in the following year. Less than 10% of those experiencing a promotion quit employment in the following year, while only 5% are laid off. Again promotion experiences of men and women appear very similar in the 1990s.

Figure 4.8: Career status in year following a promotion

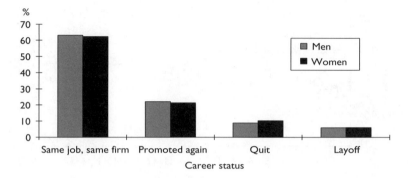

These analyses have not examined the determinants of promotion. Booth and Francesconi (1997) and Francesconi (1999) study this in some detail. They find that the probability of promotion is higher than average for both married men and married women, those with more previous work experience and longer tenure with the employer, and for those in professional, managerial and skilled non-manual occupations. The relationship between skill and promotion rates is consistent with the hypothesis that more educated workers face greater career opportunities or longer career ladders (Sicherman and Galor, 1990). Part-time work and employment in smaller workplaces are associated with lower promotion probabilities. Part-time jobs may offer greater flexibility and lesser time demands, but also offer fewer career opportunities (Preston, 1998). Interestingly, their results suggest that promotion is positively correlated with effort (measured by working longer overtime hours).

To illustrate this, Figure 4.9 plots the predicted probability of promotion by weekly overtime hours worked[8]. This figure shows that the probability of promotion is about 7% for men and women who work zero overtime hours. It is clear that a small increase in weekly overtime hours from zero results in a large jump in the predicted probability of promotion. For example, working just three hours of overtime a week increases the predicted probability of promotion by nearly 50% (from 7% to approaching 11%). For men, the probability remains relatively constant thereafter, and does not rise above 12%. For women, the increase is sustained, and the probability of promotion is almost 19% for those working 20 overtime hours per week. If overtime is a proxy for effort, then this is consistent with the hypothesis that firms reward the most hardworking employees.

This analysis of intra-firm mobility using the panel data has usefully

Figure 4.9: Probability of promotion, by overtime hours

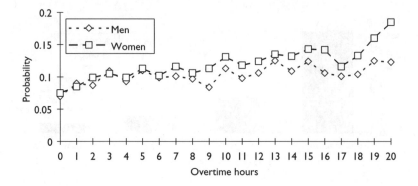

complemented the previous work using the lifetime history data. Internal promotions are strongly related to both monetary payoffs (higher wages and wage growth on promotion) and non-monetary rewards (reflected in higher job satisfaction among promoted workers). It is important to understand the incidence and determinants of promotions to obtain a more complete description of mobility in the labour market. The gender differences in the incidence of promotion are surprisingly small. This contradicts the common belief that women are promoted less frequently than men. The largest effect on the probability of promotion is through the effort put into a job (measured by working longer overtime hours). The greater the effort in the job, the higher the chances of promotion. This is of policy interest, given that workers in Britain on average work longer hours than those in the rest of Europe.

Labour market transitions

The previous sections have explored job and career mobility. However, to gain a complete picture of the state of the labour market, it is necessary to consider movements between other states. Are, for example, part-time employment and self-employment transitory states for men and women, acting as stepping stones between economic inactivity and full-time employment? Given the large increase in the female labour market participation rate, are women adopting traditionally male patterns of full-time employment, and more men adopting traditionally female patterns of economic inactivity and part-time work?

Five labour supply choices will be considered: full-time employment, part-time employment, self-employment, unemployment, and out of the labour force. The distribution of the sample across the five labour market states and six waves of data reflect economy-wide trends. Approximately 60% of working-age men in Britain are in full-time employment, 3% in part-time employment and 15% in self-employment. Nearly 20% of working-age men in Britain are in these two forms of 'non-standard' employment (part-time workers or self-employed)[9]. Approximately 6% are unemployed and a further 16% are economically inactive. About two thirds of the non-employed working-age men are not looking for a job. These proportions reflect the recent decline in employment and inactivity rates among working-age men, a well documented feature of the contemporary labour market (see, for example, Gregg and Wadsworth, 1998; Campbell, 1999).

About 40% of working-age women are in full-time employment, nearly one in four are in part-time employment and a further 5% in self-employment – approaching 30% of working-age women in Britain are in these 'non-standard' employment forms. Unemployment averages at less than 5% for women, while some 26% are economically inactive. In contrast with men, female employment has risen dramatically in recent years, with a corresponding fall in economic inactivity and little change in unemployment. However, women are still less likely than men to be in paid work.

These proportions do not illustrate the extent of flexibility in the sense of transitions between employment states. This can be examined by analysing the two wave average transition matrices for the five states, shown in Table 4.1. The principal diagonal of each panel in the table shows the degree of persistence in each labour market state in terms of the proportion who remain in the same state at two consecutive interview dates.

The table reveals a large amount of persistence in labour market status. Men exhibit a greater attachment to full-time employment and self-employment than women, whereas women exhibit a greater attachment to part-time employment than men. Working full-time is the most persistent state for both men and women. While this is unsurprising, the data also highlights considerable persistence for both men and women in self-employment and economic inactivity, and for women in part-time employment. Men are more mobile when it comes to leaving part-time employment. Unemployment is the least stable state, with only 46% of men and 27% of women unemployed at two consecutive waves. However,

Table 4.1: Labour market transition probabilities, by gender, in column percentages

| | Wave t | | | | |
Wave t+1	Full-time	Part-time	Self-employed	Unemployed	Out of the labour force
Men					
Full-time	92	35	7	29	6
Part-time	1	40	1	5	3
Self-employed	2	3	87	9	2
Unemployed	3	7	3	46	7
Out of the labour force	2	15	3	13	83
Women					
Full-time	87	12	5	18	4
Part-time	6	74	8	23	8
Self-employed	1	2	74	4	2
Unemployed	2	3	3	27	7
Out of the labour force	4	9	10	29	80

the flows into full-time work from unemployment are substantially greater for men than women.

To investigate how the likelihood of experiencing 'non-standard' forms of employment varies across life-cycle stages, Table 4.2 shows the predicted probabilities of being in part-time work and self-employment by age and number of children, for men and women[10]. The first two panels of the table focus on the probability of part-time employment, and reveal that this is substantially higher for women than men at all life-cycle stages. For men, the highest probability of part-time work is 6% for those below the age of 25 with no children. The probability of part-time work is relatively constant across all ages, although it is smallest for those men aged 35 to 44. In contrast, for women the probability of part-time work is strongly correlated with both age and the number of children. Women with two children, for example, are twice as likely to be in part-time work at all ages than those with no children. Similarly, women aged 45 to 54 are twice as likely to be in part-time work than those aged below 25. Women aged below 25 with no children have the smallest probability of part-time work at 10%, while those aged 35 to 44 with three or more

Table 4.2: Probability of working part-time or being self-employed, by age and number of children (1991 to 1996), in cell percentages

	Age <25	Age 25-34	Age 35-44	Age 45-54
Men in part-time work				
No children	6.0	2.6	1.6	2.0
I child	2.9	1.7	1.2	1.8
2 children	2.6	1.6	1.3	2.1
3 or more children	2.7	1.8	1.5	2.1
Women in part-time work				
No children	10	11	17	24
I child	16	23	29	33
2 children	18	33	39	41
3 or more children	10	31	42	41
Men in self-employment				
No children	7	11	15	20
I child	8	14	18	22
2 children	8	15	20	25
3 or more children	6	16	22	25
Women in self-employment				
No children	2.0	3.4	5.8	6.7
I child	1.5	4.9	6.8	7.8
2 children	1.2	4.6	7.6	8.9
3 or more children	0.4	3.0	6.4	6.7

Source: Author's own calculations based on multinomial logit analysis of labour market status, BHPS waves 1-6

children have the highest (at 42%). It would seem that part-time work is a response to labour supply preferences of women with children, enabling them to combine family care with paid employment.

The final two sections of Table 4.2 focus on the probability of self-employment by age and the number of children. After the age of 25, men with three children are consistently five percentage points more likely to be in self-employment than those with no children. Men aged between 45 and 54 are three times more likely to be self-employed than those aged below 25. Women are noticeably less likely to be in self-employment (for all categories) and, interestingly, there appears to be little correlation between the probability of self-employment and the number of children for women. Women appear to use part-time work rather than self-employment as a flexible response to combining childcare and labour market participation.

The transition matrix has revealed the extent to which there is persistence in labour market states and mobility between states across the period 1991-96. Female part-time work is not a transitory state between economic inactivity and full-time work. Men exhibit more flexibility than women between the states of full-time and part-time work, while self-employment is a more stable state for men than for women.

Part-time employment is much more probable for women, especially older women with more children, indicating that family responsibilities remain an important determinant of women's labour supply choices, and have a much smaller impact on men's participation decisions. Self-employment is more likely among men, and again is positively correlated with age and the number of children. It may be that self-employment and part-time employment are the means by which men and women respectively remain active in the labour market, while maintaining enough flexibility to provide care for their children.

Unemployment experiences

This chapter has so far studied in some detail the transition from education to work, the job and career mobility of those in employment, and transitions between labour market states. However, no study of the labour market is complete without detailed examination of unemployment, perhaps the most observable misallocation of economic resources. Stephen Jenkins notes in Chapter Five that moves into poverty often coincide with job loss. The discussion above on transitions from education to work has shown that an increasing proportion of young people are experiencing unemployment, while the analysis of job tenure has revealed that more recent cohorts have a higher probability of being laid off. The impact of these experiences, and information on the characteristics of individuals prone to unemployment, is important for policy purposes.

Unemployment in Britain has remained relatively high despite falling during the 1990s. The BHPS data shows that 54% of working-age men in unemployment at the interview date at a particular wave are unemployed at the date of interview one year later. For working-age men employed at the date of interview at a particular wave, the probability of unemployment at the date of interview one year later is less than 3% (Arulampalam and others, 2000). Despite falling unemployment rates, it is clear that the persistence of unemployment remains a problem. This may be because some individuals have inherent characteristics that make them more likely to experience unemployment, or it may be due to a causal link between past and current unemployment. Arulampalam and others (2000) investigate these issues by estimating dynamic panel data models of unemployment incidence; they find evidence of a strong causal relationship between past and current unemployment among men.

To illustrate this, Figure 4.10 shows the predicted probability of being unemployed by highest educational qualification and labour market status one year ago[11]. This clearly highlights the relationship between past and current unemployment, even when controlling for a large range of personal and labour market characteristics. Men educated to degree level or above, and who were employed at the date of interview at wave *t–1*, have a very small probability (less than 1%) of being unemployed at the date of interview at wave *t*. However, similarly educated men who were in unemployment at wave *t–1* have a 20% chance of still being unemployed at the date of interview at wave t^{12}. Moving down the qualification levels, the probability of unemployment increases as expected for both those in employment and in unemployment one year previously. For men with no qualifications and who were employed at wave *t–1*, the probability of unemployment has increased to about 4%, still relatively small. However, for men with no qualifications who were unemployed at wave *t–1*, the probability of unemployment at wave *t* has increased to approaching 60%, three times the probability for men educated to degree standard. That is, 6 out of 10 men with no qualifications who were unemployed one year previously are predicted to be again unemployed one year on.

There are many possible causes for such a causal relationship between past and present unemployment. Past unemployment experiences may change preferences that help to determine current unemployment (Heckman and Borjas, 1980). Alternatively, firms may judge workers' productivity by their past history of unemployment. As mentioned previously, a worker with a history of moving between jobs and of unemployment incidence may be offered less secure jobs as their unemployment experience is used as a signal by employers that they are of low productivity (Phelps, 1972; Lockwood, 1991; Pissarides, 1992; Blanchard and Diamond, 1994). Also workers may lose valuable work experience or human capital while unemployed, preventing them from securing more stable employment. Individuals in unemployment may lower their reservation wage as they search for work and are therefore more likely to accept poorer quality jobs that are more likely to be destroyed.

This relationship between past and present unemployment has important implications for policy. It suggests that policies aimed at reducing short-

Figure 4.10: Probability of being unemployed, by highest qualification and labour market status one year ago: men

run unemployment will also have longer-term implications by reducing the equilibrium unemployment rate. It also implies that unstable early years in the labour market, and an exposure to unemployment at a young age (which is becoming more common) could have repercussions for an individual's career.

This discussion has highlighted considerable persistence in unemployment among men in Britain in the 1990s. A strong causal relationship exists between past and future unemployment experiences among men. This is consistent with the scarring theory of unemployment – an individual's previous unemployment experience has implications for his future labour market behaviour. This finding has important policy implications, as it suggests that there is scope for intervention in the labour market to alter the equilibrium unemployment rate. It suggests that policies reducing short-term unemployment incidence for adult British men will have longer-run effects by reducing the natural rate. Also employment instability, particularly in the early years of a career, could have far-reaching repercussions.

Working and non-working families

Until now, this chapter has considered the labour market careers of individuals in Britain. However, it is likely that to some extent the decision to enter the labour market is made at the family level; the labour market success of individuals clearly has repercussions for other family members. Members of the household may make collective decisions to maximise their joint life-prospects by specialising in particular activities (Pahl, 1984) resulting in some interdependence in husband and wife labour supply decisions. This section examines participation in work at the family level, investigating the labour supply decisions of families and how these change year on year. Rather than look at the number of hours a family supplies to the labour market, the focus instead is on the number of earners present in each family.

Recent research has shown that twice as many households are out of work in the 1990s compared with the 1970s. It is estimated that 15% of the working-age population now resides in jobless households (Gregg and Wadsworth, 1996). There has also been an increase in the number of households where *all* members are in work over the same period. This polarisation in work has resulted in the media referring to 'work-rich' households with two or more working members, and 'work-poor' households with no working members. It is likely that this change in distribution of work across households has contributed to the increase in income inequality in Britain in recent years (Gregg and Wadsworth, 1996; Jarvis and Jenkins, 1998). This position is self-perpetuating in that work-rich households almost exclusively live in their own homes and therefore benefit from an appreciating asset. Work-poor households are increasingly marginalised into social housing, from which it is difficult to escape (see Chapter Six for further details).

Figure 4.11 illustrates the distribution of work across working-age families[13]. This shows, for example, that two thirds of single adults are in work, compared with only one in four single-parent families. This illustrates the problems that lone parents have in entering employment, and helps to explain the high prevalence of poverty among single-parent families (see Chapter Five). There is a much smaller difference in the distribution of work across couples with and without children[14]. Both husband and wife are working in almost one half of couples without children, while in a further 40% either the man or the woman is in work. Less than 15% of couples are without work. Although this may appear low, Gregg and Wadsworth (1996) report that as recently as 1975, less than 4% of two-adult households were without work[15]. Both husband and wife are working in a smaller proportion of couples with children (44%), although there is a higher proportion in which either the man or woman is working (45%).

The real interest in examining the distribution of work among families lies in transitions between the states of work and non-work. Tables 4.3 and 4.4 present these transition probabilities for single-adult families and couples respectively[16]. These tables reveal differences in transition rates between single-person families and couples, and also between those with

Figure 4.11: Distribution of work across families

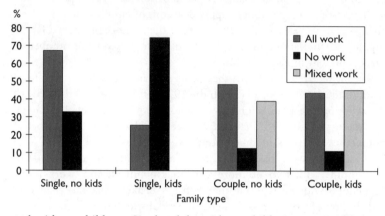

and without children. Single adults without children are more likely to remain in work than lone parents (91% compared with 82%) and are also more likely to enter work if not working (24% compared with 6%). Single-adult families without children are four times more likely to enter work in a 12-month period than lone parents. Not only are lone-parent families much less likely to be in work than single-adult families, they are less likely to both remain in work or to enter work if not in employment (see Chapter Five for details of poverty among lone parents). Iacovou and Berthoud (2000) report that the strongest positive influence on the probability of a lone parent entering employment is finding a partner with a job.

The presence of children has little impact on the work status of couples where both are in work (Table 4.4). For example, for couples without children where both are in work in a given year, 86% are still both in work in the subsequent year, 13% have one individual in employment and less than 1% have become 'work-poor' families with no employed adult. The corresponding proportions for couples with children are 84%, 15% and less than 1% respectively. There are rather larger differences between couples with and without children where one adult is in work, or both are out of work. In childless couples with one working adult in a given year, 11% become dual income couples, 8% move to the other extreme and become jobless couples while the other 81% remain couples with one earner. Contrast this with similar couples with children, in which 18% become dual income couples and 6% become couples without an earner.

Some 85% of childless couples with no earners remain in the same situation in the following year, while in 12% of cases one adult finds a job

Table 4.3: Work status transition probabilities for single-adult families, in column percentages

	Wave t	
Wave t+1	Working	Not working
Without children		
Working	91	24
Not working	9	76
With children		
Working	82	6
Not working	18	94

Note: Percentages shown are the average of five two-year transition matrices

Table 4.4 Work status transition probabilities for couples, in column percentages

	Wave t		
Wave t+1	All working	Mixed working	None working
Without children			
All working	86	11	3
Mixed working	13	81	12
None working	1	8	85
With children			
All working	84	18	6
Mixed working	15	76	25
None working	1	6	69

Note: Percentages shown are the average of five two-year transition matrices

and in 3% both enter work. These transition rates are noticeably higher for couples with children, among which 25% become single earner couples and 6% dual income couples. It would appear that couples with children have a more unstable family work status than childless couples, although much of this is caused by an additional earner rather than losing an earner[17]. Iacovou and Berthoud (2000) find that both men and women in workless couples with children are much more likely to move into work if their partner also moved into work, suggesting some interdependence or complementarity between husband and wife's labour supply decisions. This may arise due to the benefit system, with the threat of withdrawal of means–tested benefits, or because the enjoyment of leisure requires the input of both partners.

This section has provided some information on the labour supply of families in Britain in the 1990s. Recent debate has focused on the rise in the proportion of dual income and jobless families at the expense of the traditional single earner couple. Although data from the BHPS does not provide sufficient years of data to examine this trend, it does allow an analysis of transitions between dual income couples, single earner couples and jobless couples, and the impact of children on these transitions.

The analysis has described the stark differences in the labour supply of single childless adults and lone-parent families, and in their transitions between work and non-work, highlighting the disadvantages that lone parents have in the labour market. Couples with children appear to have a more flexible labour supply than childless couples, possibly caused by one parent returning to the labour market as dependent children become older and start school.

Retirement

The transition from employment into retirement typically signals the final labour market activity of an individual. Advances in technology might be expected to extend working lives through negating the impact of ageing at the workplace. Despite this, recent trends in both Britain and the US suggest that, among men, this transition is occurring on average at an earlier age (Tanner, 1997, 1998; Blundell and Johnson, 1998; Gruber and Wise, 1999), and this section provides some stylised facts associated with the retirement decision. There are two aspects to the decision to retire: the first concerns when (and how much) to reduce the amount of labour supplied to the market, and the second concerns when to start drawing on the pension rights accumulated during the working life. Many individuals may not face a retirement 'choice', but be forced into it through ill-health or a lack of employment opportunities. Possible explanations for earlier withdrawal from the labour market include occupational pension schemes or reduced labour supply (suggesting voluntary withdrawal), or shifts in relative demand for labour against older men, or against the skills embodied in older men, and age discrimination (suggesting involuntary withdrawal).

To examine labour market withdrawal of older men and women, Figure 4.12 plots the probability of entering retirement by age for men and women aged 55 and above at wave 1. These probabilities are conditional on individuals' being in employment (full-time, part-time or self-employment) in the previous year. For men, the probability of entering

Figure 4.12: Probability of entering retirement, by age

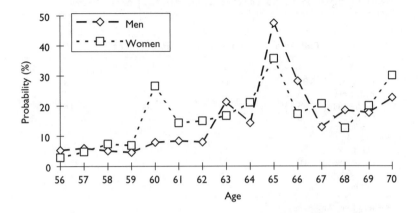

retirement remains constant at 5% to the age of 59, indicating that 1 in 20 men in work retire each year between the ages of 56 and 59. This doubles between the ages of 60 and 62, and increases to more than 20% by the age of 63. As would be expected, a large increase occurs at the age of 65, with nearly 50% of men in work retiring at this age. After the statutory retirement age, the probability drops to 13% by the age of 67 before increasing again. For women, a similar pattern emerges with the probability of retiring reaching 27% at the age of 60. Interestingly, the probability of entering retirement among women is also highest at the age of 65, at 35%.

To investigate transitions between retirement and other labour market states, six waves of panel data are used, focusing on the cohort of men and women approaching retirement age at wave 1. In particular, subsequent analysis focuses on individuals aged 55-60 at wave 1, who will be aged 61-66 at wave 6. Table 4.5 examines transitions between full-time and part-time employment, retirement and other labour market states for men and women. The figures in each cell show the percentage of transitions from the origin to destination state (column percentages). These show a high level of stability in labour market status among those aged 55-60 at wave 1, particularly among the retired. Approaching 85% of those retired at a given date of interview remain in retirement at the subsequent wave. There is a relatively large inflow into retirement from other non-employment states for both sexes, while a similar proportion enter retirement from full-time employment as from part-time work in a given year. There is little evidence suggesting that men or women remove

Table 4.5: Labour market transition probabilities: men and women aged 55 to 60 at wave 1, in column percentages

| | Year t | | | |
Year t+1	Full-time	Part-time	Retirement	Other
Men				
Full-time	82	16	1	3
Part-time	4	67	2	2
Retirement	8	10	84	18
Other	6	7	12	77
Women				
Full-time	74	5	*	*
Part-time	10	77	3	4
Retirement	14	15	82	31
Other	2	4	15	65

* = less than 0.5%

themselves from full-time work to part-time work as a step towards eventual retirement; the transition rates from full-time to part-time work are low.

Analysis of the determinants of being in retirement relative to employment of any type highlights a number of interesting relationships[18]. Retirement is positively related with education attainment for men, suggesting that highly qualified men retire at earlier ages. Education has no predictive power for women. Having a health condition that limits the type or amount of work possible increases the probability of retirement for both men and women, as does home ownership without a mortgage. However, by far the most powerful predictor of retirement for both men and women is age, with the probability of retirement increasing continuously with age. By the age of 65, almost all men and women are, and are predicted to be, in retirement. There is a large increase in the probability of retirement for women between the ages 59 and 60, and between the ages 64 and 65 for both men and women. About 45% of women are in retirement by the age of 60, compared with 20% of men. Almost 80% of men are in retirement by the age of 65. The relationship with age is not surprising, and reflects ill-health and labour demand effects, as well as legal and institutional factors.

Analysis of the probability of retiring from work has shown the expected increases at the statutory retirement ages. The transition rate into retirement is similar among full-time and part-time workers aged 55-60 in 1991 for both men and women. The data does not support the hypothesis that withdrawal from the labour market is a gradual process. Multivariate analysis confirms that retirement is an increasing function of age, and also of poor health for both men and women. Education attainment is an important predictor of retirement for men but not for women.

Given the large proportion of government expenditure accounted for by retirement pensions, the retirement patterns of ageing members of the labour force have public expenditure implications. Despite early retirement becoming more common and mortality rates falling, age remains the most important predictor of retirement. This finding is significant for the reform of pension policies and the reduction of public expenditure.

Conclusions

This chapter has studied changes in economic activity and job and career mobility in Britain using panel and retrospective lifetime history data from the BHPS. It has examined the important labour market transitions that individuals experience as their career and lives develop, as well as the working decisions of families. Some interesting and important patterns emerge from this analysis of the transition from full-time education into the labour market, job changes and career progression, movements between full-time, part-time, self-employment, unemployment and economic inactivity and retirement.

A common theme throughout this analysis is the increasingly uncertain nature of the British labour market in the 1990s. A larger proportion of men and women in recent cohorts do not enter full-time employment on leaving education. Instead, increasing proportions are entering part-time or self-employment. On leaving education for the first time, one in three now enter unemployment. This should be of particular concern given that strong causal links between past and future unemployment appear to exist among men throughout their working life. The declining job tenure also reflects this escalating instability. More recent cohorts have, on average, shorter job tenure than older cohorts. They are also more likely to be laid off from their jobs.

Some commentators are concerned that more transitions are associated with less human capital investment, and low quality short-term jobs. This has repercussions for the motivation and wellbeing of workers in such jobs. High levels of turnover and job instability could imply an increasing number of dead-end jobs with poor pay and career prospects, or it could be a means through which workers secure more stable and rewarding employment. It may also imply greater levels of employment and geographical mobility, with individuals being willing and able to relocate to areas of greater labour demand. Increased turnover in the labour market may mean that workers are continually searching for new employment that better suits their skills and requirements, and as such could be indicative of a healthy economy. This would appear to be a natural direction in which to concentrate future labour market research.

Notes

[1] This chapter summarises research undertaken by and in collaboration with ISER colleagues René Böheim, Alison Booth, Marco Francesconi and Stephen Jenkins.

[2] There are small differences between men and women. Men have a slightly higher probability of entering self-employment and unemployment across the cohorts, while women are more likely to enter part-time work and inactivity. However, these differences are not large. Although it is likely that recall error will bias downwards the proportions entering unemployment from education in older cohorts, other sources confirm that the proportion of individuals whose initial experience of the labour market is unemployment has been continuously increasing since the 1950s (see, for example, Junankar, 1987).

[3] Multivariate analysis suggests that the probability of entering unemployment on leaving education has increased from 4% for the 1960s cohort to more than 16% for the1980s cohort. The increases in the probabilities of entering inactivity and part-time work are of similar magnitude. This is allowing for differences in gender, ethnicity, unemployment rates, date of labour market entry and parents' occupation.

[4] These probabilities are calculated from multinomial logit analysis of first labour market status using the lifetime employment histories. The models also control for gender, ethnicity, and unemployment rates in the year of labour market entry and parents' occupation.

[5] Analysis excludes self-employment. Details of self-employment experiences in Britain and the determinants of the length of self-employment spells can be found in Taylor (1996, 1997, 1999).

[6] These figures are based on Cox proportional hazard model estimates published in Booth, Francesconi and Garcia-Serrano (1999), where further information and details on the procedure and results can be found. The estimation controls

for age at job start, ethnicity, the unemployment rate in the year of job termination, and industry and occupation of employment.

[7] This section draws on work by Booth and Francesconi (1997) and Francesconi (1999), and the reader is referred to these papers for further and more detailed discussion.

[8] This figure is based on multinomial logit results presented in Booth and Francesconi (1997). The model also controls for marital status, number of children, region, previous work experience, tenure, union membership and coverage, part-time work, public sector work, firm size, occupation and the unemployment rate.

[9] This is an underestimate of the proportion of men in 'non-standard' forms of employment. For example, those in temporary work or on fixed-term contracts, which can also be considered as non-standard, are included among full-time employees. The classification of self-employment as non-standard employment for men is debatable. However, given that it is an employment option for a minority of occupations, it is regarded here as non-standard.

[10] These predicted probabilities are calculated from multinomial logit results similar to those published in Booth, Jenkins and Garcia-Serrano (1996). The estimation procedure also controls for health status, marital status, education, region of residence, housing tenure and the unemployment rate.

[11] These calculations are based on random effects probit models (controlling for unobserved individual heterogeneity and initial conditions) presented in Table 3 of Arulampalam and others (2000). The models also control for the unemployment rate, age, ethnicity, housing tenure, health status, marital status and age and number of children. For more detailed analysis and evidence of unemployment persistence among working-age men in the BHPS, see Arulampalam and others (2000).

[12] It is possible for individuals to be observed in a single, unbroken spell of unemployment across two consecutive dates of interview, and this would bias these results. However, Arulampalam and others (2000) investigate several ways to control for this in their estimation procedure, and these dramatic results remain unchanged.

[13] In this context, the term 'family' refers to benefit units, as defined in *Households Below Average Income* (HBAI), rather than households. It is defined as a person or a group of persons living at the same address who are assessed as a single unit for

means-tested benefit purposes. Therefore, each household may contain multiple families. Children refer to dependent children as defined by the Department of Social Security. Pensioner families and students have been omitted. All work refers to families where all adult members are in employment, no work to where no adult members are in employment, and mixed work to where one adult member is in employment.

[14] Childless couples refer to couples who have yet to start a family as well as to older couples whose children may have left home.

[15] Drawing direct comparisons between findings of this study and those of Gregg and Wadsworth (1996) are difficult because of differences in definitions. Gregg and Wadsworth refer to households, while for this study benefit units are used.

[16] In each case, the samples are restricted to those who have not changed their family status across two consecutive waves.

[17] Note that this analysis does not control for other observable characteristics such as age or education.

[18] This analysis takes the form of a multinomial logit model, controlling for age, education, health, the unemployment rate, region of residence, marital status and housing tenure. The sample is again restricted to men and women between the ages of 55 and 60 at wave 1, so that the panel covered the period when these individuals were most likely to be making retirement decisions.

References

Arulampalam, W., Booth, A.L. and Taylor, M.P. (2000) 'Unemployment persistence', *Oxford Economic Papers*, vol 52, no 1, pp 24-50.

Banks, M. and Jackson, P. (1982) 'Unemployment and the rise of minor psychiatric disorders in young people', *Psychological Medicine*, vol 12, no 4, pp 789-98.

Blanchard, O.J. and Diamond, P.A. (1994) 'Ranking employment duration and wages', *Review of Economic Studies*, vol 61, no 3, pp 417-34.

Blundell, R. and Johnson, P. (1998) 'Pensions and retirement in the UK', in J. Gruber and D.A. Wise (eds) *International social security comparisons*, Chicago, IL: University of Chicago Press.

Böheim, R. and Taylor, M.P. (1999) 'Residential mobility, housing tenure and the labour market in Britain', *Working Papers of the ESRC Research Centre on Micro-social Change*, 99-16, Colchester: Institute for Social and Economic Research, University of Essex.

Booth, A.L. (1995) *The economics of the trade union*, Cambridge: Cambridge University Press.

Booth, A.L. and Francesconi, M. (1997) *Career mobility in Britain*, Institute for Labour Research Discussion Papers, 97/16, Colchester: Institute for Labour Research, University of Essex.

Booth, A.L., Francesconi, M. and Garcia-Serrano, C. (1999) 'Job tenure and job mobility in Britain', *Industrial and Labor Relations Review*, vol 53, no 1, pp 43-70.

Booth, A.L., Jenkins, S.P. and Garcia-Serrano, C. (1996) *New men and new women: Is there convergence in patterns of labour market transition?*, Institute for Labour Research Discussion Papers, 96/01, Colchester: Institute for Labour Research, University of Essex.

Burgess, S. and Rees, H. (1996) 'Job tenure in Britain 1975-1992', *Economic Journal*, vol 106, no 435, pp 334-44.

Campbell, N. (1999) *The decline in employment among older people in Britain*, CASEpapers, 19, London: Centre for the Analysis of Social Exclusion.

Crystal, S., Shea, D. and Krishnaswami, S. (1992) 'Educational attainment, occupational history and stratification: determinants of later-life economic outcomes', *Journal of Gerontology*, vol 47, no 5, pp S213-21.

Elias, P. (1996) *Who forgot they were unemployed?*, Working Papers of the ESRC Research Centre on Micro-social Change, 97-19, Colchester: University of Essex.

Feinstein, L. (1998) *Pre school education inequality? British children in the 1970 cohort*, Centre for Economic Performance Discussion Papers, 404, London: Centre for Economic Performance.

Francesconi, M. (1999) *The determinants of promotions in Britain: Evidence from panel data*, Working Papers of the ESRC Research Centre on Micro-social Change, 99-6, Colchester: Institute for Social and Economic Research, University of Essex.

Gregg, P. and Machin, S. (1997) 'Blighted lives', *Centre Piece*, vol 2, no 1, February, pp 14-17.

Gregg, P. and Wadsworth, J. (1995) 'A short history of labour turnover, job tenure, and job security, 1975-93', *Oxford Review of Economic Policy*, vol 11, no 1, pp 73-90.

Gregg, P. and Wadsworth, J. (1996) 'More work in fewer households?', in J. Hills (ed) *Income and wealth: new inequalities*, Cambridge: Cambridge University Press.

Gregg, P. and Wadsworth, J. (1998) 'Unemployment and non-employment: unpacking economic inactivity', *Economic Report*, vol 12, no 6.

Gruber, J. and Wise, D.A. (1999) *International social security comparisons*, Chicago, IL: University of Chicago Press.

Heckman, J.J. and Borjas, G. (1980) 'Does unemployment cause future unemployment? Definitions, questions and answers from a continuous time model for heterogeneity and state dependence', *Economica*, no 47, pp 247-83.

Iacovou, M. and Berthoud, R. (2000) *Parents and employment: An analysis of low income families in the British Household Panel Survey*, DSS Research Report, 107, Leeds: Corporate Document Services.

Jarvis, S, and Jenkins, S.P. (1998) 'How much income mobility is there in Britain?', *Economic Journal*, vol 108, no 447, pp 428-43.

Junankar, P. (ed) (1987) *From school to unemployment? The labour market for young people*, Basingstoke: Macmillan Education.

Lockwood, B. (1991) 'Information externalities in the labour market and the duration of unemployment', *Review of Economic Studies*, vol 58, no 4, pp 733-53.

ONS (Office for National Statistics) (1999) *Annual abstract of statistics*, London: The Stationery Office.

Pahl, R. (1984) *Divisions of labour*, Oxford: Blackwell.

Paull, G. (1996) *The biases introduced by recall and panel attrition on labour market behaviour reported in the British Household Panel Study*, Centre for Economic Performance Working Papers, 827, London: Centre for Economic Performance.

Phelps, E.S. (1972) *Inflation policy and unemployment theory: The cost benefit approach to monetary planning*, London: Macmillan.

Pissarides, C. (1992) 'Loss of skill during unemployment and the persistence of employment shocks', *Quarterly Journal of Economics*, vol 107, no 4, pp 1371-91.

Preston, A.E. (1998) 'Sex, kids, and commitment to the workplace: employers, employees and the Mommy track', Mimeo, SUNY – Stony Brook, NY.

Sicherman, N. and Galor, O. (1990) 'A theory of career mobility', *Journal of Political Economy*, vol 98, no 1, pp 169-93.

Stigler, G.J. (1962) 'Information in the labor market', *Journal of Political Economy*, vol 70, no 1, pp S94-105.

Tanner, S. (1997) 'The dynamics of retirement behaviour', in R. Disney and others (eds) *The dynamics of retirement*, DSS Research Report, 72, London: The Stationery Office.

Tanner, S. (1998) 'The dynamics of male retirement behaviour', *Fiscal Studies*, vol 19, no 2, pp 75-196.

Taylor, M.P. (1996) 'Earnings, independence or unemployment: why become self-employed?', *Oxford Bulletin of Economics and Statistics*, vol 58, no 2, pp 253-67.

Taylor, M.P. (1997) *The changing picture of self-employment in Britain*, Institute for Labour Research Discussion Papers, 97/12, Colchester: Institute for Labour Research, University of Essex.

Taylor, M.P. (1999) 'Survival of the fittest? An analysis of self-employment duration in Britain', *Economic Journal*, vol 109, no 454, pp C140-55.

FIVE

Dynamics of household incomes[1]

Stephen P. Jenkins

Introduction

This chapter is about the changes in people's incomes from one year to the next in Britain. It aims to establish salient facts about income dynamics in general and poverty dynamics in particular, and their socio-economic correlates, drawing on new evidence for the 1990s derived from the British Household Panel Survey.

A household's income level is strongly associated with two main characteristics: the composition of the family and the employment of its members. So this chapter follows logically from previous contributions to this book, especially Chapters Two and Four. As will be shown later in this chapter, movements in and out of poverty are related to both demographic and economic changes.

The pattern of income changes from one year to the next is one of much mobility, but most of the changes are short-range. For example, of those who are poor in one year, almost one half are not poor the following year – but those who escape poverty often remain on low incomes and have a high risk of returning to poverty in future years. Income mobility also means that the proportion of the population that is touched by poverty over a six-year period is twice as large as the proportion that is poor in any one year.

Income and poverty dynamics have intrinsic social relevance and policy significance. The extent of mobility and poverty persistence are important social indicators to be placed alongside information about the income distribution at a point in time. For example, the former Secretary of State for Social Security Peter Lilley discounted the rising incidence of low income during the 1980s with reference to new evidence about income mobility:

Social mobility is considerable. Discussion about poverty is often based on the assumption that figures for households on low incomes describe a static group of people trapped in poverty unable to escape and getting poorer. However, this picture has been blown apart by recent studies. They show that the people in the lowest income category are not the same individuals as were in last year, still less fifteen years ago. (Peter Lilley, speech in Southwark Cathedral on 13 June 1996, cited by Hills, 1998, p 52)

Regardless of whether the conclusions Mr Lilley drew from the evidence were correct (they are debatable), the point is that the evidence is seen as important by many. That it is of interest to a wide range of people is underlined by the fact that mobility findings by Sarah Jarvis and myself (Jarvis and Jenkins, 1996) were reported not only in the *Financial Times*, but also on the front page of the *Socialist Worker*.

Longitudinal analysis is an essential ingredient in policy formulation. Researchers in the United States and the UK have long since drawn attention to the differences between the poverty experience of the population over a period of time and the poverty at one particular time. They have also emphasised that the design of antipoverty policy measures should depend on whether poverty is a short-duration event that most people experience at one time or a long-duration event concentrated among particular identifiable groups in the population[2]. A dynamic perspective leads to different antipoverty strategies, as David Ellwood, a leading researcher recruited as welfare reform advisor by President Clinton, has pointed out:

[D]ynamic analysis gets us closer to treating causes, where static analysis often leads us towards treating symptoms.... If, for example, we ask who are the poor today, we are led to questions about the socioeconomic identity of the existing poverty population. Looking to policy, we then typically emphasise income supplementation strategies. The obvious static solution to poverty is to give the poor more money. If instead, we ask what leads people into poverty, we are drawn to events and structures, and our focus shifts to looking for ways to ensure people escape poverty. (Ellwood, 1998, p 49)

The New Deal and other 'welfare-to-work' policies for the unemployed, disabled people and lone parents that have been introduced by Tony Blair's Labour government are an example of this change in focus.

Defining income

Before starting on the analysis itself, it is necessary to explain briefly how income has been calculated. In most of the results discussed in this chapter, the unit of analysis is the individual – that is, we count how many men, women and children there are in each income group 'this year', and how many move from one group to another between 'this year' and 'next year'. However, each person's income has been calculated on the basis of the money coming into the household in which s/he lives. The implicit assumption is that all the members of the household enjoy the same living standards. That is the almost-universal assumption of income distribution analysis, although it may be questioned (Chapter Three contributes to this literature).

Income is calculated on the basis of the total of earnings, pensions, social security benefits, investment income and other sources received by each member of the household. Most of the data refers to the most recent week or month so is an estimate of the household's 'current' income rather than income over a whole year. This is important to bear in mind when considering changes over time: year-on-year comparisons actually contrast a week or month in the autumn of (say) 1991 with a week or month in the autumn of 1992[3]; this should be borne in mind later on in the chapter when changes in income from one year to the next are referred to.

All the figures reported here are estimated net of income tax, National Insurance contributions and council tax. They refer to household income without housing costs being deducted. This is the net income definition most commonly used in most countries, although some people have argued that an after-housing-costs measure provides a more reliable picture.

Each household's total net income has then been adjusted to take account of the needs of the household using an equivalence scale (the so-called McClements one), which reflects the number and ages of the people living there, and among whom the income is assumed to be shared.

The income concept used is: 'current household net equivalent income before housing costs'. It is the same as the one used by the Department of Social Security when compiling the official income distribution statistics (see, for example, DSS, 1998).

Changes over time in the patterns of inequality and poverty

Although the emphasis in this chapter is on year-to-year changes in the income received by the same people, it is helpful to set this in the context of the overall distribution of income in Britain, and of changes in that distribution during the past two decades. These have been analysed very thoroughly on the basis of the Family Expenditure Survey and the Family Resources Survey (Jenkins 1994, 1996; Goodman and others, 1997; DSS, 1998). These are traditional cross-section surveys that provide reliable estimates of the position each year, without revealing the underlying dynamics as only the BHPS can. Figure 5.1 illustrates the income distribution in 1996/97[4]. The mean income for the population as a whole was £307 per week (income has been adjusted for differences in needs using an equivalence scale). The median for the poorest tenth of the population was £108; for the richest tenth it was £649. It is a characteristic of income distributions that income differences are much wider at the upper than at the lower end of the scale, and this is illustrated in Figure 5.1 by the way in which the highest group towers above all the others.

Figure 5.1: Average (median) income for the poorest tenth through to the richest tenth of the population for 1996/97

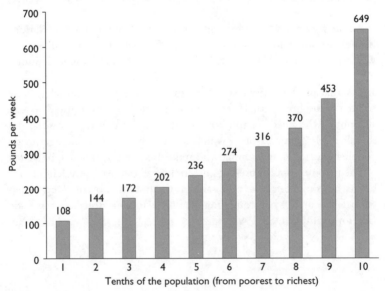

A convention has developed over the years that people whose income is below half the national average should be labelled 'poor': according to this measure, 19% of the population was in poverty in 1996/97, representing 10.5 million individuals (DSS, 1998). This proportion is substantially higher than that observed in many other comparable countries. For example, according to the first wave of the European Household Panel Survey, the proportion of individuals living in households with incomes below half the national average income in 1994 was 22% in the UK, the second highest rate for the 12 countries for whom data was available, and almost one third higher than the EU-12 rate of 17% (Eurostat, 1997).

The striking feature of the income distribution is that it changed very rapidly between the late 1970s and the beginning of the 1990s, although the pattern was broadly stable before then, and remained stable during the first half of the 1990s. It was not so much that the incomes of the poor went down, but that the incomes of the rich went up. One way to describe the change is to say that half of all the growth in the national income went to the top 15% of the population (Jenkins, 1994, Table 5). The other half of the increase was distributed fairly thinly across the middle of the distribution. The income of the poorest 15% of the population did not increase at all over that period. This means that the range of inequality between rich and poor widened sharply during the 1980s. In 1979, the median income of the richest tenth was just under four times the equivalent figure for the poorest tenth. In 1996/97, as Figure 5.1 shows, the ratio between the top and bottom groups was 6:1. The proportion of people whose income was below half of the national average swelled from 8% to 18%. The degree of income inequality as measured by the Gini coefficient (which varies between zero and one; higher values indicate higher inequality) rose from 0.250 in 1979 to 0.338 in 1990/91 (Jenkins, 1994) and has hardly changed in the following six years (see below). The rise in inequality in the UK during the 1980s was larger than the increase for virtually all other industrial countries (inequality actually fell for some nations) (see Hills, 1998).

This large change in the degree of inequality and the extent of poverty in Britain arose because of a complex combination of reasons and the mix of these changed over time (Atkinson 1994, 2000; Goodman and others 1997; Hills, 1998; Jenkins 1994, 1995, 1996, 2000a). Changes in the labour market had the largest impact (and factors such as the growth in the number of lone parents or elderly people had only a minor effect). In particular, there was a rapid rise in the earnings of better-paid workers while the earnings of low-paid workers lagged well behind. This growing differential arose from higher rewards to skills and qualifications and a decline in the importance of institutions such as unions and wage councils. Changes in the distribution of work itself also had an impact, especially at the beginning of the 1980s. It was not so much the rise in unemployment that was important; rather the rise in the number of workless households – many families now have two people working, many others have none at all working (Gregg and Wadsworth, 1996). The gap between the incomes of working and workless households also grew because benefit increases were linked only to increases in prices rather than (the higher) increases in average earnings. Particularly important contributions to the rise in inequality in the second half of the 1980s came from substantial growth in the inequality of income from self-employment and income from investments and savings. (The income tax cuts during this period also had an effect, but not large compared to the other factors.) Inequality has not grown further in the first half of the 1990s because there has been a halt in the growth in earnings differentials and in the importance of self-employment and investment income in family income packages. Also, the extent of polarisation in the distribution of work has fallen a little.

As Table 5.1 shows, the proportion of pensioners in poverty rose slightly over this time, but the proportion of poor non-pensioners more than doubled. A large body of research has analysed the economic and demographic characteristics associated with high risks of poverty. For example, 62% of families classified as unemployed were below the poverty line, according to the standard DSS analysis. An astonishing 60% of Pakistani and Bangladeshi families are poor (Berthoud, 1998). Of particular concern is the number of families with children in poverty: 3.3 million of all the poor in Britain are dependent children. It is well known that one-parent families have an exceptionally high risk of poverty; less well known that the risk is if anything even higher for children whose parents are cohabiting (Adelman and Bradshaw, 1998). However, the majority of poor children live with legally married parents – in most cases, neither parent is in work.

Longitudinal flux amid cross-sectional stability

The growth in inequality and poverty took place almost entirely in the 1980s. The number of people in poverty, according to the conventional definition, has stabilised or perhaps even declined slightly during the period in the 1990s during which the BHPS panel has been studied. As

Table 5.1: Proportion of individuals in households below half average income in 1979 and 1996/97, by family type, in cell percentages

Family type	1979	1996/97
Pensioner couple	16	20
Single pensioner	16	23
Couple with children	7	19
Couple without children	4	10
Lone-parent family	16	38
Single without children	6	16
All persons	8	19
(Number of persons below half average income)	(4.4 million)	(10.5 million)

Source: DSS (1998, Table F1[BHC], p 129 and p 170). Family type refers to an individual's family rather than to an individual's household. A family (or 'benefit unit') is defined to be a single person living alone or a couple, with or without dependent children. A household may contain more than one family

a result, the analysis of changes affecting individuals refers to a time when the number of people moving into poverty and the number moving out was approximately in balance.

Table 5.2 provides a standard cross-sectional view on the income distribution for each year between 1991 and 1996 as measured, this time, by the BHPS. One striking feature is the stability in the shape of the distribution over this period. The Gini coefficient, a measure of the degree of inequality, changed hardly at all, and nor did the proportion of the population with income below half the contemporary average income. Along with the stability in distribution shape, there was some increase in real income, as shown by the rise in mean income by about one tenth between 1991 and 1996, and the decrease in the number of persons with incomes below a fixed half-1991 mean cut-off (equal to about £130 per week).

There is a remarkable degree of longitudinal income mobility that coexists with the cross-sectional stability in the shape of the income distribution – see Table 5.3. Each person has been classified into one of six income groups, from highest to lowest, according to their income 'this year' (wave t), and then classified again in the same way, but according to their income 'last year' (wave $t-1$). Table 5.3 shows the outflow rates from each of last year's income groups to the six different income groups this year.

There is a lot of mobility because, for all income groups but one, the

Table 5.2: Trends in mean income, inequality and low income (1991 to 1996)

	1991	1992	1993	1994	1995	1996
Mean income (per week)	£259	£269	£272	£274	£288	£290
Gini coefficient	0.31	0.31	0.31	0.31	0.32	0.32
Percentage below half contemporary mean	17.8	16.6	17.3	16.6	17.1	16.4
Percentage below half 1991 mean	17.8	15.3	15.1	14.1	12.4	12.0

Source: Income is needs-adjusted household net income per person in January 1997 pounds per week

Table 5.3: Outflow rates from this year's income group origins to next year's income group destinations, in column percentages

	Income group, wave *t*						
Wave *t+1*	**< 0.5**	**0.5-0.75**	**0.75-1.0**	**1.0-1.25**	**1.25-1.5**	**>1.5**	**All**
< 0.5	54	15	5	3	2	1	12
0.5-0.75	30	56	19	6	3	2	22
0.75-1.0	9	21	48	20	8	4	20
1.0-1.25	4	5	20	44	25	6	17
1.25-1.5	2	1	5	20	35	12	10
>1.5	2	2	3	7	27	75	19
Row %	(13)	(22)	(21)	(16)	(10)	(18)	

Note: Income is needs-adjusted household net income per person in January 1997 pounds per week. Persons are classified into income groups according to the size of their income relative to fixed real income cut-offs equal to 0.5, 0.75, 1.0, 1.25, and 1.5 times the mean wave 1 income = £259 per week. Transition rates are average rates from pooled BHPS data, waves 1-6

proportion of persons in last year's group who are in the same group this year is about one half or less. For example, only about one half (54%) of those with incomes below the low-income cut-off last year also have incomes below the same cut-off this year. (The exceptional group is the richest one where the stayer proportion is nearer three quarters, although this large figure is in part due to the fact that the richest cannot move to a still-richer group.) On the other hand, it is also clear that most year-to-year income mobility is short-range: observe the clustering of observations about the main diagonal of Table 5.3. For example, of those with incomes below the low-income cut-off last year, 84% have incomes below 75% of the average income this year. This finding of 'much mobility but mostly short-range' is robust to the choice of income group category and income. For example, if you use deciles rather than fixed real income values to define the income groups the same finding emerges (Jarvis and Jenkins, 1998).

The pattern of year-to-year mobility revealed in Table 5.3 (and other related work) can be summarised in terms of the 'rubber band' model of income dynamics. Think of each person's income as fluctuating about a relatively fixed 'longer-term average'. This value is a tether on the income scale to which people are attached by a rubber band. They may move away from the tether from one year to the next, but not too far because of the band holding them. They tend to rebound back towards and around the tether over a period of several years. Over a longer period the position of the tethers will move with secular income growth, career developments or family change. Also rubber bands will break sometimes if 'stretched' too far by 'shocks' – perhaps negative ones such as death of a breadwinner or positive ones such as a big lottery win – leading to long-term changes in relative income position.

The degree of income mobility affects how often people experience low income over a period of time. Someone may not be poor this year but if incomes fluctuate, he or she may move into poverty next year. The longer the window of observation, the greater the chances of experiencing low income at least once. Income mobility also affects perceptions of how much income inequality there is. Taking the longitudinal average of each person's income will smooth out intertemporal variations in income. Because these fluctuations are a factor contributing to differences in income between individuals in any given year, the smoothing process means that inequality is lower if you look at longer-term (smoothed) income rather than inequality this year. This still leaves open the question of how large the effects of mobility on poverty prevalence and inequality reduction are in practice. Let us look at each issue in turn.

Quite a lot of people experienced low income at least once during a six-year period, relative to the proportion poor in any single year (cf Table 5.1). This is shown by Table 5.4. More than two thirds of persons in the sample never had a low income at any of the six annual interviews during 1991-96, and just 1.7% had a low income at every interview. On the other hand, almost one third (32%) had low income at least once

Table 5.4: Prevalence of low income

Number of interviews out of six (m)	% of sample with low income at m interviews out of six	% of sample with low income at m or more interviews out of six
0	68.0	100.0
1	12.9	32.0
2	8.0	19.1
3	3.9	11.1
4	2.7	7.2
5	2.8	4.5
6	1.7	1.7

Note: Income is needs-adjusted household net income per person in January 1997 in pounds per week. The low income threshold is £130 per week (half 1991 average income)

during this six-year period and almost one fifth (19%) had low income at least twice.

The upshot is that many more people are affected by low income over an interval of several years than have low income at a point in time. This also means that the social security system helps a rather larger number of people than a focus on the current caseload would suggest.

Consider now how much inequality is reduced if each person's income is smoothed longitudinally. The effect is not large: see Table 5.5. The statistics in the first column refer to incomes for just one year, 1991; the second column refers to incomes longitudinally averaged over 1991 and 1992, and so on through to the last column, in which the figures refer to the six-year 1991-96 average. Inequality falls the more the income accounting period is extended – which is expected because the averaging smoothes fluctuations – but the decrease levels off relatively quickly. The reduction in the Gini coefficient from six-year smoothing is roughly equivalent to the redistributive effect of direct taxes, as measured by the difference between the pre- and post-tax income Gini coefficients. The second row of the table expresses the same information differently. Standardising the Gini coefficients by averaged cross-sectional inequality provides a natural measure of income immobility: the more incomes are longitudinally smoothed the less immobility (or more mobility) there is. The statistic in the bottom row of the last column can be interpreted as saying that longer-term (six-year) income inequality is about 88% of inequality in an average year. Just as inequality does not disappear with

Table 5.5: Income mobility as reduction in inequality when the income accounting period is extended

| | Income accounting period | | | | | |
	1991	1991-92	1991-93	1991-94	1991-95	1991-96
Gini coefficient	0.30	0.29	0.28	0.27	0.27	0.27
Immobility index*	1.00	0.95	0.92	0.91	0.89	0.88

Note: Income is needs-adjusted household net income per person in January 1997 in pounds per week.
* Immobility index = Gini coefficient of income cumulated m periods expressed relative to weighted average of Gini coefficients for income in each of the m periods

longer-term income smoothing, nor does the incidence of low income. If incomes are averaged over six waves, then the proportion of persons with smoothed income below the low-income threshold is about 8% (compared with an average of 14.5% using single-year measures).

Poverty exit rates and re-entry rates

Table 5.3 showed that 46% of the people who were poor last year were no longer poor this year. This is the exit rate from low income for all the people who were poor last year (the exit rate from the 'stock' of poor people), and it takes no account of the fact that exit rates may vary according to the length of time already spent in poverty. Some of the individuals entered poverty one year earlier, but others would have entered two, three, four, or more years earlier. Also, poverty exit rates typically decline the longer the time spent poor, which means that the stock of poor people contains a relatively high proportion of people who have been poor for a long time (since high exit-rate people will already have left poverty). There are important distinctions to be made between exit rates from the stock of poor people and exit rates for a cohort of persons beginning a poverty spell, and it is also useful to investigate how exit rates vary with the spell length.

By similar arguments, we should distinguish between the entry rate into poverty for all the people who are not currently poor (the stock of non-poor people) and the entry rate for cohorts of people who are finishing a poverty spell (beginning a spell of non-poverty). The poverty re-entry rate differs from the rate of entry to poverty for all non-poor people, and each rate may vary with the length of time at risk of becoming poor.

Table 5.6: Proportion remaining poor, and exit rates from poverty, by duration, for all persons beginning a poverty spell, in cell percentages

Number of interviews since start of poverty spell	Total number of persons at risk of poverty exit at start of period	Cumulative proportion remaining poor (%)	Annual exit rate from poverty (%)
I	2,067	100	0
2	1,514	53	47
3	436	35	34
4	181	27	22
5	44	18	32

Note: These are Kaplan-Meier product-limit estimates based on all non-left censored poverty spells, pooled from BHPS waves 1-6. 272 exits have been recoded as censored if needs-adjusted income rises to not more than 10% above the poverty line. 375 spells with poverty exits apparently due to benefit income measurement error have been excluded from the calculations.

Table 5.6 shows estimates of poverty exit rates for a cohort of persons starting a poverty spell, together with estimates of the proportions remaining poor after given lengths of time. Table 5.7 provides similar information, but about re-entry rates to poverty for those people who end a poverty spell[5].

The tables immediately reveal some of the problems that arise in empirical implementation. The amount of information is relatively limited. Because there are only six waves of data, exit rates at long durations cannot be estimated. Also, relatively small subsample numbers constrain breakdowns by population subgroups.

There are potential measurement error issues. The poverty line used to delineate the states of 'poor' and 'not poor' is arbitrarily defined, like virtually all low-income cut-offs. It is implausible to treat small income changes – for example, from one pound below the line to one pound above or vice versa – as a genuine transition out of or into poverty, when it is as likely due to transitory variation or measurement error. To avoid these threshold effects, a rise in income is counted as a poverty exit only if the post-transition value is at least 10% higher than the poverty line. Similarly, income must fall below 90% of the poverty line to count as a transition into poverty. Adjustments such as these have been implemented in most previous studies (see, for example, Bane and Ellwood, 1986; Duncan and others, 1993). Preliminary analysis revealed that a non-trivial number of poverty transitions were accounted for by implausible changes in benefit income from one year to the next; as a further measurement error adjustment to the data, transitions in these cases have been omitted from the analysis.

Consider now the substantive estimates, beginning with poverty exits. By construction (the exclusion of spells that were already in progress at the start of the sequence – 'left-censored' spells), all persons starting a poverty spell are poor for at least one year. However, almost one half (47%) of this cohort leave poverty the following year, and the exit rate falls further to about one third and one fifth for the subsequent two years; it appears that the longer you have been in poverty, the less likely you are to escape. The exit rate for the fifth year is not lower still, but higher (32%) – although this may be a reflection of sampling error (note the small number of exits after five interviews).

The exit rates imply a median poverty spell duration for people beginning a spell of between two and three years; after five years, almost four fifths of an entry cohort would have escaped poverty. Equivalently – more pessimistically and emphasising poverty persistence – about one fifth of those starting a period of poverty are still poor after five years. Without a longer panel, and thence estimates of exit rates at longer durations, it is only possible to speculate about the incidence of very long poverty spells. Assuming that the exit rates were 0.25 for all years after the fifth, would mean that just more than one twentieth (6%) of those beginning a spell would be poor for at least 10 years and the average duration would be about 3.8 years.

This picture of poverty persistence describes the experience of those beginning a poverty spell. However, as many have emphasised, the length of completed poverty spells for those who are currently poor is rather different. Although only a small fraction of people entering poverty have long spells, the stock of poverty is dominated by those with long spells because those with short spells leave. It is straightforward to illustrate this, assuming a no-growth steady-state in which the poverty entry rate is constant. In this case, and assuming the exit rate is 0.25 for all years after the fifth, then, of those who are poor in a given year, the fraction with a poverty spell length of at least 10 years is almost one fifth (18%). The median completed spell length is between four and five years, and the average completed spell length is 5.9 years.

These calculations underestimate people's total experience of poverty over a given period because they ignore the fact that a significant fraction of people experience multiple spells of poverty: those who leave often

Table 5.7: Proportion remaining non-poor, and poverty re-entry rates, by duration, for all persons ending a poverty spell

Number of interviews since start of non-poverty spell	Total number of persons at risk of poverty re-entry at start of period	Cumulative proportion remaining non-poor (%)	Annual re-entry rate to poverty
1	2,834	100	0
2	2,187	89	11
3	1,159	84	5
4	616	82	3
5	277	79	3

Note: These are Kaplan-Meier product-limit estimates based on all non-left censored non-poverty spells, pooled from BHPS waves 1-6. 308 re-entries have been recoded as censored if needs-adjusted income falls to not more than 10% below the poverty line. 147 poverty re-entries apparently due to benefit income measurement error have been recoded as censored (see text for further details)

return. Stevens (1999), using data from the US Panel Study of Income Dynamics, has shown most effectively that combining information on poverty re-entry rates with poverty exit rates provides much better predictions of poverty experience than does relying on single-spell estimates (as above).

Table 5.7 provides information about poverty re-entry rates for all persons ending a poverty spell (again people who were already out of poverty at the start of the period have been excluded from the calculations). Re-entry rates fall from 0.11 in the second year after leaving poverty to less than one third of that rate after five years, 0.03. (The number of persons 'at risk' at the start of the period is larger than in Table 5.6 because of the high prevalence of left-censored poverty spells in this short panel.) The re-entry rates imply that about one fifth of those leaving a poverty spell will have experienced another spell within the subsequent five years. This reiterates the point made by Jarvis and Jenkins, using BHPS waves 1-4, that "the path out of low income is not a one-way up-escalator: ... there is a not insignificant chance of finding oneself on the down escalator to low income again" (1997, p 131).

The different pictures about persistence provide different impressions about the concentration among the poor of people in receipt of Income Support and other benefits. A focus on the poverty stock tells us that the persistently poor receive most of the total resources devoted to poverty alleviation at a point in time. However, a focus on flows, both out of and (back) into poverty, reminds us that the number of people who are ever helped by poverty alleviation measures is many more than those currently poor.

This is the same message as provided by the US literature. In this connection it is interesting to note that the exit rates shown in Table 5.6 are broadly similar to the estimates reported by Bane and Ellwood (1986) for the US in the 1970s. On the other hand, the poverty re-entry rates shown in Table 5.7 are noticeably lower than those reported by Stevens (1994) using PSID data for 1970-87. Taken at face value this cross-national comparison suggests greater poverty turnover in the US than in Britain. However, this conclusion must remain tentative given the differences in periods covered, definition of income, equivalence scale and the poverty line, and in the population subsamples examined.

Movements into and out of poverty by family type

Given the variation in the incidence of poverty between pensioners and non-pensioners and between those with and without children (cf Table 5.1), it is relevant to ask what the relationship is between family structure and the chances of moving in and out of poverty. Because family composition may also change from one year to the next, investigation of this issue has to be done in two stages. The analysis starts with those individuals whose family composition (defined in terms of the six categories listed in the table) remained the same between one year and the next. It will then look at movements in and out of poverty that occur at the same time as changes in family type.

Table 5.8 shows, for those whose family type did not change, what proportion of poor people escaped from poverty between 'last year' (t-1) and 'this year' (t), and then what proportion of non-poor people fell into poverty over the same period. (The number of people making the change in each direction is roughly the same, with a small net movement out of poverty; but the entry rate is much lower than the exit rate because there are far more non-poor people across whom the risk is spread.) The fairly substantial differences between types of family are complementary, in that groups with a high exit rate tended to have a low entry rate, and vice versa. Longitudinal analysis seems to point to the susceptibility of all groups, rather than indicating that persons in some family types have stable incomes and rarely cross the poverty line, while others are volatile and cross the line often.

Table 5.8: Annual transition rates into and out of poverty, for individuals who remained in the same family type, in row percentages

Person's family type	Annual exit rate from poverty	Annual entry rate into poverty	Steady-state annual poverty rate	Steady-state poor for three consecutive years
Single pensioner	36	10.4	22	9
Pensioner couple	46	4.9	10	2.8
Single non-pensioner	57	6.7	12	0.3
Couple without children	63	2.9	4	1
Lone parents	34	19.5	37	16
Couple with children	48	6.4	13	3

Note: Annual exit rate = number not poor at year t as a percentage of the number poor at $t-1$; Annual entry rate = number poor at year t as a percentage of the number not poor at $t-1$. The steady-state annual poverty rate is the percentage poor assuming that each person's family type does not change and annual exit and entry rates remain the same indefinitely. The steady-state percentage poor for three consecutive years is the steady-state poverty rate times the square of one minus the exit rate

High escape rates were shared by non-pensioners with no children, while single pensioners and one-parent families had low chances of exiting poverty. Members of one-parent families had easily the highest entry rates. One fifth of the small number of lone parents who were not poor in one year had become poor the next year (assuming they were still lone parents). Couples with children had the lowest risk of falling into poverty.

The third and fourth columns of Table 5.8 are intended to indicate the long-term implications of these entry and exit rates. Imagine that these poverty transition rates remained the same for a long period of time, and that each person's family type also stayed the same. Column three shows what the annual poverty rate would be for each group in this 'steady-state' scenario. It is also possible to calculate the proportion of persons in each family type who would be poor for three consecutive years in this situation. While these are artificial calculations, they might provide a useful picture of the underlying extent of poverty.

The ranking of different family types by steady-state poverty rates is much the same as their ranking by current poverty rates (cf Table 5.1), with the exception of pensioner couples (who have relatively high exit rates and low entry rates compared to single pensioners). The fourth column of Table 5.8 shows that only 1% of non-pensioner couples (with or without children) would spend three consecutive years poor in the steady-state scenario. For other groups (single non-pensioners excepted) the three-year rate is between 2.8 and 16%. For single pensioners (many of them widows), the rate is 9%; for lone parents (and their children) it is 16%. All these estimates are derived on the assumption that the family's structure does not change.

However, many people do move between one type of family and another because of (re)partnership formation and dissolution, childbirth, or ageing (as shown in Chapter Two). Some of these changes in family structure might be directly instrumental in a move into or out of poverty. The family type of only a minority of the BHPS sample changed from one year to the next, and some transitions were so uncommon that it was impossible to calculate transition rates.

Table 5.9 identifies the low-income transition rates that could be calculated, broken down by family type in two consecutive years. The type of family the respondent started in is listed on the left-hand side of the table, and the type he or she ended up in is listed in the column headings. The figures in bold represent the poverty entry and exit rates for those whose family type did not change, which have already been shown in Table 5.8. The top panel of the table shows the entry rates and the bottom panel shows the exit rates.

Look, for example, at people who started off as part of a pensioner couple and ended up as a single pensioner. Most of these were probably widowed. Of those in this group who had started non-poor, 9.2% fell into poverty at the same time. However, 86% of those who started in poverty when they were in a couple, ceased to be poor when they were widowed – a rather unexpected finding. The transition from pensioner couple to single pensioner is associated with higher rates of movement across the poverty threshold, in both directions, than were experienced by pensioner couples who remained together.

Moving on down the list of starting positions:

- single non-pensioners who became part of a couple with children (either by partnering and having a baby, or by joining a step-family) also had high rates of movements, in both directions;
- couples without children seemed to increase their risk of entering poverty if they made any change in their family position (compared with the very low risk if they remained as they were);

Table 5.9: Annual transition rates into and out of poverty, by family type, in column percentages

	Person's family type in first year					
Person's family type next year	Single pensioner	Pensioner couple	Single non-pensioner	Couple without children	Lone parent	Couple with children
Annual entry rate into poverty						
Single pensioner	**10.4**	9.2	7.0			
Pensioner couple		**4.9**		9.5		
Single non-pensioner			**6.7**	8.8	14.0	8.5
Couple without children			5.4	**2.9**		3.9
Lone parent					**19.5**	22.1
Couple with children			11.3	6.5	16.2	**6.4**
Annual exit rate out of poverty						
Single pensioner	**36**	86	57			
Pensioner couple		**46**		72		
Single non-pensioner			**57**	65	29	54
Couple without children		72	72	**63**		71
Lone parent					**34**	54
Couple with children			83	82	66	**48**

Note: See notes to Table 5.8 for definition of annual poverty exit and entry rates. Cells left blank are those for which cell sizes were too small to calculate transition rates.

- lone parents and their children greatly improved their chances of escaping poverty if they became part of a couple with children;
- conversely, a couple with children had a high risk of becoming poor if they became a lone parent.

What accounts for transitions into and out of poverty from one year to the next?

The discussion that follows, about the factors associated with transitions into and out of poverty, draws on methods pioneered by Bane and Ellwood (1986).

It is important to be clear how a change in a person's income is measured from year to year. If the person continues to live in the same household with exactly the same people, then all the people in that household will experience the same change in equivalent income, if the earnings or other resources of any one of them increases or decreases. If someone enters the household or leaves the household, the income of all of them will be affected by the change in the equivalence scale by which actual money income is divided. If someone moves from one household to another (for example, a young person leaving home, or a couple setting up together), then the change in that person's income is measured as the difference between the (needs-adjusted) income of the old household and the income of the new household. This is why it is essential to measure income transitions at the individual level, rather than for whole households.

Changes in equivalised net incomes can arise via changes in household money incomes ('income events') and changes in household composition ('demographic events'). The correlates of low-income transitions will be considered by examining the relative frequency of different event types. The analysis is based on a classification of event types according to a mutually exclusive hierarchy. This was done using the definitions summarised in Figure 5.2. Table 5.10 summarises the relative frequency of the different event types for transitions out of low income and transitions into low income[6]. The table provides a link between income changes and family formation and dissolution (addressed in Chapter Two) and labour market dynamics (addressed in Chapter Four).

The breakdowns suggest that income events are more important than demographic events for accounting for low-income transitions, although demographic events are relatively more important for movements into low income than for movements out. More than four fifths (83%) of transitions out of low income were income events of various types, which compares with about three fifths (62%) of transitions into low income. A person's earnings can change because they receive a different amount while staying in the same job, or because they get or lose a job altogether. Both are important. For example, among the persons for whom a rise in the household head's labour earnings was the main event associated with a transition out of low income, the household head moved from not working to working in 51% of the cases. Among the persons for whom a fall in the household head's labour earnings was the main event associated with a transition into low income, the household head moved from working to not working in 56% of the cases. (These statistics are drawn from Jenkins, 2000b.)

The breakdowns in Table 5.10 also draw attention to the relative importance of different types of income events. In particular, they highlight

Figure 5.2: Classification of 'income events' and 'demographic events' associated with a low income transition between 'last' year and 'this' year

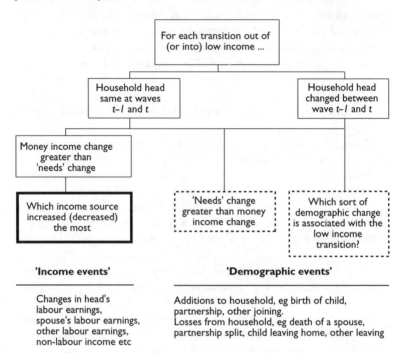

'Income events'	'Demographic events'
Changes in head's labour earnings, spouse's labour earnings, other labour earnings, non-labour income etc	Additions to household, eg birth of child, partnership, other joining. Losses from household, eg death of a spouse, partnership split, child leaving home, other leaving

the relevance of earnings changes for persons other than the head of household. For example, for movements out of low income, changes in the labour earnings of a spouse or other person in the household besides the household head are almost as important as changes for the head. Non-labour income changes also play an important role.

There are variations in the relative importance of different types of events when you focus on different subgroups of the population. For example, demographic rather than income events account for the majority of the low-income entry transitions among those currently in one-parent households. However, the broad conclusions drawn in the last paragraph are fairly robust across household types (Jenkins, 2000b). The findings that demographic events and non-labour income dynamics play a significant role for many echoes those reported by Bane and Ellwood (1986) for the US during the 1970s.

Table 5.10: Movements out of and into low income, broken down by type of event, in column percentages

Main event associated with low-income transition	Transitions out of low income	Transitions into low income
Household head's labour earnings change	34	31
Spouse's or other labour earnings change	29	16
Non-labour income change	20	16
Demographic event	18	38

Note: Income changes are money income rises for movements out of low income and money income falls for movements into low income. The analysis is based on net income transitions between one year and the following year, using pooled data for BHPS waves 1-6. Movements out of low income are only included if net income rose to at least 10% above the low income threshold; movements into low income are only included if net income fell to at least 10% below the threshold. See earlier for definitions of income and low income threshold and of the hierarchy of event types

Conclusions

The now conventional view about the British income distribution is that there was a large increase in inequality and relative poverty during the 1980s but with no further increase (or decrease) in the first half of the 1990s. This chapter has shown that even when the overall shape of the income distribution remains much the same, there is much change going on underneath the surface. From one year to the next, there is a lot of income mobility, although the typical income change is not large.

Recognition of these intertemporal dynamics puts the social security system in a new light. Although the current caseload of benefit recipients (and the current stock of poor people) is dominated by long-stayers, many more people are 'touched' by poverty and receive short-term help from the benefit system than might at first glance appear. Assessments should not only consider how well long-term income maintenance is being provided but should also measure for assisting transitions out of low income (and preventing falls into low income). The current British government's New Deal strategy is a step in this direction, although it is too early yet to judge how successful the dynamic focus has been. The reality of fluctuating incomes also raises questions about the balance between social assistance and social insurance benefits in the social security system. In principle, insurance benefits provide a means for protecting living standards from adverse short-term shocks. On the other hand, it is difficult to establish contribution records and thence eligibility if the chances of a repeat unemployment or sickness spell are high.

To move people out of poverty, and to keep them out, requires information about the driving forces behind such transitions. The results from the previous section are a reminder that movements into and out of poverty are not just about what is happening in the labour market and to primary earners. Even where earnings events and low-income transitions are relatively closely associated, it is important to recognise that earnings dynamics are often a mixture of earnings dynamics for several persons (observe the role of a spouse's and others' earnings). Demographic events also play an important role.

There are limitations to the Bane and Ellwood method used here. It is useful for identifying the salient facts to be explained but does not reveal anything about causation or provide a means for dynamic simulation for policy analysis. One specific limitation is that an hierarchical classification of events does not allow the unravelling of the impact of simultaneous events. Another feature is that the classification demands that every individual is recorded as having some kind of change (even if it is only a small one). An alternative approach has been to look for major events (such as gaining or losing a job, or a partnership forming or dissolving). Berthoud and Böheim (1998) found that people experiencing such a major event had a high chance of crossing the poverty line, but that a large proportion of those crossing the line did not appear to have experienced such an event.

One complementary direction in future work is likely to be more detailed study of the processes of entry into or exit from poverty for particular groups and particular types of transition. Jarvis and Jenkins (1999), for example, looked in detail at couples who split up. They found that the income of the man tends to increase, while the income of the woman, and of any children, tends to decrease. However, the social security system is quite effective at moderating the extent of the losses experienced by the new one-parent families. Another example has been an analysis of the prospects of low-income families with children with no job (Iacovou and Berthoud, 1999). Again, this emphasises the need to consider both demographic and employment transitions, and the links between the employment of different family members.

Notes

[1] This chapter incorporates the results of research undertaken in collaboration with ISER colleagues Elena Bardasi, Richard Berthoud, René Böheim, Sarah Jarvis and John Rigg. Sections of the text have been drawn from previous papers, especially Jenkins (1999, 2000b).

[2] See *inter alia* Duncan and others (1984) and Bane and Ellwood (1986) for the USA, and Walker with Ashworth (1994) for the UK.

[3] However, Böheim and Jenkins (2000) have compared estimates of poverty and inequality based on current and annual income measures and found that there is little difference between them.

[4] 1996/97 refers to the financial year between April 1996 and March 1997; this convention is applied throughout the chapter.

[5] The estimates are subject to a number of technical caveats, discussed in Jenkins (2000b). For more extensive analysis, based on BHPS waves 1-4, see Jarvis and Jenkins (1997).

[6] Not all low-income transitions were included in the analysis; some were excluded to reduce the impact of potential measurement error (see the note to Table 5.10).

References

Adelman, L. and Bradshaw, J. (1998) 'Children in poverty in Britain: an analysis of the Family Resources Survey 1994/95', mimeo, York: University of York.

Atkinson, A.B. (1994) 'What is happening to the distribution of income in the UK?', in *Proceedings of the British Academy: Lectures and memoirs*, vol 82, 1992, Oxford: Oxford University Press.

Atkinson, A.B. (2000) 'Distribution of income and wealth in Britain over the twentieth century', in A.H. Halsey and J. Webb (eds) *British Social Trends*, Basingstoke: Macmillan.

Bane M.J. and Ellwood, D.T. (1986) 'Slipping into and out of poverty: the dynamics of spells', *Journal of Human Resources*, vol 21, no 1, pp 2-23.

Berthoud, R. (1998) *Ethnic minority incomes*, ISER Research Reports, 98-1, Colchester: Institute for Social and Economic Research, University of Essex.

Berthoud, R. and Böheim, R. (1998) 'Predicting problem debt', mimeo, Colchester: Institute for Social and Economic Research, University of Essex.

Böheim, R. and Jenkins, S.P. (2000) *Do current income and annual income measures provide different pictures of Britain's income distribution?*, ISER Working Papers, 2000-16, Colchester: Institute for Social and Economic Research, University of Essex.

DSS (Department of Social Security) (1998) *Households below average income 1979-1996/7*, Leeds: Corporate Document Services.

Duncan, G.J., Coe, R.D. and Hill, M.S. (1984) 'The dynamics of poverty', in G.J. Duncan and others (eds) *Years of poverty, years of plenty: The changing economic fortunes of American workers and families*, Ann Arbor, MI: Institute for Social Research, University of Michigan.

Duncan, G.J., Gustafsson, B., Hauser, R., Schmauss, G., Messinger, H., Muffels, R., Nolan, B. and Ray, J.C. (1993) 'Poverty dynamics in eight countries', *Journal of Population Economics*, vol 6, no 3, pp 215-34.

Ellwood, D. (1998) 'Dynamic policy making: an insiders account of reforming US welfare', in L. Leisering, and R. Walker (eds) *The dynamics of modern society: Policy, poverty and welfare*, Bristol: The Policy Press.

Eurostat (1997) 'Income distribution and poverty in EU12 – 1993', *Statistics in Focus: Population and Social Conditions*, no 6, pp 1-6.

Goodman, A., Johnson, P. and Webb, S. (1997) *Inequality in the UK*, Oxford: Oxford University Press.

Gregg, P. and Wadsworth, J. (1996) *It takes two: Employment polarisation in the OECD*, Centre for Economic Performance Discussion Papers, 304, London: Centre for Economic Performance.

Hills, J. (1998) *Income and wealth: The latest evidence*, York: Joseph Rowntree Foundation.

Iacovou, M. and Berthoud, R. (1999) *Parents and employment: An analysis of low income families in the British Household Panel Study*, DSS Research Reports, 107, Leeds: Corporate Document Services.

Jarvis, S. and Jenkins, S.P. (1996) *Changing places: Income mobility and poverty dynamics in Britain*, Working Papers of the ESRC Research Centre on Micro-social Change, 98-19, Colchester: University of Essex.

Jarvis, S. and Jenkins, S.P. (1997) 'Low income dynamics in 1990s Britain', *Fiscal Studies*, no 18, pp 1-20.

Jarvis, S. and Jenkins, S.P. (1998) 'How much income mobility is there in Britain?', *Economic Journal*, vol 108, no 447, pp 428-43.

Jarvis, S. and Jenkins, S.P. (1999) 'Marital splits and income changes: evidence for Britain', *Population Studies*, vol 53, no 2, pp 237-54.

Jenkins, S.P. (1994) *Winners and losers: A portrait of the UK income distribution during the 1980s: Report to the Joseph Rowntree Foundation*, University of Swansea Department of Economics Discussion Papers, 94-07, Swansea: University of Wales at Swansea.

Jenkins, S.P. (1995) 'Accounting for inequality trends: decomposition analyses for the UK, 1971-1986', *Economica*, vol 62, no 245, pp 29-63.

Jenkins, S.P. (1996) 'Recent trends in the UK income distribution: what happened and why', *Oxford Review of Economic Policy*, vol 12, no 1, pp 29-46.

Jenkins, S.P. (1999) 'Income dynamics in Britain 1991-6', in HM Treasury *Persistent poverty and lifetime inequality: The evidence*, CASEreports, 5, and HM Treasury Occasional Papers, 10, London: London School of Economics and HM Treasury.

Jenkins, S.P. (2000a) 'Trends in the UK income distribution', in R. Hauser and I. Becker (eds) *The personal distribution of income in an international perspective*, Heidelberg: Springer-Verlag.

Jenkins, S.P. (2000b) 'Modelling household income dynamics', *Journal of Population Economics*, vol 13, no 4.

Stevens, A.H. (1994) 'Persistence in poverty and welfare: the dynamics of poverty spells: updating Bane and Ellwood', *American Economic Review (Papers and Proceedings)*, vol 34, no 3, pp 557-88.

Stevens, A.H. (1999) 'Climbing out of poverty, falling back in: measuring the persistence of poverty over multiple spells', *Journal of Human Resources*, vol 34, no 3, pp 557-88.

Walker, R. with Ashworth, K. (1994) *Poverty dynamics: Issues and examples*, Aldershot: Avebury.

SIX

Housing, location and residential mobility

Nick Buck

Introduction

People's housing situation changes through stages of their life-course – the way in which this occurs in Britain is the focus of this chapter. In keeping with the rest of this book, the chapter is concerned with the dynamics of the housing situation, and not simply cross-sectional snapshots. It considers not only the nature of the moves that people make from year to year, but goes beyond this to look at the cumulative impacts of these moves. It then describes housing careers as they develop over the life-course.

The housing career may be considered as not unlike the work career. It starts with leaving the childhood situation, a process of relatively active search. It then leads to relatively high mobility, and a process of investment to obtain or keep better jobs or housing, although in the case of the work career the investments are mainly in human capital, while in the housing career they are financial investments. These processes of career building in both housing and work tend to lead to a stabilisation in middle periods of the life-course. It is at the later stages of the life-course that the patterns diverge, since although there is sometimes a scaling down of housing requirements, it is nothing like as deterministic as the disengagement from the labour market.

However, there are three important reasons for elaborations to this view of the housing career. The housing career is:

• substantially shaped by the work career, both because the investments which people can make in housing will depend on their incomes (and on the stability of their incomes) and also because work career mobility will often require housing mobility;

- directly influenced by the movements through various stages of the life-course: there are changing housing space and location requirements from different stages of the process of family building;
- strongly influenced by the pattern of state intervention, perhaps even more so than the work career, leading to much greater differences in housing careers in different countries, and greater changes over time within a single country.

Some will question whether it is appropriate to argue, as this chapter does, that housing can have an independent effect on the life chances of families. From one point of view housing is simply another consumption good, satisfying a set of needs, such as shelter, and is not intrinsically different from a range of other consumption goods, such as food, clothing, transport and services. From this viewpoint, the housing that individuals or families consume will depend simply and straightforwardly on their incomes and their preferences, and on the supply of housing. There would be no reason to expect housing consumption to have effects on life chances, independent of the processes that generate income and family formation.

There are a number of reasons for thinking that this view of housing as a simple consumption good is profoundly wrong. The housing market is substantially different from the markets for most other goods and services. This is both for economic reasons concerned with the distinct nature of housing as a good, and for social and political reasons. From the economic point of view, the peculiarity of housing is caused in part because it may be purchased in two different ways, by renting the use of accommodation or by purchasing it as an asset. The choice between these two will depend both on the level of income, and its stability, since the costs of owner-occupation tend to be higher, as do the risks associated with default on payment. Renting may be preferred when higher mobility is expected. The fact that housing is purchased as an asset that has tended to appreciate in value also has the consequence of generating large differences in individual wealth, and hence to underpinning further levels of inequality. Housing is also somewhat unusual in that people do not move house (change their pattern of housing consumption) very frequently. Essentially, this is because there are substantial transaction costs involved. Some of these are financial. Even in rented housing there may be costs associated with searching for new accommodation, furnishing and fitting it out.

These costs are likely to be much higher in owner-occupied housing. Beyond this, there are costs that follow from a house having a fixed location, so there may be costs associated with the disruption to local networks of friends, services and employment, which may need to be rebuilt. Finally, housing provides a major part of social identity, and there may be psychological costs in moving (although of course there may be benefits if the housing was particularly unsatisfactory). As a result, people move relatively infrequently, and may often find themselves in housing that is not ideal in relation to their current needs and income.

However, housing is also distinctive in terms of the degree of state involvement that has characterised most societies. Over the longer period of time, the manifest failure of the market alone to provide adequate housing for people on all income levels has led to substantial state intervention in housing, which has either regulated it, or structured it through the provision of subsidised housing. This has also led to variations in the balance between owning and renting. In Britain, where the pattern of state intervention in the 20th century was largely through state provision of housing, over time different tenures acquired very distinct social identities. State-provided (or social) housing eventually acquired a degree of stigma which meant that it was not normally a preferred tenure for anyone who could afford to live in a different sector. In somewhat less class-divided societies, tenure divisions have been perhaps less important, but in Britain they have turned into major lines of social and political cleavage.

In Britain during the last three decades there has been a profound change in the pattern of state involvement in housing, essentially a scaling back in state intervention through provision of rented housing. The more recent growth of owner-occupation has also been strongly supported by state policy, in particular through tax subsidies to mortgage payments, although these are now being terminated. Owner-occupation was also actively supported through the subsidised sale of social housing to tenants. This change provides one important element of the context for this chapter, and one aim is to investigate what the evidence from the BHPS about housing careers of the population of Britain in the 1990s shows about the adequacy of the current housing system.

Because of this centrality of housing tenure divisions in British housing, the chapter will first examine how these tenure divisions interact with life-course, with the development of housing careers, and with dynamics of tenure change revealed by the panel study. It will then be possible to examine the effects of locality differences, and the patterns of migration and residential mobility in more detail. A summary on the cumulative impacts of seven years of change on individuals will conclude the chapter. Throughout, the concern is with the way in which the housing system may mediate and exacerbate social inequalities, and with the adequacy of the current system in the face of greater turbulence in family life, employment and incomes discussed in other chapters of this book.

Housing tenure and the life-course

Before considering the impacts of the policy changes referred to above, it is helpful to understand the way the British housing system worked in an earlier period – although such an analysis is restricted to cross-sectional data. Table 6.1, drawn from the General Household Survey, shows the tenure distribution in 1973, by major life stage groups. It is based, like all tables in this chapter, on individual level data. It suggests major variation in housing tenure through the life-course. It suggests that the use of private renting was especially concentrated among younger single people, and to a degree young couples. In 1973 there was still some over-representation of elderly people in private renting, reflecting the fact that this used to be the dominant tenure. Public sector renting, which accounts for more than one third of the sample, still accounted for a substantial proportion of family and couple-based households. It had only slightly below average representation of couples with dependent children, and above average representation of older couples below retirement age, and non-dependent children still in their parents' home. It had a substantial over-representation of lone parents, but at this period this group accounted for a tiny proportion of the population. However, younger couples without children were markedly under-represented in this sector. This group was given relatively low priority under housing allocation policies. However, their lack of representation in the public rented sector may also reflect a tendency among younger age cohorts to move away from the sector, especially as they already had the highest representation in owner-occupation.

At the beginning of this chapter the idea of a housing career was introduced. The data in Table 6.1 supports this idea of housing through the life-course, of expected housing careers, given owned and rented housing, where there may be some form of state subsidy to renting, and when owning is not necessarily affordable to the whole population. In this model young people stay in the parental home until they can afford to set up an independent home, so that the age at which young people

Table 6.1: Housing tenure, by life stage (1973), in row percentages

	Owner-occupation	Public renting	Private renting
Child <16	50	39	11
Child 16-29 with parents	42	48	10
Young adult alone <30	24	16	60
Couple, no children <45	55	21	24
Couple, with children	55	34	12
Lone parent	26	56	19
Single 30-59	38	41	22
Couple, no children 45-59	47	39	14
Couple, no children 60-74	50	33	16
Single 60-74	40	39	21
Aged 75+	47	33	20
Total	**49**	**37**	**15**

leave the parental home will depend in part on the availability of housing but also on norms of youth independence. Some young people will move directly from the parental home into owning, especially if they have stayed there relatively late to save the costs of a deposit, or if they move in with a partner who already owns. However, a substantial proportion of young people will move into rented accommodation, since this is likely to be more affordable. It is also more compatible with their expected high residential mobility, which follows both from high job mobility, and because they may still be searching for a partner. Progressively, as these people form partnerships, become established in work careers and build savings the more secure of them will move into owned accommodation. This is likely to be accelerated as couples start to have children. This means there will be an increasing proportion of owner-occupiers at each later life stage, but it is also to be expected that some will remain renting, either because they remain relatively mobile, or because their incomes do not reach a level to make owner-occupation affordable. It is also possible that at the latest stages of the life-course older people may move into rented accommodation, to release capital, or because it provides care.

In Britain during the post-war years, up to around the period of which Table 6.1 represents, this model operated with a substantial state-subsidised sector, which if certainly not preferred over owner-occupation, was not wholly unacceptable even in the middle life-stages. The model is complicated by the fact that there were also processes of movement from the private rented sector into the state rented sector based on allocation. In their effects these were not entirely unlike the processes by which people entered owner-occupation: a period on a waiting list (equivalent to a saving period), accelerated by the arrival of children.

There is an important complication to the easy progression of this model, and this is that it may be seriously destabilised by shocks. Unemployment may make previously affordable housing no longer affordable. Even more directly, the breakdown of partnerships will lead at least one member of the couple to seek new accommodation, and perhaps to begin again in establishing a housing career. These problems can be mitigated in the subsidised housing sector. To the extent that the people at risk of economic shocks are concentrated in this sector, the risk that economic accidents might lead to loss of housing is reduced. In principle, the larger the sector, the more likely that shelter for those exposed to economic shocks is provided. The situation with regard to family fission is less clear, since it requires flexibility of allocation within the subsidised sector to provide new housing for departing members of a couple, which was not always available. There has also been concern that inflexibility of allocation may have led to difficulties in adjusting to labour market change.

Contrasting the situation in 1973 with data from the first wave of the BHPS in 1991 (Table 6.2) reveals a pattern of substantial change. In the first place, owner-occupation has expanded at the expense of both other tenures, with the proportion in private renting falling by almost one half, and that in public renting by more than one third. In spite of falling to less than 8%, private renting remains an important tenure for young single people below the age of 30. For most other groups it is very much a minority tenure. For all but two of the groups, public sector housing has fallen back, and fallen rather sharply. The exceptional groups are the single elderly, and those aged 75 and above. In part this reflects the ageing of the middle-aged cohorts with high representation in public sector housing observed in the 1973 data, but it also reflects the relative poverty of many people in these age groups. By contrast, public sector renting had declined very sharply in some of the life-stages where it had been important in earlier decades, for example the pre-retirement couples without dependent children. It had also declined, although not quite as sharply, among couples with children. However, children below the age of 16 were more likely than average to live in this sector. This reflects in

Table 6.2: Housing tenure, by life stage (1991), in row percentages

	Owner-occupation	Public renting	Private renting
Child <16	68	27	5
Child 16-29 with parents	77	19	4
Young adult alone <30	40	10	50
Couple, no children <45	79	9	12
Couple, with children	76	19	6
Lone parent	43	50	7
Single 30-59	59	30	12
Couple, no children 45-59	84	12	4
Couple, no children 60-74	72	24	4
Single 60-74	51	44	5
Aged 75+	53	40	8
Total	**70**	**23**	**7**

part the growth in the overall proportion of lone parents, but also, the greater likelihood of large families living in this sector.

John Ermisch and Marco Francesconi in Chapter Two focus on the emergence of cohabitation as a rather different form of partnership to marriage. The distinctiveness of cohabitation is confirmed if some of the couple categories are split up. Among younger couples without children, more than twice as many cohabiting couples are in private renting compared with married couples. This may be explained by age differences, but there are more striking differences among couples with children, with 46% of cohabiting couples in social housing, compared with 16% of married couples, confirming that cohabiting couples are markedly less affluent than married couples.

This is evidence of the process which some writers have described as the residualisation of the social rented sector (Forrest and Murie, 1988), that is to say that it now predominantly houses those with no access to any other sector, and hence a large proportion of its residents are in receipt of state welfare benefits. The introductory chapter to this volume (Table 1.5) has already shown the impact of this process in relation to employment status. It is argued that this concentration of unemployed people and other welfare recipients within the social rented sector further reduces the attractions of council renting for those who have any choices. The continued contraction of private renting has further reduced alternatives to owner-occupation. The latter's share has increased to around

Table 6.3: Housing tenure, by income decile group (1991), in row percentages

Income decile group	Owned outright	Owned with mortgage	Social renting	Private renting
Lowest	18	21	53	8
Second	24	21	46	10
Third	26	27	37	9
Fourth	25	40	28	7
Fifth	20	51	23	7
Sixth	19	61	14	6
Seventh	19	66	9	6
Eighth	17	72	6	5
Ninth	11	74	6	9
Highest	12	79	3	6
Total	**19**	**50**	**23**	**7**

70%, much higher than the share found in most other European countries, and means that more younger people and people on lower relative incomes are to be found owning their homes in Britain than in most other countries.

Table 6.3 shows the relationship between housing tenure and income level (here separating those who own outright from those who own with a mortgage, since the former tend to include a high proportion of elderly who may have relatively low incomes). The concentration of lower income households in social housing is quite clear, with very few in the higher deciles in this tenure. However, there do exist significant numbers of owners with mortgages at lower income levels.

This raises one of the key questions that this chapter aims to address: the sustainability of the British housing system where there is now one clear preferred tenure. Owner-occupied housing is likely to be more expensive than subsidised renting, and most of the state subsidies to owning have been removed. It depends on a more regular flow of income than renting. Under what conditions is owning affordable at the lower end of the income distribution? Are there groups for whom income instability, or instability of family circumstances makes owner-occupied housing inappropriate, but for whom alternatives are highly unsatisfactory? How far does the home-ownership-for-all model work in the face of transformations in the worlds of work and family?

Rates of tenure change

Up until now the use of the BHPS in this chapter has been essentially cross-sectional – but the panel data on transitions can be used to explore these issues, by establishing rates of tenure change and mobility, and showing how these are associated with initial states and other life events. The BHPS design, which follows movers, and also interviews new household members who join with original sample members, makes this particularly appropriate.

We start by looking at tenure changes, between wave 1 and wave 2 of the BHPS. Table 6.4 is based on the whole sample, and as with other tables, the units are individuals, rather than households since the latter are inappropriate in a longitudinal context. For example, the tenure changes include those of children leaving their parental home. It includes not just those who moved; some tenure changes can occur without a move. The table shows some of the gross flows through which the overall change in the tenure distribution occurs. The most striking feature is the difference between private renting and the other tenures in the rate of outflow. Only just about three quarters of private tenants remain in the sector from one year to the next. In effect, this shows the process of early housing career mobility, in which people use the private sector as a stepping stone into one of the other two main tenures (see Ermisch and others, 1995, on this process). A substantial majority of exits from the private rented sector are into owner-occupation, but there is still a significant flow into social housing (the ratio of social housing entrants to owner-occupier entrants is higher than the ratio of the whole social housing stock to the owner-occupied stock). However, when looking at flows from the main tenures, the level of exit from social housing is significantly higher than that from owner-occupation, and while exits from owner-occupation are mainly to the private rented sector, those leaving from social housing are relatively more likely to enter owner-occupation.

Table 6.4: Housing tenure at wave 2, by tenure at wave 1, in column percentages

| Wave 2 tenure | Wave 1 tenure | | | Total |
	Owned	Social renting	Private renting	
Owned	97.6	3.0	15.6	**70.4**
Social renting	0.5	94.3	8.5	**21.9**
Private renting	1.9	2.7	75.8	**7.7**

Table 6.5: Tenure change, by mobility status, in column percentages

Wave 2 tenure	Owned outright	Owned with mortgage	Social renting	Private renting	All tenures
			Wave I tenure		
Whole-household movers					
Owned outright	65	6	1	2	8
Owned with mortgage	19	78	11	31	43
Social renting	8	3	76	16	26
Private renting	8	14	12	50	23
Children leaving parental home					
Owned outright	5	3	0	5	3
Owned with mortgage	46	39	24	28	37
Social renting	12	11	51	15	19
Private renting	37	47	25	53	41
Separating couples					
Owned outright	18	112	5	6	10
Owned with mortgage	24	39	17	39	34
Social renting	0	12	56	13	21
Private renting	59	36	21	41	35
Other movers					
Owned outright	27	6	2	5	7
Owned with mortgage	32	58	19	31	38
Social renting	13	8	56	6	13
Private renting	29	28	23	58	43

Table 6.4 is based on both movers and non-movers. The patterns are rather different when we look only at movers as in Table 6.5. This table is based on combining the data from each single-year period between successive waves in the panel up to wave 7.

Among whole-household movers, there are substantial and perhaps surprising proportions of moves from owner categories to renting, which run counter to some of the assumptions of the ineluctable rise of owner-occupation. Among outright owners, who include a large proportion of older people, the major process appears to be elderly people moving into forms of sheltered or similar rented accommodation, but mortgagee movers are much younger, and appear from other evidence to be a mixture of evictions and repossessions, and those moving for job reasons. This points to some of the strains imposed by the rapid rise in owner-occupation in the 1980s, and difficulties of moving within the owner-occupied sector in the early 1990s. More than three quarters of whole-household movers from council renting remain in the sector, but there is a small flow into owner-occupation, and private renting. Around half of movers from private renting stay in the sector, and a majority of the remainder move into owner-occupation, but there is a significant flow into social renting, probably the majority from the major categories of housing need, such as lone parents.

As to movement associated with composition change, the largest single category consists of children leaving the parental home. Because of the dominance of owner-occupation among households with children, this dominates the tenures of origin. However, renting accounts for 60% of first destination tenures, reflecting the important continuing role of the private rented sector for this group. However, 40% of this category do move directly into owner-occupation. The latter group was somewhat older – median age 23, compared with median age 20 for movers to renting. However, this age would still be very young by European standards for starting to purchase a house. It is not clear if this level of movement into owner-occupation is likely to have fallen since the late 1980s, but if anything the housing market conditions in the early 1990s have favoured this group. If we analyse men and women separately, we find that women are less likely to leave home to private renting (37% compared with 45%) and more likely to move directly into one of the major tenures. This is probably because they are more likely to leave home directly into a partnership, rather than to live alone.

The figures on individual movers from separating couples do show very high levels of tenure mobility. In particular, there is a substantial move from owner-occupation to renting, and also a substantial move in the reverse direction, reflecting perhaps a return to the parental home, or movement in with a new partner who may be an owner. There are some differences between men and women, with women, again, less likely to end up in private renting (33% compared with 38% of men), and more likely to end up in social housing (24% compared with 18%).

Other household composition changes are more heterogeneous, but they also imply high levels of tenure mobility. In particular, they lead to some of the larger flows from private renting to the owner-occupied sector, including, for example, the next step up the housing ladder for those children who left the parental home into renting in earlier years.

Area deprivation, preferences and the life-course

One critical feature of housing not covered so far is that, with exceptions which are relatively minor in Britain, it is fixed in location, and from an economic perspective the opportunities this location affords are a major part of the housing service being purchased. However, because housing requires land, and the supply of land is fixed, there are likely to be substantial variations in housing price according to the opportunities and amenities different locations provide – hence the estate agent's view of location as the primary determinant of house price. This means, fairly obviously, that an individual's income and housing cost calculation will not only determine the physical characteristics of housing they can afford, but also the locations they can afford. It also means, given the transaction costs referred to earlier, they may also find, as their circumstances change, that they are in a sub-optimal location in relation to their needs. They may also find that area opportunities and amenities deteriorate. There is another contrast between a naïve economistic view of the role of location in life chances, which says that location should not have an independent role, since people can 'get on their bikes', and a view that sees constraints on mobility as potentially generating further disadvantage.

Housing and location may jointly contribute to variations in life chances and patterns of inequality, through a number of routes, including a reinforcement of other inequalities, for example, through:

• unequal opportunities for wealth acquisition;
• unequal opportunities provided by different localities;
• the stigmatisation associated with particular tenures;
• constraints on mobility that may have negative subsequent consequences in other life domains.

This chapter shows how panel data that track the economic and housing circumstances of individuals over time may contribute to an understanding of these effects.

The ways in which the characteristics of areas in which people live may shape their life chances, raises many complex issues, particularly in establishing the exact causal links; treatment here is intended only to be indicative of possible associations. It is possible to match characteristics of areas to the individual data from the BHPS, including, for example, measures of area deprivation. There are a number of possible indicators, and here the Carstairs index (Carstairs and Morris, 1989) is used. This

Table 6.6: Area deprivation, by housing tenure (1991), in column percentages

Quintiles of area deprivation score	Owned	Social renting	Private renting
Best	26	8	19
Second	23	13	17
Third	22	18	24
Fourth	16	26	12
Worst	14	35	27

index is often used in health research, but it is used here for two pragmatic reasons: it is available for the whole of Great Britain, and it does not use housing tenure as one of the constituents of the index. This is important since the analysis here is concerned in part with the relationship between housing tenure and area deprivation. The Carstairs index is a score based on the following characteristics of areas drawn from the 1991 Census, the:

- unemployment rate;
- percentage with no access to a car;
- percentage in overcrowded housing;
- percentage in lower social classes.

The index is divided into quintiles based on proportions of the Census population, and BHPS respondents are assigned on the basis of their local area characteristics. This index measures characteristics of the population, and not, for example, of the physical characteristics of an area which themselves may be another source of inequality.

Table 6.6 shows the association between housing tenure and area deprivation. Even though tenure is not included in the index, it is quite clear that it has a strong association. Tenants of social rented housing are much more likely to be living in the worst 20% of areas than owners. Nevertheless, there are a significant number of owners in the worst areas. However, rented housing is overall more likely to be in deprived areas, so that if there is a negative effect of being in a deprived area on life chances, then rented housing may confer an additional disadvantage. The association between area deprivation and household income level is also relatively strong, with 32% of households in the lowest decile living in the worst 20% of areas, compared with 11% in the best 20% of areas. In

Table 6.7: Preferences for mobility and reasons for wanting to move, by housing tenure, in column percentages

		Owned	Social renting	Private renting	Total
Prefer to stay		61	57	56	60
Prefer to move	Housing reason	15	15	19	15
	Dislikes current area	8	14	10	9
	Other area reason	8	5	7	8
	Other reason	7	8	8	8

terms of life-stages, young adults tend to be living in the worst areas (38% in the worst quintile), followed by lone parents (30%), and singles aged 30-59 (27%). For all the other groups, divergences from the average are relatively small. The extent to which there might be barriers to mobility out of the more deprived areas is examined later in the chapter.

In addition to area data, the survey also collects information on subjective attitudes to respondents' housing. At each wave the panel asks about preferences for moving. The question wording is 'If you could choose, would you stay here in your present home or would you prefer to move somewhere else?' This is a preference question, rather than asking about intentions or whether active steps are being taken to move; it is quite possible that respondents believe that they are not able to move, but may have some preference for doing so. There is a very high level of moving preferences (around 40%) compared with the level of those who typically say they are seriously considering moving (15% of a GHS 1983 sample used by Gordon and Molho, 1995). This measure can be taken as some indication of dissatisfaction with current housing or neighbourhood. A follow-up question on reasons for wanting to move gives some indication of the nature of this dissatisfaction. Table 6.7 shows data for 1991 on these preferences. The reasons for wanting to move have been grouped into four categories: reasons related directly to housing (such as wanting somewhere bigger), indications of disliking aspects of the current neighbourhood, other area preferences (especially a preference to move to a particular place or type of place), and a residual category. While in general, the distribution of reasons within each tenure are rather similar, some differences do stand out. Not surprisingly, the highest proportion wanting to move is found in the private rented sector. Since this group is likely to have aspirations to move into owner-occupied housing, it is not surprising that housing-related reasons are rather more important.

In the social rented sector, with a slightly lower level of preference for moving, it is the dislike of the current area which stands out, particularly in contrast with owners, who are more likely to express positive area preferences. This suggests that the neighbourhood characteristics of public housing estates are a significant contribution to dissatisfaction with social housing, rather than necessarily the conditions of the housing itself. It may also reflect the relative lack of choice over location within the social housing sector.

A multivariate analysis of these mover preferences (see Buck, 2000) suggests that in addition to tenure a number of other factors are important. Duration of residence is strong and negative, with a 3% decline in the probability of expressing a preference for moving with each year at the address, reflecting growing inertia as individuals became settled. There are substantial life-stage effects, with much stronger preferences for leaving an address at younger ages, including especially the early stages of family formation. There is a strong association with housing density (persons per room) in the expected direction. On the other hand, there is a negative association with numbers of children, perhaps reflecting the higher perceived disruption costs associated with moving children. The unemployed also expressed stronger preferences for movement. There is no association with income or with qualification levels.

This provides some evidence for a higher preference for mobility among those in the worst housing situations, as measured by density; among those in what is widely seen as the least favoured housing tenure (public sector renting), and among those in a disadvantaged labour market position. This is additional to the preferences related to life-cycle stage as indicated by the age effects. These associations tend to suggest that at least at the subjective level, unsatisfactory housing conditions are reinforcing disadvantage in other domains, particularly in the labour market.

Housing mobility

The BHPS data can also be used to explore how often people actually move. We start by examining the patterns of change during a single year, to look at comparative mobility rates for different groups. Table 6.8 shows rates of single-year mobility by life-stage. The table is based on pooling the evidence from each of the first six pairs of adjacent waves, in order not to bias the results by looking only at the rather exceptional housing market conditions of the early 1990s. It confirms very clearly the hypotheses outlined above, that of relatively high mobility in earlier

Table 6.8: Single-year mover status, by life stage at earlier wave, in row percentages

	Non-mover	Mover
Child below 5	87	14
Child 5-15	92	8
Child 16-29 with parents	82	18
Young adult alone	50	50
Couple, no children <45	84	16
Couple, with children	90	10
Lone parent	84	16
Single 30-59	89	11
Couple, no children 45-59	96	4
Couple, no children 60-74	97	3
Single 60-74	96	4
Aged 75+	95	5
Total	**90**	**10**

life-stages. Almost half of young adults living away from the parental home and not in a partnership move each year, compared with around 10% for the population as a whole. Adult children still living with their parents are also relatively mobile, along with younger couples with no children and lone parents. At the other extreme are the older life-stages, including, for example, the couples aged above 45 with no dependent children.

The survey also asks a set of retrospective questions about the reasons for moving. In Table 6.9 these reasons are related to the distance moved, measured by whether the move crossed a local authority (LA) or a regional boundary. The sample is restricted to adults who were interviewed after the move, and focuses on the first move made after wave 1 up to wave 6. Multiple reasons could be given, so that the percentages in the final column sum to more than 100%. Considering this column first, housing-related reasons are clearly the most substantial, especially when involuntary housing reasons, such as evictions and repossessions, are included. Job-related moves make up around one sixth of the total. This is not dissimilar from the share of job moves found in earlier studies (see Coleman and Salt, 1992, p 420). The formation and dissolution of partnerships accounts for almost the same proportion. Other family formation behaviour accounts for around 10%, with a similar proportion giving reasons related to area preference.

Table 6.9: Distance moved, by reason for move, in row percentages

Reason for move	Within LA district	Between LA district within region	Between region	% of all moves
Job related	22	37	42	16
Partnership	70	24	6	16
Other family	57	23	20	10
Education	12	29	59	6
Eviction	71	22	7	6
Housing	81	14	5	38
Area	68	23	9	11
Other	76	15	9	9
All moves	63	21	15	100

There are marked differences in the distance moved by reason given. Housing-related moves are predominantly local. Partnership-related moves are also more local than average, as, surprisingly, are area-related moves – suggesting that it is local neighbourhood characteristics that are prompting the move. At the other extreme job-related moves and education-related moves are, as expected, substantially more likely than average to be inter-regional.

Household composition is almost by definition likely to be related to residential mobility. Births and deaths are the only sources of change that are not directly dependent on mobility. One striking finding of the BHPS has been the extent of household composition change. Buck (1994) showed that 14% of households experienced some form of composition change over a single year. So it is reasonable to expect to find a substantial proportion of migration events associated with household composition change.

The potential range of household composition change events that may be associated with migration is very large, and here just a subset of them will be examined. Table 6.10 shows the distance of move of migrations associated with different types of household change, again focusing on the first move up to wave 6, but in this case including children. Because some types of household change are more associated with non-response than others, the distribution of move types should be treated with some caution (for example, children leaving home to join with a partner may be over-represented compared with children leaving home to other

Table 6.10: Distance moved, by household composition change, in row percentages

	Within LA district	Between LA district within region	Between region	% of all moves
No change	71	18	11	54
Partnership split	65	22	13	6
Child leaving home to partner	69	24	7	6
Child leaving home for other reason	52	21	27	12
Partnership formation	55	36	9	4
Return to parent	58	23	20	3
Child birth	71	24	5	3
Other joins	69	23	8	4
Other separations	71	15	14	9
All moves	67	20	13	100

destinations). Taking this into account it is still clear that children leaving the parental home, and the formation and dissolution of partnerships do make up well over half of the migrations associated with composition change. However, there remain significant numbers of other types of change, including returns of children who had previously left, and other miscellaneous movements, mainly involving unrelated people or more distant relatives. The category 'Child birth' refers to situations where there has been a birth as well as a move by the parent(s). Moves involving household composition change are likely to take place over a longer distance than those involving no change. Moves involving adult children either leaving or returning to the parental home are particularly likely to be long distance, except where children leave home to form a partnership. Moves involving partnership splits are more likely to be interregional than moves involving joins.

Cumulative impacts of multiple years of change

Up until now the chapter has focused on what the panel data suggests about changes from one year to the next. However, in looking at careers it is the cumulative impact of several years of change that is of more interest. We want to know how many people will have changed their state over a longer period, making allowance for the possibility that some

Table 6.11: Chances of moving within a six-year period, taking into account initial life-stage, in row percentages

	Non-mover	Mover	Expected % moving assuming independence between years
Child 16-29 with parents	30	70	69
Young adult alone	19	81	99
Couple, no children <45	46	54	64
Couple, kids	65	35	46
Lone parent	55	45	65
Single 30-59	63	37	52
Couple, no children 45-59	78	22	23
Couple, no children 60-74	86	14	16
Single 60-74	82	18	23
Aged 75+	78	23	27
Total	**63**	**37**	**48**

individuals are much more mobile than others and make repeat moves, and also that people may return to their original situation. In principle, it is possible to estimate what the mobility rate should be if moving at one wave was independent of previous wave moves. In effect this would be the annual mobility rate applied each year to those who have not yet moved (arithmetically this would be one minus the proportion not moving raised to the power of the number of years of exposure). If it is assumed that each person (including previous year movers) had a 10% chance of moving each year, then 47% would have moved after six years. This is more realistic than the assumption that there were no multiple moves, which would lead simply to the figure of 60% having moved during the six-year period. However, there are reasons for thinking that the assumption of independence is unlikely. In particular, it may be that certain individuals are more mobile than others, and are especially likely to be make multiple moves. When considering movement through states, such as tenure, when there may be moves in and out, it is even less clear *a priori* what cumulative impacts are likely to be.

Looking at what has happened in the six years between wave 1 and wave 7, taking the initial situation into account, Table 6.11 shows the percentage who move at least once during this period, by life-stage. The final column shows the estimated six-year mobility rate based on the one-year data in Table 6.8, and assuming that the probability of moving in one year was independent of previous moves. This estimate provides an average of mobility conditions during the period. As anticipated, the six-year mobility rate for the whole sample is substantially less than would arise if mobility was independent in this way, indicating that there is a strong probability of repeat mobility. Comparing the life-stage groups does confirm the sharp differences by age, seen earlier, with more than 80% of young single adults moving during this period. Mobility of adult children in the parental home is most closely in line with the independence assumption, which is what is to be expected for a process where repeat moves are rather rare. The differences by life-stage above the youngest age ranges do seem essentially to be related to age rather than family structure, and single people above the age of 30 do not seem especially mobile. The difference between the cumulative mobility rate and the expectation based on the independence assumption is greatest among lone parents, suggesting a considerable heterogeneity in this group between those who make multiple moves and a more stable group.

A multivariate analysis of residential mobility (reported in Buck, 2000) identifies some of the factors which influence it. There is a relatively high duration dependency (the longer individuals have lived at an address, the less likely they are to leave it). Duration will interact with age, and some large part of the falling probability of migration with age found in many data sources will be captured here by the duration variable. Having taken this into account there is a significantly higher probability of migration from addresses entered when below the age of 30. The effect is strongest for addresses entered when below the age of 20. These age effects reflect the rapid turnover characteristic of younger adults at this stage of the life-cycle. Above the age of 30 there are no significant age effects when age is measured as here. There is no significant gender difference in the probability of moving.

There has been substantial research on the association between tenure and migration, mainly focused on the question of whether the housing system contributes to labour immobility (for example, Hughes and McCormick, 1981, 1985). The main focus has been on long distance (that is, inter-regional) migration. This research has found that council tenants have much lower probabilities of making inter-regional moves, but rather higher probabilities of making local moves. The analysis suggests that for all moves there is a significantly higher mobility associated with public sector renting compared with ownership, and still higher levels associated with private renting. However, separate analyses of inter-regional and intra-regional moves suggest that it is local moves to which public sector tenants are more prone.

There is a significant positive association between income and mobility, with people in the highest income decile group more than twice as likely to move as those in the lowest decile group. Those single, cohabiting, divorced or separated are all more mobile than the married. High housing density also has a substantial positive effect on the likelihood of moving. Those in intermediate and working-class jobs are significantly less mobile than the economically inactive. While the unemployed appeared to be somewhat more mobile, the difference is not significant. In general, those with qualifications are somewhat more mobile than those without, although the effect is only statistically significant for those with middle level qualifications but not degrees.

It is possible to use these results to estimate the distribution of completed durations at addresses for respondents with different characteristics. For example, a married man with median income, a working-class job and no qualifications who started living in council accommodation between the ages of 20 and 24 would expect a median duration of 51 months. By contrast, a similar man in owner-occupied housing would expect a median duration of 111 months. A similarly aged man in owner-occupation with a higher-paying service class job, and with a degree would expect a median duration of 45 months. These examples show that lower income families in council housing have comparable mobility rates to higher income owner-occupiers. It is lower income owner-occupiers who have very low mobility rates. To some degree at least this must reflect the situation of the British housing market in the early 1990s, where there was both very low overall mobility, and a relatively large number of lower income purchasers who may have been trapped by falling house prices.

If these findings are contrasted with the factors that explained preferences to move, discussed in the previous section, then the disadvantaging preference factors (density, unemployment and public sector housing) are all positively associated with actual mobility. It is not possible to tell whether the higher mobility of these groups represents stronger preferences or greater opportunities (or greater levels of involuntary mobility). There are also positive associations between mobility and indicators of higher social and economic status (for example, income, qualifications, and the negative association with working-class jobs). This suggests a relatively complex social structuring to mobility, so it is only possible to answer in a limited way the question of the nature of social and economic constraints on mobility.

Table 6.12: Housing tenure at wave 7, by tenure at wave 1, in column percentages

		Wave 1 tenure		
Wave 7 tenure	Owned	Social renting	Private renting	Total
Owned	92	14	42	71
Social renting	2	81	17	21
Private renting	6	5	41	8

The cumulative impacts of tenure change can be examined in a similar way to that in which we looked at migration. From the one-year data in Table 6.4 it is possible to estimate the proportion who would remain in each tenure assuming that the departure processes remained fixed, applied uniformly to all members of the tenure and that there was no return to the tenure. This would imply that by wave 7, 86% of wave 1 owners would still be owning and 70% of social housing tenants would still be in that sector, compared with only 19% of private renters. Table 6.12 shows that these assumptions do not hold, with much lower overall departures from each tenure. However, there are differences in the cumulative impact of the processes. Overall, there is a much higher probability of remaining in owner-occupation than in social housing. Social housing takes a rather higher share of those leaving owning than it did in a single-year period, but the scale of the flow is modest. In the longer period a much larger share of those leaving social housing are entering owner-occupation compared with private renting than in the single-year period. In effect, this is evidence that private renting acts as a short-term intermediate tenure for people either moving between the main tenures, or who will eventually return to their previous tenure. While the cumulative rate of loss from private renting itself is high, it is nowhere near as high as might be assumed from the single-year figure, implying that within this tenure there is a group with relatively long durations.

Analysis by life-stage suggests that apart from children leaving the parental home the groups most likely to leave owner-occupation during this seven-year period were lone parents and those older than 75. This suggests financial difficulties in the first case, and either equity release, or the need for care in sheltered housing in the latter. Analysis by wave 1 income also suggests that owners in the lowest income quintile were much more likely to leave the sector than those in higher quintiles, implying difficulties of affordability for owner-occupation.

Table 6.13: Wave 7 tenure for wave 1 owner-occupiers, by experience of social and economic 'shocks', in row percentages

| | Wave 7 tenure | | |
	Owned	Social renting	Private renting
Number of waves unemployed			
0	95	1	4
1	84	6	10
2	76	7	17
3 or more	71	8	21
Experienced partnership split between wave 1 and wave 7			
No	94	1	5
Yes	77	10	14

However, the panel data on other events can be used to explore how far they are related to moves out of owner-occupation. This addresses the question of whether owner-occupiers subject to external shocks are subject to particular risks of losing their housing. Here we focus only on the working-age population, and exclude children still living in their parents' home. Table 6.13 shows the wave 7 tenure situation of those who were owner-occupiers in wave 1. The first part of the table compares people who have experienced unemployment (strictly speaking, reported themselves as unemployed at one of the intermediate waves), with those who have not. While the overall departure rate from owner-occupation is very low, it rises progressively and substantially with experience of unemployment, suggesting that some of the labour market instability and insecurity, which Mark Taylor discusses in Chapter Four, feeds through into housing market effects. We saw earlier that partnership splits were associated with departures from owner-occupation, with around 45% leaving the tenure immediately, a rather direct effect because the split necessarily implies a move. The second half of this table suggests that while some people do return to owner-occupation after the split, it also suggests that people cannot necessarily return rapidly and some remain renting after several years. Interestingly, there is no major difference between men and women in departure rates. Overall, this again suggests that owner-occupation has limitations in the face of family instability.

In terms of life-stage, the highest departure rates from social housing were from children leaving the parental home, suggesting that part of the decline in the role of social housing works through intergenerational

Table 6.14: Whether moved to less deprived areas by wave 1 tenure: wave 1 residents of most deprived 20% of areas, in column percentages

	Owned	Social renting	Private renting	Total
Stayed in worst quintile	79	87	47	79
Moved to fourth quintile	6	6	16	7
Moved to top three quintiles	15	8	37	14

changes. There are also high departure rates among young adults and couples with no children. On the other hand, the departure rate for couples with children is only about average. There is a strong association between departure rate and wave 1 income level. Income also seems to make a difference to the destination of those leaving private renting. Thus 50% of private renters in the lowest income quintile in wave 1 were in social housing by wave 7 (compared with 24% in owner-occupation), while 70% of private renters in the highest income quintile were in owner-occupation by wave 7 (compared with 22% in social housing).

The earlier analysis of mobility patterns suggested that social housing tenants have higher mobility than owners and are also more likely to live in deprived areas. This raises the question of whether social housing tenants were able to use their mobility opportunities to leave more deprived areas. Table 6.14 looks at the mobility between area-type of people who were in the worst 20% of areas at wave 1; it includes non-movers. Overall, 21% left such areas. However, there are marked tenure differences. More than half the private renters moved to less deprived areas. This reflects life-cycle processes such as the concentration of younger single people in rented housing in more deprived inner urban areas, who relatively soon move into owner-occupation in less deprived areas. Contrasting the other tenures, it is clear that owners, in spite of their lower mobility, are more able to leave deprived areas, and in particular are twice as likely to establish a significant improvement in conditions by moving to an area in the top three quintiles. The mobility of social housing tenants appears to recycle them within the more deprived areas.

Establishing a housing career

In the previous sections, evidence about tenure change patterns for the whole population has been used to compare the different opportunities

Table 6.15: Tenure change for young people leaving the parental home, in column percentages

	Wave 1 tenure		
Wave 7 tenure	Owned	Social renting	Total
Owned	66	45	61
Social renting	5	39	12
Private renting	29	17	27

and life chances of individuals in different tenures and with different resources. This has provided information on trajectories through the housing career at different life-stages. This section looks at more direct evidence specifically on the early stages of the housing career, examining in particular the processes by which young adults enter one of the main tenures.

Table 6.15 shows tenure change for the group who were living in the parental home at wave 1, and have left by wave 7; it excludes people whose parental home was in the private rented sector, because their numbers were so small. A more detailed analysis of this data would also take account of the age at which young adults were leaving the parental home, but some inferences can be drawn from this table. The distribution between the origin tenures, not shown, is almost identical to that shown in the second row of Table 6.2, suggesting that there are no great differences in the rate of departure from the parental home by tenure of origin. On the other hand, there are clearly significant differences in tenure destinations, which implies a degree of inter-generational tenure succession, in a situation where social housing may have become a residual tenure largely catering for those with few other choices. While owner-occupation is the largest destination tenure for both groups, almost 40% of individuals whose parents were in social housing find themselves in social housing when they leave the parental home, and people from owner-occupied backgrounds are one and a half times as likely to find themselves in owner-occupation. Very few end up in social housing, but substantial numbers are private renting, suggesting in particular longer periods of career mobility before entering one of the main tenures, compared with people from social housing origins.

The dominance of owner-occupation as a desirable tenure raises questions about its affordability, as stressed throughout the chapter. The analysis above implicitly used exits from owner-occupation as a measure of difficulties of affordability. However, it is also possible to use the panel

Table 6.16: Household incomes of first-time purchasers compared with other young households, in £s per month

Percentiles of income distribution	First-time purchasers	All households with head <30	Renter households with head <30
Lowest decile (10)	£931	£393	£297
Lower quartile (25)	£1,287	£834	£499
Median (50)	£1,885	£1,600	£993
Upper quartile (75)	£2,601	£2,529	£1,622
Highest decile (90)	£3,727	£3,500	£2,347

data to look at entrants to owner-occupation, and compare them with non-entrants. In the late 1980s in the UK, as house prices rose steeply there was considerable concern about the affordability of the sector to the majority of younger people, and a concern that the ratios of mortgage debt to income were rising to dangerous levels. Falling prices in the early 1990s made the situation more benign for the group of potential entrants, although not for those who did buy in the late 1980s. Examining BHPS first-time buyers in the period 1991-97 reveals a median ratio of mortgage debt to income of 1.78, well below the long-term standard ratio ceiling operated by mortgage lenders of three times your income. This ratio is only reached at the ninth decile of ratios for BHPS purchasers. However, it ignores the situation of non-purchasers. Table 6.16 compares average monthly household income for first-time purchasers aged below 30 (at the wave after the purchase) with all households with a household reference person aged below 30, and with similar rented households. Although the distributions for purchasers and renters do overlap considerably, and it is likely that many renters could in principle afford to buy, the median renter income is around the same level as the lowest decile of purchaser income. It is likely that these low-income purchasers will have special circumstances (such as additional unmeasured contributions from parents, exceptional savings). This data suggests that at least half the renters have incomes that would make purchase extremely difficult.

Conclusions

Panel data permits some distinctive new analyses of the housing career. In many ways it is required for a full and satisfactory account of that career, since retrospective recall will capture only imperfectly some of the economic correlates of the housing career. Recall data also has significant limitations for the exploration of the relationship between housing careers and family formation and dissolution, since it is unlikely that data from all the people involved can be collected. This chapter has only scratched the surface of the possibilities for use of panel data in the analysis of housing careers. It has, for example, said little about the impacts of exogenous shocks from the labour market. Longer runs of panel data will be required to analyse some sorts of housing trajectories, for example to look at processes of equity accumulation over the long term, and its association with circumstances of origin.

Nevertheless, the analyses have shown how life-stage is related to the processes of tenure mobility, and have confirmed the processes of housing career stabilisation associated with movement out of the earlier life-stages and with entry into one of the main tenures. The evidence also confirms the residualisation of social housing in the sense that there is a high level of exit from the sector, and little entry into the sector by those who have the resources to make a choice. The evidence also suggests that the disadvantages associated with renting, and especially social housing, may be reinforced by its concentration in more disadvantaged areas, and the difficulties social housing tenants have in leaving such areas. However, the evidence also suggests difficulties associated with a housing system in which owner-occupation is universally preferred. There are significant parts of the population who would have difficulties in entering owner-occupation. The analyses also present evidence that people are more likely to leave owner-occupation if they are on a low income or experience unemployment or family break-up. Owner-occupation alone cannot provide adequate housing for all in a world of income inequality and increasing instability in family and work life.

References

Buck, N. (1994) 'Housing and residential mobility', in N. Buck and others (eds) *Changing households: The British Household Panel Survey 1990-92*, Colchester: University of Essex.

Buck, N. (2000) 'Using panel surveys to study migration and residential mobility', in D. Rose (ed) *Researching social change*, London: UCL Press.

Carstairs, V. and Morris, R. (1989) 'Deprivation, mortality and resource allocation', *Community Medicine*, vol 11, no 4, pp 364-72.

Coleman, D. and Salt, J. (1992) *The British population: Patterns, trends and processes*, Oxford: Oxford University Press.

Ermisch, J., Di Salvo, P. and Joshi, H. (1995) *Household formation and housing tenure decisions of young people*, Occasional Papers of the ESRC Research Centre on Micro-social Change, 95-1, Colchester: University of Essex.

Forrest, R. and Murie, A. (1988) *Selling the welfare state*, London: Routledge.

Gordon, I.R. and Molho, I. (1995) 'Duration dependence in migration behaviour: cumulative inertia versus stochastic change', *Environment and Planning A*, vol 27: 1961-1975.

Hughes, G.A. and McCormick, B. (1981) 'Do council housing policies reduce migration between regions?', *Economic Journal*, no 91, pp 919-37.

Hughes, G.A. and McCormick, B. (1985) 'Migration intentions in the UK: which households want to migrate and which succeed?', *Economic Journal*, no 95 (supplement), pp 113-23.

SEVEN

A measure of changing health[1]

Richard Berthoud

Purpose

The BHPS data on family structures, employment, income and housing, on which previous chapters are based, have been the subject of detailed analysis ever since the panel data first came on stream in the mid-1990s. Much of the material covered so far has summarised work that has already been published in a series of more detailed, and sometimes more technically complex, papers. However, the survey also includes a substantial set of questions about respondents' state of health, and their use of health services. These have not been analysed in anywhere near as much detail, and certainly not in a way that takes full advantage of the longitudinal structure of the data. The purpose of this chapter is to develop the analysis of the dynamics of ill-health. However, because the analysis of this part of the BHPS data is at a much earlier stage, it is necessary to start by considering some more technical issues than needed to be addressed in other chapters.

The most commonly used survey-based measures of ill-health and impairment in Britain are derived from cross-sectional surveys. A sample of respondents is interviewed once, and asked questions about their current state of health. This provides an estimate of the number of people ill or impaired at any time, but it provides no direct indication of the rate at which people become ill or recover. This is true of the self-reported health measures obtained by, for example, the General Household Survey (ONS, 2000) and the 1996 Health Survey for England (Prescott-Clarke and Primatesta, 1998); and of the impairment measures obtained by the 1985 Disability Survey (Martin and others, 1988), the 1995 Health Survey for England (Prescott-Clarke and Primatesta, 1997) and the Disability Follow-up to the Family Resources Survey (Grundy and others, 1999).

It is easy to assume that ill-health and impairment are long-term, perhaps irreversible, conditions. Two statistical features of the cross-sectional data just described encourage this assumption. First, when comparing the notional 'stock' of periods of ill-health in progress at any point, with the notional 'flow' of all episodes of ill-health starting in the course of a period, there is an obvious tendency for long-term and permanent conditions to dominate. If someone is ill for only a short period, the odds are that their interview will not coincide with the illness, whereas permanent conditions are bound to be recorded, whenever the interviewer calls. Second, all sources agree that the prevalence of ill-health and impairment increases steadily with age. This must mean that more people become ill than recover, and it is easy to translate this into the idea that ill-health is something that arrives as you age, and continues till death.

That may be true for many cases, and especially for certain conditions that are intrinsically irreversible. However, the possibility that people might move in and out of ill-health, or move up and down a scale ranging from fully fit to very ill, tends to be obscured by the types of cross-sectional data just described. A measure of changing health over time would be of value for four reasons:

- it is important to measure the rate at which people become sick and/ or recover;
- it is important to distinguish analytically between permanent and temporary conditions;
- it is valuable to analyse the rate at which people enter (or leave) ill-health on the basis of characteristics that were observed *before* the event in question; this is likely to give much more insight into predispositions and potential causes of ill-health than analysis of characteristics observed *at the same time as* the problem under consideration;
- the answers to survey questions about illness and impairment cannot provide a precise classification; for example, one form of imprecision would occur if the same person gave different answers on different occasions – year-on-year comparisons of responses given by the same people provide some indication of the reliability of the data.

There have been a number of studies of the rate at which people become impaired or disabled as they move into old age (for example, Disney and others, 1997). However, it is difficult to find any analysis of changes from year to year in levels of ill-health across the full age range.

This chapter has two objectives:

- to review some of the methodological issues that need to be addressed in the development of a longitudinal measure of health from the BHPS, describing the analytical steps, so that other colleagues – specialists either in health data or in longitudinal analysis – can comment on the methods used;
- to provide substantive analysis of the correlates of changing health.

These early findings are of interest in themselves, but also help to show how the measures adopted perform in practice. Because this analysis is at a much earlier stage of development than the work summarised in previous chapters, the narrative focuses rather more on issues of measurement and reliability than has been the case so far.

The analysis is based on 7,336 adults (16+). The sample was confined to those who gave a full interview every year from 1991 to 1997, or who entered the survey at age 16 in the course of that period, or left it on death (and gave an interview every year that they were eligible). The analysis was also limited to those who answered all three of the health questions used to develop the longitudinal measure. Much of the longitudinal analysis is based on pooling waves: there were 46,886 person-waves, and 39,552 transitions between wave *t* and wave *t+1*, falling to 6,118 sequences of seven consecutive years. However, the cross-sectional analysis is based on a single wave (the middle of the sequence, wave 4), containing 6,673 cases.

Three questions and an index

Rather than ask people to compare their health now with this time last year, the BHPS asks respondents to describe their health at the time of each annual interview. A measure of changing health is therefore a two-stage process: to develop a measure of current health and then to compare each year's answers with the responses to the same questions the year before or the year after.

The BHPS contains three main questions that can contribute to a measure of ill-health and impairment. Other questions in the health section cover such ground as experience of accidents, levels of stress, receipt of care and use of health services. These are all candidates for cross-analysis against the overall measure of ill-health, without directly contributing to it.

One question is a subjective assessment of the respondent's general state of health:

Please think back over the last 12 months about how your health has been. Compared to people of your own age, would you say that your health has on the whole been …

Excellent 23%
Good 49%
Fair 20%
Poor 6%
Very poor 2%

Such a broad question has the disadvantage of being vague and imprecise; it carries the converse advantage of being all-inclusive and evaluative in a way that narrower and more explicit questions are not. The question asks respondents to compare their health with that of other people of their own age but (as Table 7.1 shows) this comparison seems to have been partly discounted: the older they were, the more likely they were to report poor health.

A summary measure of subjective ill-health based on this question was derived by assigning a score of 0 to 'excellent', 1 to 'good' through to 4 for 'very poor'.

The second question asked whether the respondent had health problems of any of 12 broad types:

Do you have any of the health problems or disabilities listed on this card?

Arms, legs, hands, feet, back or neck	26%
Difficulty in seeing	5%
Difficulty in hearing	9%
Skin conditions/allergies	11%
Chest/breathing problems, asthma, bronchitis	12%
Heart/blood pressure or blood circulation problems	14%
Stomach/liver/kidneys	6%
Diabetes	2%
Anxiety, depression or bad nerves	6%
Alcohol or drug related problems	0.3%
Epilepsy	0.8%
Migraine or frequent headaches	9%
Other health problems	4%

The list of problems varied in its precision: some categories related to parts of the body; others to physical functions; others to specific medical conditions. As discussed earlier, there is probably something of a bias towards long-term rather than short-term conditions: most people experiencing acute episodes will have recovered (or died) by the time of their interview.

A total of 58% of the BHPS sample reported at least one of these health problems; 27% reported more than one. A summary measure was derived by counting the total number of such problems reported. However, the upper range of the summary measure was limited by treating five or six problems as *five*, and seven problems or more as *six*.

A third pair of questions asked for details of five types of impairment, defined as normal activities that individuals might not be able to do:

> Please look at this card and tell me which of these activities, if any,
> you would normally find difficult to manage on your own?
>
> | | |
> |---|---|
> | Doing the housework | 6% |
> | Climbing stairs | 6% |
> | Dressing yourself | 2% |
> | Walking for at least 10 minutes | 7% |
>
> Does your health limit the type of work
> or the amount of work you can do?
>
> | | |
> |---|---|
> | Yes | 18% |

It is important to maintain a conceptual distinction between ill-health and impairment. The one often causes the other, but they are not the same thing. Some serious illnesses may cause little or no impairment, at least until they reach a terminal stage. Some severely impaired people may be in the best of health – someone who had both legs amputated many years ago, for example. The items on the list included in the BHPS are only a small sample of all the impairments that are examined in specialist surveys (for example, Grundy and others, 1999), but may nevertheless provide a broad indicator of disability.

A total of 19% of the sample had at least one impairment; 9% more than one. A summary index of impairment was derived simply by counting up the number of impairments; thus the maximum was *five*.

As Table 7.1 shows, all three of these questions indicated a steady worsening of health and an increase in impairments with age. This relationship is entirely consistent with other cross-sectional measures of health from the GHS and other sources mentioned earlier. In detail, the problems and impairments questions were much more strongly correlated with age ($R = 0.42$ and 0.32 respectively) than the subjective question (R

Table 7.1: Answers to three BHPS health questions, by age group (wave 4), in row percentages

	Health fair, poor or very poor	Any health problems	Any impairments
16-19	18	25	4
20-29	24	28	7
30-39	22	32	9
40-49	26	43	16
50-59	31	58	25
60-69	35	71	33
70-79	41	80	37
80+	44	87	54

= 0.17). This may be because the subjective health question invited respondents to take their age into account when assessing their position.

The analytical hypothesis is that there is some underlying concept of 'ill-health', which each of these questions approximates, but which none of them measures exactly. If that were the case, it would be normal to expect a substantial overlap between the answers to the questions, so that people with many 'problems' also had 'poor' health and some 'impairments'. At the same time, the different formulation of the questions means that they each capture a slightly different aspect of 'ill-health'.

A key test of the validity of a single index combining the answers to three questions is that people should tend to answer them in similar ways – this would suggest that they are all measuring roughly the same thing. Before showing the results of that test for the questions as a whole, it is necessary to discuss the robustness of the inclusion of individual items from the health problems question. Table 7.2 shows the regression coefficients based on multivariate analysis which tested the associations between each separate health problem and subjective ill-health and impairments. Most of the problems in the list were associated with a substantial increase in the level of ill-health suggested by both of the other two indicators. However, there were some exceptions. Sight problems were associated with impairment, but not with subjective ill-health. Hearing problems, skin conditions and migraine were not associated strongly with either of the other two indicators. The conclusion drawn from this is that these latter three problems (however serious they may be in their own right) do not contribute to the same concept of ill-health as the other items and so they have been removed from the count

Table 7.2: Multiple regression equation between specific health problems and the other health questions (wave 4), given as regression coefficients

	Subjective ill- health	Impairments
Arms, legs, hands, feet, back or neck	0.49	0.80
Difficulty in seeing	0.20	0.53
Difficulty in hearing	0.03	0.16
Skin conditions/allergies	0.08	0.00
Chest/breathing problems, asthma, bronchitis	0.47	0.43
Heart/blood pressure or blood circulation problems	0.40	0.47
Stomach/liver/kidneys	0.53	0.37
Diabetes	0.34	0.28
Anxiety, depression or bad nerves	0.60	0.33
Alcohol or drug related problems	0.46	0.40
Epilepsy	0.44	0.40
Migraine or frequent headaches	0.16	0.03
Other health problems	0.60	0.41
R^2	29.5%	33.4%

Note: The analysis used ordinary least squares regression. An ordered logit equation produced very similar results

of health problems. All the remaining results shown in this chapter are after this correction has been made.

Table 7.3 shows that there was a strong tendency for survey respondents to give similar answers at each of the three questions, without the association being so strong that they could be considered simply as identical questions. The correlation coefficients between each pair of questions were all above 0.50, which is very high for survey questions based on samples of individuals.

Most specific illnesses and impairments are clearly identifiable in an objective way: the patient can report symptoms and a doctor can diagnose a condition. Ill-health might be viewed as the existence of one or more of these conditions, and health as the absence of them. In practice, health and ill-health are much broader, and therefore fuzzier, concepts and cannot be measured so objectively by surveys:

• some illnesses cannot be diagnosed unambiguously;

Table 7.3: Cross-comparison between the three health questions (wave 4), given as correlation coefficients

	Subjective health	Number of health problems	Number of impairments
Subjective health	1.0		
Number of health problems	0.53	1.0	
Number of impairments	0.52	0.56	1.0

- the patient may not be able to give a technically accurate report on the details of their diagnosis;
- there is variation within and between conditions in the severity of their effects on the patient – common metric is needed if an underlying concept of ill-health is to be used;
- some aspects of ill-health are not specific conditions; the patient feels poorly, or is subject to a variety of small problems.

These considerations dictate that an overall measure of ill-health has to be based on some of the analytical techniques developed to study other 'fuzzy' concepts such as 'political commitment' or 'consumerism'. Since no one question is an accurate measure of the underlying concept, the answers to several questions are combined to provide an overall index. This has been done here by adding together the scores on the three questions just described. Someone would score zero if they said that their health had been excellent, they had no health problems and their health did not limit their activities in any way. The theoretical maximum was 15 (very poor health = 4, seven or more health problems = 6, all activities limited = 5). Three members of the sample did score the maximum (during at least one wave), but the numbers with extremely high scores were very small. The full distribution is illustrated in Figure 7.1.

The ill-health index has been compiled by adding together the *actual* scores on each of the three questions: 0-4 for subjective health, 0-6 for health problems, 0-5 for impairments. This may be taken to imply that one point in the subjective scale is equivalent to one 'problem', both of which are equivalent to one 'impairment'. There is no basis for those equivalencies; but then there is no basis for any other. A technical solution often adopted is to standardise each of the input variables (using Z-scores), so that each contributes the same mean and the same variance to the summary score. That would be necessary if the units of measurement

Figure 7.1: Distribution of scores on the full index of ill-health (wave 4)

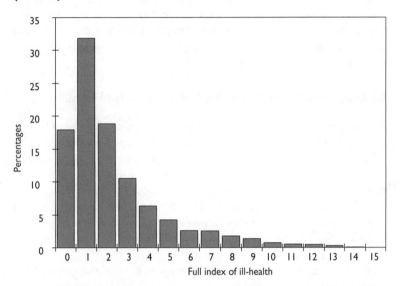

Full index of ill-health

of the contributor variables were completely different (try adding annual income to number of consumer durables in an index of prosperity, for example). However, in this case the means and variances of the raw variables were broadly similar. An index based on standardised variables was tested, but performed just the same as the non-standardised version. The latter was retained, on the grounds that it is easier to tabulate and explain an index taking 16 whole-number values, than the much more complex range of values produced by an index derived from standardised inputs.

There are various ways in which the validity of this index can be tested. Cronbach's alpha is specifically designed as a measure of the internal consistency of a multi-item index. It is calculated on the basis of number of contributory variables, and the extent of the correlation between them. It can take a value of between 0 and 1; the literature suggests that a good indicator should have a value of alpha of at least 0.6. The value of the index of ill-health derived here is 0.77, which suggests that the indicator is a very good measure of some underlying concept[2].

Another test of an index is its 'reliability'. If people answered questions at random, most of them would give a different response each time they were asked it (unless they could remember the previous answer); but they would answer consistently if the response was based on some genuine situation. The test–retest correlation coefficient for the ill-health index was 0.82. Since some of the variation between tests (a year apart) will have been caused by genuine changes in people's health (the subject of later analysis) this is a very high coefficient, and again supports the use of the index as a genuine measure.

Characteristics of those with good and bad health

A third type of test is to check that the index behaves analytically as it 'ought' to, bearing in mind the known and hypothesised characteristics of the ill-health we are trying to measure. All other cross-sectional data sources, plus common observation, suggest that ill-health is much more prevalent among old people than among younger adults. Figure 7.2 shows the pattern of ill-health by age. For men, the average increased from 1.0 in their late teens to 3.7 in their 80s; for women, the corresponding range was from 1.5 to 5.1. The index produces results that are closely in line with expectation.

Another way to validate the index is to show that those with high scores have behavioural patterns of the type expected among people with

Figure 7.2: Average score on the full index of ill-health, by age and sex (wave 4)

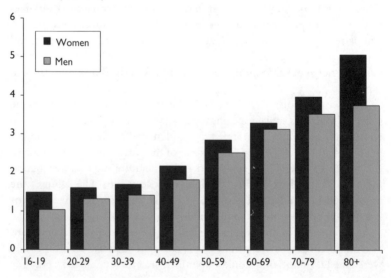

Figure 7.3: Average number of visits to the GP and average number of other health and welfare services used in the past year, by score on full index of ill-health (wave 4)

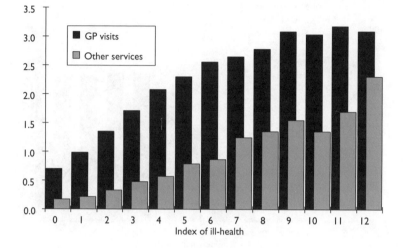

poor health. For example, they ought to make more use of health services. Figure 7.3 clearly shows that the more ill people appeared to be, according to the index, the more often they saw their doctor[3], and the more likely they were to use one or another of a range of other health and welfare services (including treatment as an in-patient in hospital)[4].

Visits to the doctor and use of health services are so obviously associated with ill-health that it may be wondered whether these measures should not also have been included in the package of variables that contributed to the overall index. They were not, for both theoretical and practical reasons. The theoretical point is that while the three questions used were directly concerned with health itself, visits to the doctor and use of health services were concerned with what, if anything, the respondent had done about it, and what services were available. If services had been included in the base index, it would not then be possible to analyse whether different groups of people (defined in terms of such characteristics as sex, ethnic group, class or region) were making more or less use of the NHS than might have been expected, given the state of their health. The practical point is that adding these two further questions did not improve the performance of the index, as measured, for example, by Cronbach's alpha.

Another way to examine the index is to see how far it related to some

Figure 7.4: Proportion of men who were unable to work because of long-term sickness, and of individuals who received care from a household member, by score on full index of ill-health (wave 4)

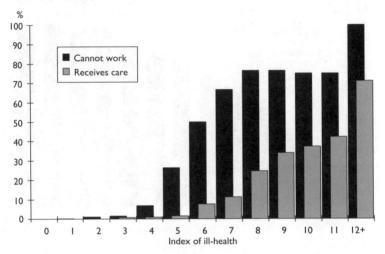

of the well-known consequences of ill-health. These are illustrated in Figure 7.4. The black columns show the proportion who answered 'long-term sick' for the question on employment. The analysis is confined to men aged between 20 and 59, because these are people who would probably be in work if they could, without alternative potential occupations in the form of childcare, study or retirement.

None of the men who scored 0 or 1 on the health index were off work long-term sick; hardly any of those who scored 2 or 3. The proportion grew rapidly across scores 4, 5, 6 and 7, so that three quarters of those scoring 8 or more were unable to work. These are very clear indications of the validity of the index.

The grey columns of Figure 7.4 show how many respondents lived in a household with another adult who said that s/he provided 'care' to the respondent in question. The analysis is confined to those who lived with other adults, since those who lived alone could not have received 'care' as measured here. Virtually no one was cared for in this way up to point 5 on the index, but the proportion increased rapidly across the rest of the range. Again, the evidence about 'caring' strongly supports the use of the index of ill-health.

As before, these two elements, cannot work and receives care, have not

Figure 7.5: Estimated risk of death in the next year, by age and score on the index of ill-health (waves I to 6)

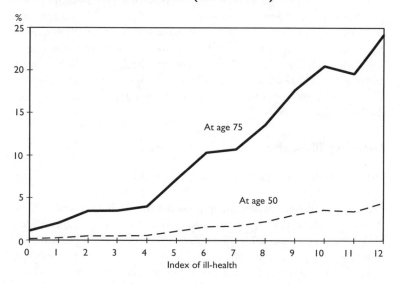

been included in the index. The theoretical point is the same: these are measures of the consequences of ill-health or impairment, not of ill-health itself. The overwhelming practical point is that these two questions cannot be measured meaningfully for all members of the sample (for example, pensioners, or those who live alone) so they cannot contribute to a measure of ill-health which should be applied universally.

A fifth measure of the consequences of ill-health is uniquely available in this survey. Because BHPS respondents are re-interviewed every year, the interviewers usually learn if a member of their sample has died within the past 12 months. This is not fully accurate, because some of those who disappeared without trace may also have been dead. Nevertheless, it provides a measure of the consequences of ill-health that is not usually available from general surveys of the population. In fact, the proportion who died each year was very low for those who scored few points on the index, and rose to about 12% in the higher ranges. Age was also strongly associated with the risk of death, as well as being associated with the onset of ill-health. A logistic regression equation was needed to sort out the independent effects. It indicated that the probability of death was explained equally by age and ill-health. The higher mortality rate of men compared with women was also significant, but less important than the other two variables. One point in the health index was equivalent to about three years of age, so that a man of 30 scoring 10 ill-health points had the same risk of dying as a man of 60 with no points. The relationships are illustrated in Figure 7.5, which plots the results of the logistic regression equation for men at two ages. It shows that 50-year-old men had a fairly low risk of dying, whatever their reported health. High risks were estimated for those who combined advanced age and serious ill-health. These are hardly surprising findings; their value lies in confirming that the health index works.

Defining 'ill-health'

Figure 7.1 showed that the index of ill-health was distributed fairly smoothly across a range of values. There was not a clear distinction between completely healthy people on the one hand and totally ill on the other. Only 18% of adults were recorded in the position of ideal health that might be considered the standard expectation. Health and ill-health appear as a continuum.

This is a finding in its own right, but it raises important technical issues for the analysis. It is possible to treat the index as a numeric variable with a mean and a variance, rather like genuinely continuous variables such as income. In that context, becoming ill or recovering would be viewed simply as movements up and down the scale (equivalent to rising and falling income). Such a treatment would offend statistical purity (because we cannot claim that a score of 4 represents twice as much ill-health as a score of 2) but in practice a 16-point scale with a reasonably smooth distribution can often yield robust results if treated in that way.

An alternative analytical approach is to treat the full range of scores as an ordinal variable. The assumption made by this approach would be that a score of 4 is worse than 3, and 3 worse than 2, but it makes no assumptions about the size of the steps between them. This is the technically ideal solution, but it involves a good deal of complex calculation to provide generalised conclusions about 'ill-health' rather than a series of specific conclusions about each point in the scale. The calculation itself is easy enough to program, but the output is not so easy to interpret, or to explain to the general reader.

A third option is to use the index to divide the population into two groups: those with ill-health and those without (who may be labelled healthy). The advantage of this approach is that it is easy to present in tables, and reflects a strong perception in many readers' minds that you are either healthy or ill. Setting a boundary line is equivalent to defining a group of people with very high or low incomes, and labelling them rich or poor. The longitudinal analytical issues then become: who falls sick and who recovers?

This third (binary) option requires a decision about the dividing line. This is bound to be arbitrary. The analysis has been based on treating people with index values of 4 or more as 'sick', leaving all those at 3 or below as 'healthy'. There are three grounds for choosing that cut-off point:

- It allocates about one fifth of the population to the sick category. This is intended to reflect a widespread perception that ill-health is an attribute of a minority of the population, but not a tiny minority. It is also of the same order of magnitude as many other binary measures of ill-health derived from surveys such as the GHS.
- The definition closely reflects the perception that ill-health is a characteristic of advancing age. Scores of 4 and higher were associated with age. A score of 3 was equally common at all ages (while lower scores were more common in younger age groups).
- A score of 4 was the point in the distribution at which the risk of being unable to work on health grounds started to appear (see Figure 7.4).

Moving to the dynamic measure

All of the analysis so far (with the exception of the risk of death) has been based entirely on respondents' answers to questions on one occasion. Having established an apparently reliable cross-sectional index of ill-health, it is now possible to move on to longitudinal measures, comparing one year with another. Typically, we want to know what changes happened in each person's health between this year (referred to as year t) and next year $(t+1)$. It will also be possible to look at comparisons over a series of years $(t, t+1, t+2$ and so on). Given that ill-health increases with age, it is to be expected that more people become ill each year than recover, but there may be a substantial turnover, depending on the nature of the conditions affecting each individual.

Table 7.4 looks at the rate of change for the seven categories of health problem that contributed to the overall index of ill-health[5], and for which

Table 7.4: Year-on-year changes in the incidence of health problems

	% of *t+1* cases which were new that year	% of *t* cases which ended the following year
Arms, legs, hands, feet, back or neck	30	26
Difficulty in seeing	52	54
Chest/breathing problems, asthma, bronchitis	30	26
Heart/blood pressure or blood circulation problems	28	23
Stomach/liver/kidneys	47	43
Diabetes	15	6
Anxiety, depression or bad nerves	51	48

the incidence was greater than 1% of all adults. The first column measures the rate at which new conditions started, the second the rate at which old ones stopped. Both entries and exits are expressed in relation to the stock of cases, as this enables direct comparison to be made between them.

For most of the problems analysed (the exception was difficulty in seeing), the rate of starting was slightly higher than the rate of stopping, implying a tendency for the caseload to increase as members of the sample grew older year by year. The most stable problem was diabetes: few started to report this condition, but very few ceased to do so. The problems with the highest levels of turnover were seeing, nervous conditions and problems with abdominal organs. It is important to remember that all these categories cover a wide range of conditions and severities.

Looking more broadly at the three questions that make up the full index of ill-health, the majority of people gave the same answers both years running (Table 7.5). The subjective question produced the most changes between one year and the next, perhaps precisely because it was so subjective that people could change their mind about exactly which option to choose. Even so, more than half stuck to their previous answer, and only 5% of respondents moved more than one position up or down the scale. The counts of health problems and of impairments were even more stable. The net movement was towards more ill-health the second year than the first (with every respondent one year older), but the general conclusion is that very little change occurred.

One of the key criteria by which the full index of ill-health was

Table 7.5: Changes in the three components of the index between t and $t+l$, in column percentages

	Subjective ill-health	Health problems	Impairments
Reduced by 3 or more	0.3	0.3	0.7
Reduced by 2	2.1	1.8	1.2
Reduced by 1	18	13	5.7
No change	58	67	83
Increased by 1	19	15	6.7
Increased by 2	2.7	2.7	1.7
Increased by 3 or more	0.6	0.4	1.2
Average increase	*+0.03*	*+0.04*	*+0.04*

developed was that each of its components should appear to be a measure of the same underlying concept. The three were closely correlated with each other, as shown in Table 7.3, and this led to the calculation of Cronbach's alpha at the high level of 0.77. The analysis in any one year shows that people with (say) many health problems also have more impairments. So it is to be expected that people who increase the number of their health problems would also report an increase in their impairments. Analysis from year to year suggests that this is much less true than the cross-sectional correlations might have led us to expect. Whereas Table 7.3 showed that in any one year the components had correlation coefficients with each other in excess of 0.5, Table 7.6 shows that from one year to the next the correlations fell to below 0.2. As a result, the measure of the reliability of the index (alpha), fell from 0.77 in a single year to 0.34 across two years.

Table 7.6: Correlations between changes in each of the health questions, t to $t+l$, given as correlation coefficients (R)

	Change in subjective health	Change in number of health problems	Change in number of impairments
Change in subjective health	1.0		
Change in number of health problems	0.17	1.0	
Change in number of impairments	0.16	0.11	1.0

Table 7.7: Changes between *t+1* and *t+2*, analysed by changes between *t* and *t+1*, in column percentages

	Number of points changed between *t* and *t+1*			
	1	2	3	4 plus
Of those who became (more) ill between t and t+1: Recovered (back to point *t* or better by *t+2*)	45	32	24	15
Partial recovery (*t+2* between *t* and *t+1*)	na	28	43	56
Stable change (stayed at point *t+1* in *t+2*)	35	22	15	13
Continued deterioration (beyond point *t+1* by *t+2*)	20	18	18	16
Of those who became (more) healthy between t and t+1: Relapsed (back to point *t* or worse by *t+2*)	46	36	20	14
Partial relapse (*t+2* between *t* and *t+1*)	na	28	39	52
Stable change (stayed at point *t+1* in *t+2*)	41	31	27	25
Continued improvement (moved beyond point *t+1* by *t+2*)	13	15	14	11

These findings suggest that while the index places each respondent fairly reliably at a position in the overall range between excellent health and serious sickness, the measurement in any one year is subject to an uncertainty which reveals itself in the form of a small wobble from year to year. A score on the index of (say) 5 should really be interpreted as 'about 5' which might sometimes be reported either as 4 or as 6 the following year, as the respondent changed just one of his or her answers without changing either of the others. On this interpretation, small fluctuations from one year to another should not be taken to signify changes in the individual's underlying health, but as oscillations around a basically stable position.

This interpretation is supported, at least in part, by comparing what happened to people in the *following* year, the year after they appeared to report a small increase or decrease in their level of ill-health (Table 7.7). Nearly half of those who moved up or down the scale a single point in the first year had returned to their original position the following year. Not surprisingly, the bigger the shift observed on the first occasion, the

Table 7.8: Distribution of changes in full ill-health index, over one year and over two years, in column percentages

	Change between t and t+1	Change between t and t+2	Biggest reduction or increase between wave 1 and later waves
Reduction of 4 or more	1.2	1.3	3.6
Reduction of 3	2.1	2.1	4.9
Reduction of 2	5.7	5.8	7.9
Reduction of 1	18	18	11
No change (in either direction)	42	39	16*
Increase of 1	19	20	15
Increase of 2	6.9	8.1	16
Increase of 3	2.9	3.5	11
Increase of 4 or more	2.3	3.5	15

* Of the 16% whose biggest reduction or increase was recorded as 'no change', 5% had not changed at all, and 10% had both a reduction and an increase of equal size

less likely it was to be wiped out entirely by the time of the next year's survey, although many of the larger initial changes were at least partially reversed.

This means that small changes in the index observed over short periods cannot be taken to demonstrate actual improvements or deteriorations in people's health. The analysis has to focus on the more robust indications provided by larger changes over longer periods. Such a conclusion is supported by measures of the reliability of the index of change. For the comparison between years t and $t+1$, the value of alpha fell to only 0.34. If the comparison was across a two-year period, though, the value improved to 0.41; if the period of measurement was extended as long as six years (that is, wave 7 compared with wave 1) the reliability of the index of change reached 0.51.

The unreliability of the index over time means that it is only possible to identify changes that were large and/or long term. This is unfortunate, because it seriously hinders our ability to identify short-term changes in health associated with acute episodes from which people recover. The full distributions of changes over one and two years are shown in the first and second columns of Table 7.8. The safest conclusion is that 15.1% of adults increased their score on the index by at least two points over a two-year period. Another 9.2% of adults decreased their score by at least two points over the same period. This confirms the small net growth in ill-health as people get older. However, it can now be seen, for the first time, that this is the outcome of a fair amount of movement in both directions.

A wider measure of changing health can be taken by looking at the full range of reports made by each respondent during the seven years of the BHPS, rather than at a one- or two-year intervals. The starting point is the score on the index of ill-health recorded in wave 1[6]. Only 5% of the sample retained exactly the same score throughout the period of the survey (a further measure of the short-range instability of the scale). As the third column of Table 7.8 shows, 42% of the sample were at some time at least two points higher on the scale than when they started, and their health can be said to have got worse; 16.4% were at some time at least two points lower in the scale, and their health can be said to have improved. (Some were recorded as having moved to the same extent in both directions, and these have been counted as no change.) So the longer run of years reveals substantially more changes in people's health than a simple year-on-year comparison seemed to indicate.

Another, and perhaps more meaningful, measure, is to calculate how many people 'fell ill' during the period, and how many 'recovered'. A threshold was suggested earlier, labelling people as 'ill' if their score on the index was 4 or higher – the worst-off fifth of adults. The longitudinal analysis shows that 21% of all adults became ill, in the sense that they were not 'ill' in wave 1, increased their score by at least two points at some later point, and were 'ill' at the time of the later measurement, or else they had died (Table 7.9)[7]. A total of 7% of adults recovered, having reduced their score by at least two points, and crossing the boundary in the opposite direction to stop being ill. As before, the movement into illness is partly offset by movement out of it. Another way of putting the same figures is to say that the risk of someone not yet ill becoming ill was 28%; while the chances of someone who was ill recovering were 35%.

Precursors of falling ill

The measures of changing health presented in Table 7.8 and Table 7.9 represent an important outcome of the longitudinal analysis, recording the rate at which members of the general population moved up and down a scale of ill-health. It can be concluded that there is a fair amount of movement; that it is not all in one direction; and that it does not necessarily happen suddenly: gradual changes in people's scores over the

Table 7.9: Movements in and out of 'illness' between wave 1 and later waves, in percentages

	As % of all	As % of those who were not ill at the start
Was not ill at any time	59	72
Fell ill or died during period	21	28
Was ill at the start	20	na
Was always ill	12	65
Recovered from illness	7	35
Was not ill at the start	81	na

Note: 'Ill' is a score of 4 or more on the ill-health index. 'Fell ill' and 'recovered' requires a movement of at least two points between wave 1 and the best/worst year

years seem more common than step changes following some catastrophic illness or accident. The precise measures of change may be somewhat arbitrary, and alternatives could be proposed. However, the broad conclusions may not be very sensitive to the choice of metric.

The next stage in the analysis may be at least as useful as the basic measure of change. One of the main benefits of a panel survey is that it can be used to describe the characteristics of the people whose health deteriorated or improved, using data collected before the change under consideration. So the analysis can identify the antecedents of change much more effectively than any source of data which identifies changes in health after the event.

'Medical' factors

Variations in the rate of falling ill and recovering are shown in Figure 7.6, analysing five factors which might be considered to have a direct physiological or psychological influence on the risk of ill-health. Socio-economic factors are discussed later. In each case, the probability of moving up or down the health scale during the seven-year period is analysed on the basis of the respondent's characteristics in 1991, the first year of the survey.

Those whose score on the index of ill-health at the start of the period of observation was just below the arbitrary boundary line between 'healthy' and 'ill' had a higher risk of crossing that boundary, than people who were in the very best of health when first interviewed (black shaded columns on the graph). In one sense, this is statistically obvious: if we

Figure 7.6: 'Medical' precursors of falling ill and recovering

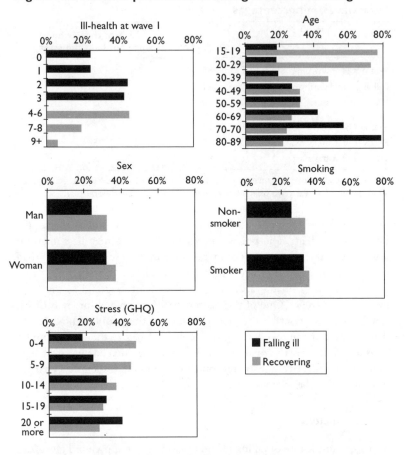

define falling ill as an increase of two points and reaching at least point 4, then respondents starting at zero had much further to go than those starting at 2 or 3. On the other hand, it reflects a conclusion indicated previously: that falling ill was often a gradual process rather than an all-at-once event. Another way to present the same figures is to say that only one eighth of all those who were observed to 'fall ill' in the BHPS had started in 'perfect' health.

The converse is that for those who were already ill at wave 1, the probability of recovery was inversely related to how ill they were to start with (grey shaded columns). Again, this may seem like stating the obvious, but it is nevertheless an important finding that those on the margins of illness had quite a good chance of getting better, while those at the top of the ill-health scale had very small hopes of returning to good health.

The first two columns of Table 7.10 show the results of logistic regression equations in which key 'medical' variables are used to 'predict' which wave 1 respondents would fall ill during the following years. The statistics themselves are not easy to interpret in lay terms, but they are designed to be as comparable as possible with each other, indicating the increase in the probability of falling sick associated with a one-standard-deviation change in the value of the predictor variable under consideration. The first column shows the effect of each variable taken one at a time, ignoring the others. The first figure (0.57) shows that the respondent's initial level of sickness was one of the most important predictors – second only to age. The second column shows the effect of each variable, after taking account of the effects of all the others. The effect of initial sickness was reduced somewhat according to this measure, but it remained second in overall importance.

The risk of falling ill was low among men and women in their teens, 20s and 30s, but this increased more and more rapidly with age (second panel of Figure 7.6). A majority of those in their 80s were already ill at the start of the period, but four out of five of those who were not had fallen ill (or died) during the following six years. The prospects of someone ill returning to good health were high for younger people, and reduced systematically with age, in a pattern neatly complementing the risk of falling ill. The rising caseload of illness with age is not simply a matter of a constant yearly excess of entrances over exits; there is a clear acceleration in the rate at which these problems occur, while the chances of recovery reduce rapidly with age.

The logistic regression equations in Table 7.10 show that age was the most important predictor of falling ill, taken on its own, and easily the most important after the mutual influence of all the variables had been taken into account. This strongly suggests that age is itself a determining factor, and that the reduction in the influence of some other variables (such as low income, see Table 7.11) may have been caused by the fact that many elderly people have below-average incomes.

Figure 7.6 also confirms that women were more likely to fall ill than men. This is consistent with the observation that women experience higher morbidity than men, even though their mortality rates are lower. However, the grey shaded columns of the graph show that women had slightly *higher*, not lower, recovery rates than men. So it seems that women's health was more variable: a high rate of risk and a high rate of recovery

Table 7.10: Logistic regression equations predicting *falling* ill (longitudinal) and *being* ill (cross-sectional): 'medical' factors, given as standardised logistic regression coefficients

	Univariate association with *falling* ill	Multivariate association with *falling* ill	Multivariate association with *being* ill
Ill-health (at wave 1)	0.57	0.44	na
Age (squared)	0.63	0.62	0.82
Sex	0.18	0.19	0.06
Smoking	0.14	0.16	0.12
Stress (GHQ)	0.18	0.10	0.67

Note: All predictor variables are measured at wave 1. Falling ill is defined as moving from healthy to ill between wave 1 and some subsequent wave (2-7). Standardised regression coefficients are the unit coefficients multiplied by the standard deviation. The results are the same as if the predictor variables had been expressed in standardised format (Z scores). All results are significant at the 95% confidence level or above. Multivariate analyses also controlled for the 'socio-economic' variables shown in Table 7.11

indicate a tendency to experience medium-term episodes of ill-health rather than permanent illnesses. The logistic regression analysis suggests that the difference between men and women is a significant influence, although substantially less important than initial health and age.

The right-hand column of Table 7.10 shows, for a comparison, a multivariate regression equation estimating the likelihood that someone should be ill at any time, based on other information collected at the same time – the standard cross-sectional analysis of current health. It is interesting to find that the difference between men and women was more important in the dynamic than in the static analysis. This probably reflects the higher entry and exit rates recorded by women, so that fluctuations in their health are an especially important feature of their experience.

The key demographic variables, age and sex, are easy to interpret, because they are predetermined and because they are objectively measured – there is no need to ask whether ill-health caused people to be old, or whether respondents varied in their interpretation of the question about their sex. However, it turns out that the interpretation of smoking is also relatively straightforward: smokers were more likely to fall ill than non-smokers. The effect was similar in scale to the difference between women and men, and held up after other explanatory variables had been considered. The effect on *falling* ill was similar to that observed for *being* ill.

Interpretation of the effects of stress requires more detailed consideration. The right-hand column of Table 7.10 confirms that people who report illnesses also report very high levels of stress. It has often been argued that this stress is one of the causes of ill-health; but, since both are measured at the same time, it could just as plausibly be suggested that ill-health causes stress. The difficulty of interpretation is compounded by the inaccurate name given to the standard measure of stress. It is called the Generalised Health Questionnaire (Goldberg, 1972), and is too easily understood to be a measure of (ill)-health. Not one of the 12 questions is directly concerned with physical health[8]. The scale is a good indicator of psychological wellbeing, which at its upper end can be interpreted as stress or as psychological ill-health[9].

Concurrent measurements suggest that stress was second only to age in the strength of its association with ill-health. The dynamic perspective (Figure 7.6 and Table 7.10) confirms that those who reported stress in wave 1 were significantly more likely to fall ill than those who were happy with the way things were going. However, the strength of the association with *falling* ill was much lower than the association with *being* ill. It has to be assumed that much of the latter is caused by the stressful experiences of falling ill, although more detailed analysis of this longitudinal data would be needed to confirm that interpretation.

Socio-economic factors

The first five predictor variables analysed have been grouped under the heading 'medical' because they all have physiological or psychological components which might be directly associated with the onset of certain conditions. On the other hand, most of them also have social components as well – for example, we cannot determine in advance whether women's higher rate of falling ill is associated with such physiological factors as hormonal balances or with social constructs such as gendered variations in lifestyles. However, there are other well-known correlates of ill-health that are unambiguously derived from social and economic conditions. Given the substantial social inequalities in health observed in many countries, it has been argued that social conditions may be the 'fundamental' causes of disease (Link and Phelan, 1995).

This is the point at which it is possible to look for links between changing health and some of the other key elements of social and economic life investigated by the BHPS and discussed in other chapters. A preliminary trawl of potential influences did not suggest that family

Figure: 7.7 Socio-economic precursors of falling ill and recovering

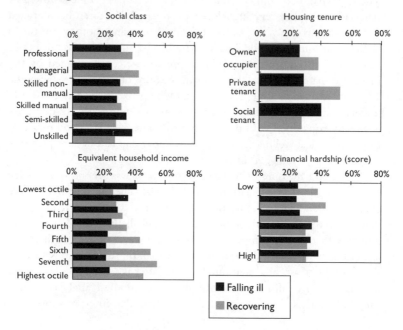

structure had any obvious effects on the risk of falling ill. Nor did an individual's employment status seem to have any direct effects. However, there were indications of a role for other factors, which can be grouped under the heading of social disadvantage. Figure 7.7 illustrates variations in the rate of falling ill, and recovering, using a selection of four variables: social class; housing tenure; equivalent household income; financial hardship.

Probably the most widely used base for the socio-economic analysis of ill-health and mortality has been 'social class'. Class is as fuzzy a concept as ill-health, and there are many ways to define and categorise it. The analysis here has adopted the definition most commonly applied in medical sociology, assigning each member of a household to a 'Registrar General's Social Class' based on the current or most recent occupation of the conventional 'head of the household'. The first graph in Figure 7.7 suggests that professional workers and their families had a lower than average chance of getting sick and a higher than average chance of recovering. At the other end of the scale, the families of semi- and unskilled workers had a higher risk of falling ill and a lower-than-average expectation of recovery. These variations are not trivial – they imply that in a steady state there would be almost twice as much ill-health among unskilled workers and their families as in the professional class. On the other hand, the 'top' and 'bottom' categories represent only a minority of the population, and the distribution of entries to and exits from ill-health is not clearly graded across the other social classes.

In a more detailed analysis, it seems that the main class difference was between the professional and managerial groups, on the one hand, and all the other classes combined. Table 7.11 uses an indicator of 'middle class' in which professional families were assigned a value of 2, while managerial families scored 1; all other families were treated as not-middle-class. The analysis confirmed that members of the middle class defined in this way had a relatively low risk of falling ill, although part of the initial relationship illustrated in Figure 7.7 was reduced when a multivariate equation took account of the effects of other factors. The class effect on *falling* ill was very similar to the relationship with *being* ill; this suggests that it is class that affects health, not the other way round.

It was shown in Chapters One and Six that there has been a sharp polarisation of housing tenure during the past 25 years, with 'social housing' increasingly being seen as a last resort for families with very poor prospects. It has been argued that tenure may even have overtaken social class as the clearest indicator of social exclusion. So it is interesting to find (from the second panel of Figure 7.7 and the second row of Table 7.11) that the residents of social housing are significantly more likely to fall ill than owner-occupiers or private tenants. A substantial share of this effect is still visible after other factors, such as age and social class, have been allowed for. The tenure effect is similar in magnitude to the class effect.

An association has also been noted between (this year's) income and (this year's) ill-health (see, for example, Webb, 1995). The association has been used to argue that low income leads to ill-health (Black, 1980; Acheson, 1998). However, another possibility is that ill-health leads (through loss of earnings) to low income. These hypotheses require far more detailed investigation than can be undertaken here[10]. Figure 7.7 shows an apparently clear tendency for adults living in households with low equivalent incomes to have high chances of falling ill and low chances of recovery. This suggests that low income precedes, and may therefore cause, illness. If variables are taken one at a time, income was as important as gender, smoking, class or housing tenure as a precursor of ill-health.

Table 7.11: Logistic regression equations predicting *falling* ill (longitudinal) and *being* ill (cross-sectional): 'socio-economic' factors, given as standardised logistic regression coefficients

	Univariate association with *falling* ill	Multivariate association with *falling* ill	Multivariate association with *being* ill
'Middle class'	-0.19	-0.11	-0.12
Social housing	0.23	0.10	0.20
Equivalent household income	-0.28	ns	-0.07
Financial hardship	0.20	0.15	0.09

Note: See note to previous table. Multivariate analyses also controlled for the 'medical' variables shown in Table 7.10. 'ns' means 'not significant'

However, the association *entirely* disappeared when other variables had been taken into account. One possible explanation is that the apparent income effect was caused by the fact that many old people, especially older women, have a high risk of falling ill and are also poor.

Another interpretation lies in the final variable considered in this preliminary analysis. An index of 'financial hardship' was measured on the basis of three BHPS questions: high scores were assigned to people who did not save from their current income, who said that they were in financial difficulties and who were behind with their rent or mortgage payments. Not surprisingly, these indicators of hardship are very highly correlated with low income, but by no means all poor people are in financial hardship on this measure, and by no means all those in hardship are also poor (Berthoud and Ford, 1996). It turned out that hardship in wave 1 was an indicator of the risk of falling ill, at least as effective as better-known factors such as gender, smoking and social class. The most interesting point is that hardship held up as a predictor of ill-health in the multivariate equation, when the apparent income effect collapsed. It is possible that the relationship between first-order income and ill-health is entirely mediated by financial stress, rather than by consumption levels, which would be the most direct outcome of variations in income.

A broad conclusion is that socially constructed variables measured at wave 1 were just as effective at predicting who would fall ill in subsequent years, as some other variables with a more obvious medical component.

Conclusions

The BHPS asks three questions about ill-health from slightly different perspectives. The three questions combine to provide a measure of current ill-health that is internally consistent. The index is closely associated with the known consequences of ill-health such as use of health services, inability to work, receipt of 'care' and death. The index stands up well as a measure of an underlying concept of ill-health. An opportunity to undertake further tests of its validity will occur in the ninth wave of the survey, when a well-established multi-dimensional measure of ill-health (known as SF36) will be included in the questionnaire.

Although the overall measure was broadly stable from year to year, small changes to the answers to one question were not always associated with changes in the other two. It has to be concluded that the index would not provide a sensitive measure of small changes in ill-health over a short period. This is a serious disadvantage, as it means that the index could not be used to analyse short-term episodes of ill-health. It could, however, provide reliable evidence about longer-term changes in people's situation. The first substantive conclusion of the analysis is that most people who become ill do not move directly from peak condition in one year to serious debility in the following year. Progressive deterioration is more common than sudden catastrophe.

A second conclusion is that movement is in both directions. Since ill-health is more common in old age than among young people, it follows that more people become ill than recover. Nevertheless, the net growth in ill-health from year to year is the outcome of substantial movement up and down the scale. For example, 15% of adults moved at least two points up the ill-health scale during a two-year period, but 9% moved at least two points down the scale.

The crucial advantage of the panel survey is that it is possible to analyse the characteristics of people who fall ill, based on data collected *before the event*. This can establish the precursors of and predispositions to ill-health much more effectively than any cross-sectional survey. It showed, not surprisingly, that those with less than perfect health to start with, have a higher risk of falling ill. A more interesting conclusion was that the risk of falling ill accelerated more and more rapidly as people grew older (and the chances of recovery declined). So the high level of ill-health in older people is a genuine ageing effect, not just a gradual accretion of chronic problems over the years.

Age and initial health were easily the best predictors of falling ill.

However, other variables were also identified. Smoking was associated with declining health, as well as with current health status. Women had a higher than average chance of falling ill, but also had high rates of recovery; their characteristic pattern seems to be medium-term episodes of illness, rather than permanent problems. Personal stress was a predictor of ill-health, but it was far less closely associated with *falling* ill than with *being* ill. It seems likely that a large proportion of the known link between stress and physical health is explained in terms of the psychological consequences of illness.

An important role for the BHPS, and especially for this book, is to show how far movements into and out of ill-health are associated with socio-economic indicators of class and disadvantage. Middle-class respondents were less likely to fall ill, and council tenants were more likely to do so, than other members of the sample. Another known correlate of illness is low income; this initially stood-up as a predictor of falling ill, but disappeared completely when other factors were controlled for. Financial hardship, though, provided a more robust explanation for changing health.

This chapter has used a small selection of predictor variables, but provides an indication of the sort of detailed analysis that will be possible, now that a longitudinal index has been established. The BHPS health data has been under-used in the past, and one of the aims of this chapter has been to encourage much wider use of this rich material.

Notes

[1] The analysis on which this chapter is based was undertaken as part of a study of social capital and health commissioned by the Health Development Agency. Thanks to James Nazroo, Antony Morgan and David Pevalin for comments on an earlier version.

[2] The more items that are available for inclusion in the index the higher is the value of alpha. 0.77 is very high given only three items. The 12-item GHQ, for example, (see below) has an alpha of 0.88, but this is equivalent to a value of 0.65 for a three-item index.

[3] The calculation of frequency of visits to the GP during the past year was based on a rough estimate by the patient, scored as follows: none = 0, one or two = 1, three to five = 3, 6 to 10 = 4, more than 10 = 5.

[4] The other health services asked about were: health visitor, home help, meals on wheels, social worker, chiropodist, alternative medicine, psychotherapist, speech therapist, physiotherapist and others.

[5] See pages 166-7 for an explanation of the omission of hearing, skin and migraine problems from the index.

[6] This measure includes the health-scores recorded before death by those who died between waves 2 and 7. It does not include the experiences of teenagers who joined the survey after wave 1.

[7] Becoming ill means moving from an index score of 2 or less to 4, or from 3 to 5 or more. Those who died in the course of the survey period are effectively judged to have been (very) ill.

[8] Among the 13 health problems recorded in the BHPS (see page 165), 'anxiety, depression or bad nerves' is *much* more closely associated with the GHQ (on a cross-sectional measurement) than any of the others. Since the GHS is often used as a clinical indicator of mental illness, it may be argued that a high score should register as a form of ill-health, rather than, as here, as a correlate of ill-health. On the other hand, stress, not mental illness, is what the questionnaire actually measures.

[9] Martin (1999) has identified stress as one of three sub-components of the 12-item GHS, the other two being self-esteem and successful coping. The single scale is used here.

[10] See Benzeval and Judge (2000) for more analysis based on the BHPS.

References

Acheson, D. (Chairman) (1998) *Independent Inquiry into Inequalities in Health Report*, London: The Stationery Office.

Benzeval, M. and Judge, K. (2000) 'Income and health: the time dimension', *Social Science and Medicine* (forthcoming).

Berthoud, R. and Ford, R. (1996) *Relative needs: Variations in the living standards of different types of household*, London: Policy Studies Institute.

Black, D. (Chairman) (1980) *Inequalities in health: Report of a research working group*, London: DHSS.

Disney, R., Grundy, E. and Johnson, P. (1997) *The dynamics of retirement*, DSS Research Reports, 72, London: The Stationery Office.

Goldberg, D. (1972) *The detection of psychiatric illness by questionnaire*, Oxford: Oxford University Press.

Grundy, E., Ahlburg, D., Ali, M., Breeze, E. and Sloggett, A. (1999) *Disability in Great Britain*, DSS Research Papers, 94, Leeds: Corporate Document Services.

Link, B. and Phelan, J. (1995) 'Social conditions as fundamental causes of disease', *Journal of Health and Social Behavior*, special issue, pp 80-94.

Martin, A. (1999) 'Assessing the multi-dimensionality of the 12-item general health questionnaire', *Psychological Reports*, vol 84, pp 927-35.

Martin, J., Meltzer, H. and Elliot, D. (1988) *The prevalence of disability among adults*, London: The Stationery Office.

ONS (Office of National Statistics) (2000) *Living in Britain: Results from the 1998 General Household Survey*, London: The Stationery Office.

Prescott-Clarke, P. and Primatesta, P. (1997) *Health Survey for England 1995*, London: The Stationery Office.

Prescott-Clarke, P. and Primatesta, P. (1998) *Health Survey for England 1996*, London: The Stationery Office.

Webb, S. (1995) 'Poverty and health', in M. Benzeval, K. Judge and M. Whitehead (eds) *Tackling inequalities in health: An agenda for action*, London: King's Fund.

EIGHT

Political values: a family matter?

Malcolm Brynin

Influence of the family: stability or flux?

Why should discussion of the family be of interest when we look at political values or behaviour? It is unlikely that voting predispositions form a part of the ritual of courtship. The family as such cannot have an opinion. It cannot vote as a unit – for this purpose it has to break up into its individual membership. Neither politicians nor political analysts have tended to view the family as a factor in politics. For the politician thinking of politics the family is only of an interest – if with a dash of wishful thinking – as a moral force. For the political analyst, unaffected by wishful thinking, the family holds no obvious interest at all: electoral preferences are measured in terms of individual characteristics. For instance, older people, people from a relatively high social class, non-trade union members – these people are predisposed towards the Conservative Party. The family is merely in the background, providing some of the characteristics, such as tenure or total household income, that might be used to predict individual political values.

However, there are several very good reasons for taking a look at the family's values and voting patterns:

- if real circumstances (income, jobs, and so on) influence individual opinions or political behaviour – and the extent to which this is the case can be tested empirically – then, because many of the factors that impinge on individuals vary by family circumstances (for example, a person remains in employment but their spouse or partner loses a job), the family can be seen as a possible mediator of values and voting;
- to what extent the family is a crucible for the formation or maintenance of particular political views is of great interest; conformity within the

family over time is likely to mean that family members influence each other in their political and other persuasions;
• related to the above, general changes in family structure could have an impact on the transmission of political values over time, and thus the family itself might have an impact on the political system.

The family is a fundamental building block of social structures, partly because it is an important basis for the transmission of social mores over time. Yet this very fact leads to a paradox in our understanding of the social role of the family. In a view that set the analytical agenda for many years, the (stable) nuclear family is perceived to be 'modern' because, with its emphasis on the individual, it is well suited to the maintenance of an industrial society (Parsons, 1964). Things can go wrong: without a balance between cohesion and adaptability pathological outcomes are possible (Olson, 1993: although quite what this balance should be has never been clear). However, in a way that cannot be dismissed merely as the result of pathological imbalances, this theory contained the seeds of its own decline. This is because the flexibility of the modern economy may actually either 'require' (perhaps an unnecessarily functionalist view) or at least encourage even more flexible family forms than the nuclear family. It has often been argued, for instance, that Western economies have evolved postmodern or post-Fordist forms that are more fragmented and flexible than the mass production processes which went before. With this change has come change to the class structure, which no longer provides a firm foundation for social or political action – the weakening of the trade union base is one example.

At the same time, the social and economic basis for the male role within the family of sole breadwinner has greatly altered. There is more labour-market opportunity for both women and young people to become independent and to split – or be forced to split – from a dominant male breadwinner. At least in the case of women, legal changes and support from the benefit system have reinforced this situation. (While young people have probably seen a slight reversal in institutional support, education opportunities have increased.) It is possible that these changes have led to greater independence of social and political views within the family.

So the functionalist view of the importance of the nuclear family within a modern society is probably already outdated. This view is now seen by many as 'traditionalist', with the result that the new family developments have been decried as heralding the 'end of the family' (Popenoe, 1988), a view often taken up by politicians and sections of the mass media. It is a

---

view that leads to 'polarisation' – the traditionalist against the modernist stance.

However, there are strong grounds for a view of the family as evolving into a range of different forms, even if the nuclear form is dominant, as might be expected in an increasingly complex society. Polarisation must give way to 'pluralisation'. The many forms of the modern family require more variety of approaches to the understanding of the relationship between the family and society (Cheal, 1991). From this viewpoint, economic, familial, and implicitly political structures are fragmenting along parallel lines, producing increasing unpredictability. There are good theoretical grounds for wishing to test the current relationship between the family and politics.

That the family is not what it used to be has been attested many times. The picture from other surveys and from the BHPS of the place of the individual within the family, and of the family within society, is one of increasing looseness or fragmentation. The building blocks from one level to the other are still there but are crumbling at the edges. A possible corollary is that this might have an impact on the stability of individual social or political attitudes. For instance, in recent decades there have been significant increases in social and geographical mobility which, as many studies have indicated starting with Rose (1980/1984), have weakened the link between social class and political loyalties. The family is the crucible through which class position is transmuted over time, and so the triangle family/class/vote has as a whole become more wobbly than previously. One aspect of this greater social mobility is the increased significance of the individual *within* the family. This implies a reduced influence of one person on another within a family relationship. This is seen in a number of ways, which can be traced in the BHPS itself. The growth of cohabitation, as attested in Chapter Two, leads to more and shorter relationships. A further aspect is that dependence is replaced by interdependence. Chapter Three shows a clear relationship within couples between female employment and equal control over and organisation of family finances, which is also stronger where women work full-time rather than part-time. In a small proportion of cases financial interdependence is replaced by substantial independence.

Politically, the household could be a destabilising rather than a cohesive force. The flux in the family might cross over to the transmission of social and political opinions or leanings, so that it encourages political unpredictability. This chapter is partly a study of voting patterns, partly a study of the family. It seeks to examine how far individual voting tendencies are influenced by the family, and at the same time, what this tells us about family integration.

Emphasis on relationships

The BHPS carries data not only on jobs, income, family formation, and health but on a range of family arrangements, views on the family, social attitudes, and political attitudes. (An adjunct to the main BHPS survey, from wave 4 onwards, also introduces a separate set of questions for young people in BHPS households aged 11 to 15.) Through these differing elements of the survey it is possible to answer questions to do with an individual's engagement with society, and – at a finer grain – to do with the family. This chapter, which takes a look at family attitudes to politics, does both of these. Its theme is the relationship between the political views of different family members.

This approach is not a common one. There has in the past been a tendency to conflate the family and the individual into what is effectively a unitary model, where there is assumed to be no within-household interaction. This conception underlies the influential theories of the economist Gary Becker (1981), whose view of the family, in particular the couple, is as a single entity. This is an entity dominated economically, and you might assume culturally, by a male 'head of household'. Empirically, this latter assumption is a direct reflection of historical survey sampling strategies that took the family as a sampling unit, selected head of household as respondent, and defined this person as the (male) chief breadwinner. So inevitably the unitary model is gendered. The empirical reaction against this is not only one of taking account of the views of women but of building more complex models of the impacts on a range of outcomes within families which were previously obscured (see, for example, Heath and Britten, 1984).

This means more than merely taking into account the views of all family members. The family, a dynamic structure, is neither a single entity nor a mere aggregate of individuals. It is more than the sum of its parts. Interactions between family members have important outcomes. In the case of inter-family comparisons, an example is the analysis of the impact of polarisation between work-rich and work-poor families discussed in Chapter Four. As other work shows, having two incomes more than doubles the relative advantage. However, there are also within-family effects. As Chapter Five shows, a change in the circumstances of, or the departure of, one family member can have a radical effect on the wellbeing of other family members. Over time, there are additions and differences in income which intensify relative advantage and disadvantage. In this sense, the effects of income are not linear over time.

When considering attitudes, rather than, say, employment or finances, then the straightforward additive model – summing the responses of individuals within the family – is particularly weak. Whether family members have the same or conflicting views there is likely to be a process of reciprocal influence, with reinforcement through cohesion or attrition through opposition over time. This leads effectively to a 'multiplicative' approach (with its obverse, the potential for divisiveness), deriving from analysis of intra-family interactions. The emphasis in what follows is therefore on *relationships* – especially the couple.

Voting patterns and the family

A number of studies of the political data in the BHPS reveal considerable fluidity at the individual level (Johnston and Pattie, 1996, 1999; Sanders and Brynin, 1999). These fluctuations in party preference seem at best poorly related to changes in current circumstances such as gains or falls in income or in housing payment problems; they are instead associated with weakly held social attitudes. There is a large core of people who, although they might lean somewhat more towards one party than to another, have little real commitment to any party. This substantial core of relative indifference results in considerable short-term 'turbulence'. While this weakening of partisanship can in particular circumstances result in a significant 'dealignment' of party identification, it does not necessarily lead to a commensurate realignment. Crewe and Thomson (1999) argue that the 1997 General Election saw a fundamental withdrawal of support for the Conservatives which was probably not matched by an equally fundamental shift towards Labour.

At the individual level there is a significant degree of instability and unpredictability in political views. Does the family promote or constrain this? The second of these seems a reasonable choice. There is after all inevitably some consensus in the family, especially within couples (who have been the main target for research). As people select their partners, and they do so partly on the basis of similarity of outlook or background, it might be expected that the views of one partner will be similar to the views of the other. Like marries or links to like. The degree of homogamy among couples (in this case defined by education) has probably been increasing in Western societies (Mare, 1991). People do not select partners only on the basis of social class but also on cultural or education similarity within this (Kalmijn, 1994). Social mobility should not be seen in any way as randomising individual relationships. The trend, as people increasingly take charge of their own destinies, is in the opposite direction, towards togetherness. As both social class and education are strongly associated with political views a fairly pronounced degree of homogamy on this latter basis might also be expected. Lampard (1997), using British Election Study data, shows a significant degree of political homogeneity within couples (which perhaps also varies by whether or not each individual's parents were themselves politically homogamous).

However, if individuals hold inconsistent views and these are volatile over time, could we not look at the other side of the family coin and ask if cross-pressures within the family (different members holding different views) adds to the general volatility? In a study using BHPS data, Zuckerman, Kotler-Berkowitz and Swaine (1998) argue that while the family should be seen as one element in the panoply of social influences at work on individuals (in whatever sphere), and is in effect a special case of this influence, what is of interest is less the degree of political consensus than the fact that it is far from total. While agreement in social views, class identification, and religious affiliation generally help to predict uniform voting, only 9% of British households comprise members who share Conservative Party identification, a Conservative vote, and middle-class identification. On the left/Labour side the figure is even less, at 7%. Rather than conformity, we may see diversity. The authors conclude:

> Individuals whose preferences are unstable at any point in time and over time can hardly produce households that display political uniformity. Politically diverse households can hardly lead individuals to consistent political attitudes and values. As a result ... large-scale social divisions display complex political patterns. (Zuckerman and others, 1998, p 491)

This implies a paradoxical conclusion. On the one hand, social and family networks must be expected to reinforce stability and consensus within those networks. However, the increasing fluidity of these networks might contribute to the already attested decline in the social underpinning of political preference, in particular as represented by the apparent decline in strength of the relationship between social class and voting. This leads to a simple question: are there sufficient cross-pressures within the family to distort the individual distribution of political views, and potentially to add to volatility in these views? The analysis that follows seeks to answer this by examining changes in party preference at the individual level that appear to be influenced by living in a partnership.

The individual and change in party preference

As already indicated, the BHPS reveals a much more fluid situation than can be observed in cross-sectional studies. Every year respondents are asked which party they support. If unable to name one, they are then asked which they feel closest to. If still unable to choose they are asked which party they would vote for if there were an election tomorrow. This fallback is not used in the following analysis, so the final variable does not even partially represent vote intention – the pollsters' standard question – although it probably functions similarly to vote intention in its ability to predict actual vote (Brynin and Sanders, 1997). It is difficult to be certain exactly what the variable used here means – party support, preference or identification (with an implicit progression in ideological commitment from the first to the third of these). However, as the focus here is on interpersonal comparisons rather than on the ideological or other foundations of voting behaviour, this matters rather little. For the sake of variety, these terms are used interchangeably in the following account.

Changes in party preference in the BHPS from 1991 to 1997 (the first seven waves) match the changing fortunes of the parties as told by the polls. In 1991, 33% of the sample supports the Conservatives and 28% Labour. In 1997, these preferences are 22% and 40% respectively. Two further aspects stand out:

- many people not identifying with a party nevertheless vote for one; for instance, 25% of the sample in 1992 identifies with no party, yet only 16% of the sample claims not to have voted in the election of that year (about six months before the interview);
- there *appears* to be a substantial crossing over of the main party lines, with the two main parties effectively swapping places in the public's affections.

However, in reality such disloyalty is not that common. This can be seen in Figure 8.1, which shows, relative to the number of waves (out of seven) that people identify with the Conservatives, how many times on average they support Labour, a third party or no party. Where Conservative

Figure 8.1: Identification with the Conservatives and competing choices

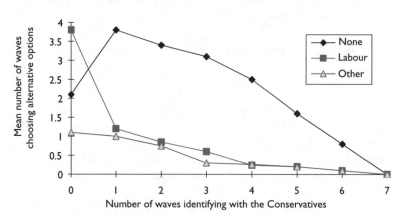

support is non-existent (number of Tory ID = 0) the average number of waves dedicated to Labour is nearly four. Where it is anything greater than zero, support for Labour declines initially to less than 1.5 waves and then lower. In other words, those never identifying with the Conservatives tend to be Labour supporters. However, identification with the Conservatives has to go up to only one wave out of the seven (still tenuous enough), for Labour support to plummet. At the same time, the number with no ID rises considerably and only falls below its initial position when Conservative support reaches five out of seven waves. The losses sustained by the Conservatives are the result of the weaker penumbra of support returning to limbo, not of a change of camp. Not even the third parties are a counter-attraction.

Although wave-on-wave switches between the two main parties are minimal, cumulatively they add up to a significant switch from Conservative to Labour. Of those identifying with the Conservatives in wave 1, by wave 7 as many as 11% identify with Labour, while only 1% of Labour supporters move the other way. Even if this explains only one quarter of the (gross) swing to Labour, well over half of which stems from previous non-identification, the cumulative transfer of support from Conservative to Labour culminates in a significant switch in actual vote. Nearly 15% of those voting Conservative in 1992 voted Labour in 1997, with only about 1% going the other way. Nearly 13% of Labour's vote in the 1997 election came from previously Conservative votes.

On the other hand, this is unlikely to reflect a fundamental shift in the inclinations of the voting public. The changes occur mostly among those with the weakest of political beliefs. These are probably people whose natural home had always been Labour but who, without necessarily dropping their weak social convictions, were attracted by the Conservative message during the heyday of the party in the 1980s. (This, however, cannot be tested through the BHPS, which began in 1991.) The shift to Labour is the net result of a great deal of fluctuation. Only 15% of the sample identifies with the Conservatives across all seven waves and only 19% with Labour. A mere 3% supports any of the third parties with the same consistency. This need not imply apathy as only 7% fails to identify at all across all seven waves, but it certainly implies a small core of consistent political support.

In the case of voting, the chances of fluctuation between two elections are obviously limited, but even then stability is tenuous. Only 59% of the sample voted the same way in the two elections. A total of 63% of 1992 Conservative voters stayed loyal in 1997; the figures for Labour and the third parties are 87% and 49% respectively. Nor are the switches between party preference and vote exactly parallel. For instance, 79% of those who changed their party *preference* to Labour between waves 1 and 7 equivalently switched their *vote* (including non-identification or non-vote as the starting position in both cases).

Year-on-year attrition is high, stability neither the exception nor the rule. It is not surprising, therefore, that change in party *preference* is not easy to predict. However, in the simpler case of voting in 1992 and 1997 it is possible to investigate a straightforward choice: whether to vote the same in 1997 as in 1992, or to change. This is the basis of the analysis reported in Table 8.1, which examines the factors associated first with voting a particular way (Conservative) in each of the two elections and, second, with switches from the Conservatives (to any other outcome) during this time. The method of logistic regression shows the log odds of making this choice given a range of background factors. The higher the coefficient the stronger the effect of that background factor on the odds of making the choice.

In the case of the first two models the dependent variables are Conservative vote (compared to all alternatives, including not voting) in 1992 and 1997 respectively. The explanatory variables in each of these two models derive from the same wave (or the previous wave in a small number of cases where a variable is unavailable in that wave or might be influenced by the current wave's responses). The third model, showing change over the period, uses the same variables as in the 1997 model.

Table 8.1: Logistic regression of the odds of voting Conservative and of switching from the Conservatives, given as logistic regression coefficients

	Tory 1992	Tory 1997	Leaves Tories 1992-97
Age	0.01***	0.02***	−0.02***
Male	−0.03	0.03	−0.04
Married/partnered	0.18***	0.16**	−0.15*
Was married	−0.01	−0.12(*)	0.11
(Never married)			
Lives in South	0.09**	0.05	−0.04
Reads no paper	0.02	0.13*	0.10
Reads Tory paper	0.57***	0.73***	−0.36***
Reads neutral paper	0.24	0.20**	−0.11
(Reads 'left' paper)			
Interested in politics	0.09**	0.10**	−0.17***
(Less interested)			
Has left-wing views	−0.89***	−0.87***	0.50***
Is pro-NHS	−0.18***	−0.20***	0.11*
Is religious	0.12***	0.16***	−0.13**
No work experience	−0.17*	0.00	−0.14
Professional/managerial	−0.07	0.03	−0.05
Routine white-collar	0.19**	0.13	−0.07
Self-employed	0.39***	0.21*	0.04
(Manual working class)			
Sees self as classless	−0.13*	−0.08	0.11
Sees self as middle class	0.33***	0.40***	−0.19**
(Sees self as working class)			
Has a degree	−0.37***	−0.23**	0.04
Is a union member	−0.08*	−0.16**	0.22***
Income	<0.00001***	0.00	<0.00001
Rent/mortgage problems	−0.09	−0.20*	0.27*
Constant	−2.44***	−3.42***	1.38***
Pseudo R²	*18.4%*	*19.4%*	*8.9%*

Note: Figures in brackets are reference categories.
* = significant at 95% confidence level
** = significant at 99% confidence level
*** = significant 99.9% confidence level

Despite the considerable attrition of the Conservative vote during the period, the profiles of Tory voters in the two elections remains remarkably similar. They tend to be older, are more likely to be married, to read a Conservative newspaper, to have right-wing views (whether generally or in respect of health policies), to affirm a religion, to be clerical workers or self-employed, to have a middle-class self-perception yet not to have a degree, and to be relatively well-off (in terms either of income or of ability to pay for housing costs).

The only substantial difference between the two models is in the impact of occupational class. A considerable attenuation of its effect occurs between 1992 and 1997. This could in part be the result of people's circumstances changing but this degree of change is likely to be minimal. It is more probable that the Labour Party's success in 1997 was so general that it cut across social class in a sweeping fashion, leaving the Conservatives with a thin and restricted support base in one or two occupational classes (perhaps ironically in the light of Conservative claims to have created a classless society). One result that is particularly interesting in view of the theme of this chapter is the stronger likelihood of people in marriages or partnerships (predominantly the former) to vote Conservative, even controlling for age. Marriage is either a conservative force or Conservatives are more likely to marry.

Moving to the final column, the last line of the table shows how much more difficult it is to demonstrate which people change parties at the individual level. After all, there is no reason why age, gender, social class, and so on should predispose people to change their views at a particular time. These switches to a large extent reflect social trends and move with aggregate perceptions of the state of the parties, the national economy, and so on. As the BHPS unfortunately lacks any indicators of these perceptions, no comment can be made about them in the case of these models.

Nevertheless, some individual factors do seem to be associated with desertion from the Conservatives. These are pretty much the inverse of the factors that are related to Conservatism in the first place. Those who leave the party are younger, less likely to be married, unlikely to read a Tory paper, have left-wing views, are unlikely to think of themselves as middle-class, and may well be members of a trade union. In other words, they are presumably on the periphery of Conservative support in the first place. They had probably in earlier years been 'captured' by the Conservatives but their underlying support was perhaps always tenuous. This impression is reinforced by the fact that (compared to Conservative loyals) these switchers are less interested in politics. On the other hand, while they appear to float they are not floating voters in the traditional sense. They are, rather, 'cross-voters': people who at some point vote in opposition to the predictions made on their behalf by regression models. They do not do what their backgrounds suggest.

Is this propensity to 'cross-vote' reinforced or undermined by cross-pressures within the family? Where conflictual opinions exist, do individuals alter their views to reduce disagreement? Do families influence voting outcomes?

Party identification and voting in the family

The focus in this section is on couples. In wave 2, 64% of couples share the same party preference, although vote agreement is much higher at 74%. The latter point suggests that families are effective when it most counts. Extreme differences (for instance, one Conservative, one Labour) are rare, whether looking at preference or vote. However, switches in support between parties among couples as units parallel the individual trend. For instance, 33% of couples voted Conservative in 1992 and 21% in 1997, while there was a rise in favour of Labour from 25% to 35%. Whether looking at individuals or at couples the same sort of trend emerges. At first glance this suggests that families make no difference.

On the other hand, this is a macro view of change. The picture is of the distribution of party support across British coupledom. From a micro point of view, the picture is different. Here the focus is neither the individual nor the family but the *relationship*. From the perspective of one half of this relationship (for the moment, male, but the same applies if the female is the unit of analysis) what now emerges is a considerable fragmentation in couple support in the case of the Conservatives but entrenchment for Labour. Looking at the party positions of couples in wave 1 and comparing to wave 7, Table 8.2 shows that this fragmentation is extreme among previously cohesive Conservative couples. In wave 7 these couples are characterised by a more complex range of outcomes than in wave 1.

The overall picture is first of a drift from the Conservatives (towards Labour) in all couple combinations, which parallels the individual trend, but secondly of far greater fragmentation of political outcomes in families where some Conservatism exists. In the case of couples where both partners are Labour supporters in wave 1, only 1% does not contain at least one Labour partner by wave 7. The equivalent for the Conservatives

Table 8.2: Change in couples' party ID, in column percentages

Wave 7	Both Tory	Both Labour	Both other/ none	One Tory, one other/ none	One Labour, one other/ none	One Tory/ one Labour
Both Tory	52	–	3	11	–	2
Both Labour	3	91	19	8	51	31
Both other/none	11	1	47	27	8	5
One Tory and one other/none	24	–	5	32	–	5
One Labour and one other/none	6	6	26	17	35	28
One Tory and one Labour	4	2	0	5	5	30

Couples' party ID in wave 1

is 20% (rows 2, 3 and 5). Where one partner is Labour in wave 1 and the other is not a Conservative, there is no Labour supporter in 8% of cases in wave 7, but the equivalent for the Conservatives is an astonishing 52%. Here is a process of intensification and attenuation of party support at the family level. This is accompanied by a change in the scope for intra-family cross-pressures through an increase in the number of homes where a Conservative supporter is isolated in this support.

Cause or effect?

We still have no idea whether these mutual shifts in party support are the result of a correlation between individually random changes (correlated because partners are similar) or whether partners influence each other – directly or otherwise – in their party support. It is possible, for instance, that in a period of decline in fortunes of a political party, having only one partner in a couple who bucks the trend is not enough to influence the overall party position. The brake on the downward slide away from a party might only operate where both members are equally resistant to change. To put this another way, shifts in support are more likely where there are cross-pressures.

As a first step it is useful to convert the changes described above among couples into individual change. Does a different proportion of individuals change politically in some voting combinations of partners rather than

Table 8.3: An aggregate index of the impact of one partner's party preference on the preference of the other partner

	Both Tory	Both Labour	Both other/ none	One Tory, one other/ none	One Labour, one other/ none	One Tory, one Labour
% Tory wave 1	100	0	0	50	0	50
% Tory wave 7	82	1	6	28	1	20
Change waves 1-7	*−18*	*+1*	*+6*	*−22*	*+1*	*−30*
% Labour wave 1	0	100	0	0	50	50
% Labour wave 7	11	91	28	24	69	67
Change waves 1-7	*+11*	*−9*	*+28*	*+24*	*+19*	*+17*

others? Table 8.3 shows the proportion of individuals supporting either Labour or the Conservatives over time by couple beliefs in a specific wave. Each column shows the relationship between party preferences within couples in waves 1 and 7. In the first row this is indexed either at zero (neither couple member chooses this option in wave 1), at 50 (only one chooses it) or at 100 (both choose it). The second row shows the position in wave 7. The third row shows the difference between row one to row two.

The first panel shows that the proportion of individuals within couples supporting the Conservatives in wave 1 falls by 18 percentage points in wave 7 where both had supported the Tories in wave 1 (column 1). But the loss of Tory support is greater where one supported the party and the other supported neither of the main parties (column 4) and greatest of all where the partner supported Labour (column 6). This suggests a certain stickiness of support depending on the partner's view.

The bottom half of the table shows the complementary analysis for Labour. It can be seen that the proportion of individuals switching to Labour where both partners were Conservative in wave 1 is relatively small. (Column 2 shows some Labour attrition where both support the party in wave 1, but this reflects little more than 'regression to the mean': if change occurs for whatever reason it can only be away from joint support for Labour.)

This mapping of the extent of individual movement in party preference by the relationship between the preferences of partners suggests that movement is more likely over time where there is cross-pressure at one point in time. Partners continue to influence each other rather than just responding as individuals to what is going on around them.

Table 8.4: Conservative partners over time, in column percentages

Female partner	Stays Tory	Male partner Tory to other/none	Tory to Labour	Total switch from Tories
Stays Tory	74	43	17	36
Tory to other/none	22	44	48	45
Tory to Labour	4	13	36	19

Again, however, this is a macro view. It is also necessary to observe these changes from the relationship point of view. This is undertaken in Table 8.4. For simplicity, this concentrates only on the contrast between loyal Conservatives and those who move away from the party. Comparing columns 1 and 4 shows that while 74% of women where their partners stay Conservative also stay loyal (the figure for men staying with the party where their partner does so is 81%), when he switches to other or none, 43% of women remain Conservative. Where he switches to Labour – a relatively rare choice – only 17% of women stay Conservative (although more than half of the switches do not go to Labour). At the very least, a proneness to switch, and also in a particular direction, is shared.

Thus far the focus has been on stable partnerships but another test of the impact of relationships on party identification is possible where relationships change: couples starting, or splitting and perhaps re-forming. The highest level of change in preferences between waves 1 and 7 is among both women and men who have entered a new relationship (whether after an old one has broken down or from fresh). A total 36% of men in a new relationship change their preference compared to 30% of those remaining in stable relationships. While this is the largest of these differences, it further suggests the possibility of intra-couple effects: there might be a slight tendency for individuals to adapt their views to new situations.

In the case of changes in support, in contrast, these are likely to move in parallel within partnerships the more stable these are (although stability itself varies with other factors such as age). Through focusing on a comparison of stable and new relationships, and only on the cases where the male partner has a particular identification in wave 7 (in this case Labour, although the pattern would look very similar with a Conservative identity), it is possible to see whether or not it makes some difference being in a new relationship. A total of 43% of women with the same partner in waves 1 and 7 stay Labour during the period compared to 14% where the partner is different (and where in both cases the partner is a Labour supporter in wave 7). Where a woman has a new partner and he is Labour in wave 7 the chances of her being a stable supporter of Labour are therefore very small. Stability is more likely where she has been living for some time with a man who is currently Labour.

The figures in this section suggest potential mutual influence between change in partners' political views. This is tested, in Table 8.5, through a number of logistic regression models where the dependent variable is again the (log) odds of vote switching from the Conservatives between 1992 and 1997. Defectors are compared to Conservative loyals. Four models are presented, using different indicators of partner's vote as explanatory variables: her vote in 1992, her vote in 1997, her vote in both years, and changes in her vote between these years. The omitted category is in brackets. With the exception of age no other variables are included, to avoid any correlation between these and both partners' vote. (While her vote in the two elections as shown in the third model must be highly intercorrelated, in the context of the other models the implications of the results are quite apparent.)

Using her vote in 1992 as a predictor shows that a man is unlikely to switch from the Conservatives where his partner is also a Conservative, but having a partner who is an adherent of either Labour or a third party creates no strong pull. However, using the partner's vote in the current election (model 2) shows that if at this juncture she supports a party other than the Conservatives then there is a move away from the Conservatives by her partner. It is the current position that counts for most, whatever the partner's previous voting pattern. This is confirmed in column 3, which shows the primacy of her current vote over her previous vote. If the female is currently Labour, whether or not she was previously, a Conservative man is likely to drop support for the party. The finding is even stronger in the final column where it can be seen that living with a stable Labour voter is unlikely to persuade men to drop their Tory vote, at least in large numbers, but where the woman switches to Labour (from whatever position, including not voting at all), this increases the probability that he will switch from the Conservatives. So, current Labour support by a partner is a stronger spoiler for Conservative men than previous Labour support, but a switch to Labour even more so. This is important because it helps to distinguish the relative influence of selection – or of 'like marries like' – from influences of one partner on the other after formation of the partnership. In the case of selection

Table 8.5: Conservative defection by men between 1992 and 1997 elections, given as logistic regression coefficients

| | Year of partner's vote | | | |
	1992	1997	Both	1992/97 Change
Age	−0.03***	−0.03***	−0.03***	−0.03***
Partner's 1992 vote				
Conservative	−0.90***		−0.27	
Labour	0.50		−0.28	
Other	0.26		−0.06	
(None)				
Partner's 1997 vote				
Conservative		−1.05***	−1.03***	
Labour		0.96***	1.00***	
Other		0.67*	0.51	
(None)				
Partner's vote change				
Stays Conservative				−1.45***
Stays Labour				0.52
Tory to Labour				0.81*
Tory to other/none				−0.28
Labour to all other				0.01
Other/none to Tory				−0.75
Other/none to Labour				0.82*
(Stay other/none)				
Constant	1.40***	1.19***	1.18***	1.18***
Pseudo R²	7.6%	13.3%	14.0%	14.0%

* Significant at 95% confidence level
** Significant at 99%
*** Significant at 99.9%

effects, where a Conservative man lives with a non-Conservative woman he might be more likely to change his vote because he is a weak Conservative supporter, as a result of which he finds he can also live with a non-Conservative supporter. However, if selection is the sole explanation then the 1992 effect should be the same as in 1997. In fact, however, it is recent cross-pressuring that counts. It would appear that there are real effects of one person on another within couples.

Finally, it is possible to test the core theme directly – the impact on voting of cross-pressured couples. Table 8.6 defines cross-pressured couples as those where party ID is not shared. (This is measured one wave prior

Table 8.6: Logistic regression of 1992 Conservative vote, analysed by own and partner's party ID in 1991, given as logistic regression coefficients

| | Men | | Women | |
| | Votes for: | | Votes for: | |
	Tories	Labour	Tories	Labour
Self Tory				
Partner:				
Tory	2.97***	−3.19***	2.86***	−2.69***
Labour	2.12***	−1.42*	1.74***	−0.36
Other	2.08***	−1.43*	2.00***	−2.35**
None	2.24***	−1.44***	2.26***	−2.62***
Self Labour				
Partner:				
Tory	−0.79*	2.02***	−0.52	2.15***
Labour	−2.57***	2.65***	−3.27***	2.78***
other	−1.41**	1.91***	−1.91*	1.74***
none	−1.74***	2.16***	−1.19***	2.47***
Self other				
Partner:				
Tory	0.26	−1.56*	0.52	−0.94
Labour	−1.23	0.31	−1.00*	0.64*
Other	−1.26***	−1.00**	−1.35***	−1.51***
None	−0.90*	−0.02	−0.51	−0.11
Self none				
Partner:				
Tory	1.36***	−0.45	1.44***	−0.85***
Labour	−0.54	1.60***	−0.45*	1.33***
Other (both none)	−0.47	−0.58	−0.08	−0.08
Constant	−2.50***	−1.40**	−3.57***	−0.23
Pseudo R²	*44.0*	*42.0*	*42.3*	*42.8*

* Significant at 95% confidence level
** Significant at 99%
*** Significant at 99.9%

to the election year, a matter of months before the election. Again, the control variables are not shown.)

The hypothesis is that homes where cross-pressures exist (for instance, identification with the Conservatives but living with a Labour partner) are less likely to vote in the direction of their previous identification. The results are shown for both the Conservative and the Labour vote, and for men and women.

Table 8.7: Children's votes, by parental votes (1992), in column percentages

Child's vote	Mother's vote			Father's vote		
	Tory	Labour	Other/ none	Tory	Labour	Other/ none
Tory	50	6	14	54	7	10
Labour	9	53	9	10	57	10
Other	12	9	34	9	7	36
None	29	32	43	26	29	44

The hypothesis is confirmed. Where some sort of cross-pressure exists, the log odds of a man voting for the party he appears to prefer are reduced relative to cases where his partner shares his preference. The same applies in the case of her vote. Radical cross-pressuring (Conservative and Labour supporters living together) is rare, and residence with a partner who has no party ID while the respondent has an ID is far more common. Generally, though, this also lowers the propensity of the respondent to vote for the party identified with.

Voting across the generations

In concluding this chapter it is worthwhile looking across the generations. To what extent are young people influenced by their parents' political ideas? Given that these must surely be the original influence on young people's formative notions, the answer, shown in Tables 8.7 and 8.8, is rather surprising. Looking at voting in 1992, of the 358 people aged 30 or below who were living with their parents at that time, only about half in the case of the two main parties follow their parents' lead. This is somewhat different for the same sample in 1997 (when many of these people will have left home).

However, although young people who still live at home give their parents only half-hearted political support (precisely this in 1992), they do not often oppose them. Few young people vote for the opposite camp; they are simply less likely to vote at all. (While more than 90% of parents voted in 1992, less than 70% of their resident adult children did so. Surprisingly, perhaps, this latter figure does not change by 1997, even though these young people are five years older and many have left home. While nearly 60% of parents stayed in either the Conservative or Labour

Table 8.8: Children's votes, by parental votes (1997), in column percentages

Child's vote	Mother's vote			Father's vote		
	Tory	Labour	Other/ none	Tory	Labour	Other/ none
Tory	42	5	19	42	6	12
Labour	14	56	26	15	60	27
Other	14	7	22	15	9	25
None	29	32	33	27	25	36

camp over the two elections, only just more than 30% of their adult children did so.)

Recalling that more than 70% of couples vote the same way, it seems that families are less cohesive across the generations than within. If partners competing for political allegiance help to create political flux, filial allegiance does little to constrain this over the generations.

Conclusions

The first section of this chapter has demonstrated through longitudinal analysis that there is a considerable degree of fluctuation in party identification at the individual level over time, which is also reflected among couples. Couples are to some extent a political unit and the distribution of their party support broadly mirrors the individual distribution. The middle section undermines this conclusion by suggesting that members of couples pull each other's party ID and vote out of the path that might be otherwise chosen, that is over and above what might be expected from purely individual choices. Several tests of the impact of political cross-pressures within the family (lack of agreement in party preference) on voting choice reinforce this finding. Finally, cross-generational transmission of political inclinations seems weak, although, since few young people actually vote for a party diametrically opposed to the parental choice, it is likely that the effect is merely lagged over time.

There is no doubt that family members tend to have similar political views and behaviour. However, this is a given and does not mean that family members influence each other. Nevertheless, political preferences and voting dispositions do seem to be pulled about within relationships through the influence of one person on another. In particular, where homogamy is low (agreement fails to occur, or when agreement comes to an end), one member appears to make the preferences of other members' position vulnerable to change. Families add to rather than constrain the political instability observed at the individual level. Families create tiny knots of stability in society, but when looking at political behaviour, these very knots possibly contribute to political instability.

It would seem that fundamental changes to the social fabric, whether in work or family formation (as attested by other chapters in this book), are associated with a greater level of instability not only of the family as a unit but of relationships, and the interdependence of individuals within relationships. These changes are in turn associated with a greater unpredictability in individual attitudes to how society should be organised, whether reflected in political preferences or in voting behaviour. The argument of this chapter is that these changes are reciprocal rather than merely running in parallel. It is not claimed that this has a significant impact on the electoral system (though families *might* contribute to political volatility). More to the point is that families both contribute to and reflect a greater volatility in social life.

References

Becker, G. (1981) *A treatise on the family*, Cambridge, MA: Harvard University Press (reprinted in 1991).

Brynin, M. and Sanders, D. (1997) 'Party identification, political preferences and material conditions: evidence from the BHPS, 1991-92', *Party Politics*, vol 3, no 1, pp 53-78.

Cheal, D. (1991) *Family and the state of theory*, New York, NY: Harvester Wheatsheaf.

Crewe, I. and Thomson, K. (1999) 'Party loyalties: dealignment or realignment?', in G. Evans and P. Norris (eds) *Critical elections: British parties and voters in long-term perspective*, London: Sage Publications.

Heath, A. and Britten, N. (1984) 'Women's jobs do make a difference', *Sociology*, vol 18, no 4, pp 475-90.

Johnston, R. and Pattie, C. (1996) 'The strength of party identification among the British electorate', *Electoral Studies*, vol 15, no 3, pp 295-309.

Johnston, R. and Pattie, C. (1999) 'Aspects of the interrelationships of attitudes and behaviour as illustrated by a longitudinal study of British adults', *Environment and Planning*, vol 31, no 5, pp 899-923.

Kalmijn, M. (1994) 'Assortative mating by cultural and economic occupational class', *American Journal of Sociology*, vol 100, no 2, pp 422-52.

Lampard, R. (1997) 'Party political homogamy in Great Britain', *European Sociological Review*, vol 13, pp 79-100.

Mare, R. (1991) 'Five decades of educational assortative mating', *American Sociological Review*, vol 56, no 1, pp 15-32.

Olson, D. (1993) 'Family continuity and change', in T.H. Brubaker (ed) *Family relations: Challenges for the future*, Newbury Park, CA: Sage Publications.

Parsons, T. (1964) *The social system*, New York, NY: Free Press.

Popenoe, D. (1988) *Disturbing the nest: Family change and decline in modern societies*, New York, NY: Aldine de Gruyter.

Rose, R. (1980/1984) *Do parties make a difference?*, London: Macmillan.

Sanders, D. and Brynin, M. (1999) 'The dynamics of party preference change in Britain, 1991-1996', *Political Studies*, vol 47, no 2, pp 219-39.

Zuckerman, A., Kotler-Berkowitz, L. and Swaine L. (1998) 'Anchoring political preferences: the structural bases of stable electoral decisions and political attitudes in Britain', *European Journal of Political Research*, vol 33, no 3, pp 285-321.

NINE

Seven years in the lives of British families

Richard Berthoud and Jonathan Gershuny

A paradox: individual dynamics versus social trends

The panel survey provides a moving picture of people and families. It could be thought of as a form of timelapse photography in which we see beards sprouting or hairlines receding, in which partners and children move into the frame and out of it, in which the decoration and furniture become, as we view successive snaps, more lush and expensive or increasingly pinched and shabby.

The book began by thinking about social change in the aggregate over recent decades, comparing 'cross-sectional' survey evidence from the 1970s through to the 1990s. However, in subsequent chapters the focus on change over time tended to fall away – despite the fact that longitudinal data from the BHPS has been used throughout. The lives of the same people at successive points in time have been analysed, revealing the changes in conditions of life that they experience. However, these individual experiences of life events do not necessarily add up to social change viewed in the aggregate. On the contrary: the micro-dynamics of life, the processes through which individuals' and households' circumstances are maintained or transformed from year to year – what might be thought of as life chances – may simply be the best, the most informative and the most powerful way to describe the current workings of the society. Individual dynamics can sum to social statics.

The contrast between micro-dynamics and macro-statics can be illustrated by thinking about the 'movement' of a river. If you stand on the bank, you can see the water flowing downstream. If you come back a year later, the water passing by is a completely different set of molecules to the ones you saw last time. Yet the same river is still there! So is the flow; so are the waves. Similarly, it is different people flowing each year from the source of the river of life, down the turbulent rapids of childhood and adolescence, through the broadening stream of education, marriage, employment and parenting, into the slow-moving estuary of old age and, eventually, to the ocean that awaits us all. Lives are always changing, but life may continue unchanged.

The river may remain stable, even though the water flows rapidly on. Or the river *itself* may change. The flow may be faster one year and slower another, depending on rainfall. Over the decades, the banks may fall in, or the river's course may be altered, perhaps dramatically, either as a result of natural forces or through man-made intervention. Similarly, over time differences occur in the course of social and economic life, which may or may not be the result of public policy. These include changes in marriage and childrearing patterns, in employment structures, in mortality rates and so on. The key to 'dynamic' analysis is that events experienced by individuals do not necessarily create trends in society as a whole. On the other hand, the major trends that have occurred during the past generation are made up of altered life experiences for individuals, and it is only by studying those personal experiences, and the influences on them, that it is possible to understand the trends fully.

The successive chapters of this book look in turn at a range of separate aspects of people's lives – they add up to a comprehensive account of life experiences through the 1990s. Comprehensive, but not yet integrated. None of these aspects or 'domains' of life proceeds in isolation. An employment event may have marital consequences – losing a job may impose strains on a relationship that lead, after an interval, to the split from a spouse. Both events might involve a loss of income and lead to poverty. The various aspects of people's lives, that for analytical convenience have been treated separately in the chapters of this book, are in fact joined up.

This study has focused on two particular perspectives. First there is the life-course progression. Shakespeare's 'seven ages of man' may now seem over-determined (as well as unacceptably sexist and ageist), but the idea of distinct life-stages remains useful. The standard life-course progressions are the regular and expected events of anyone's life. They bring with them various changes in life experiences. As we grow older, we expect to become richer at first, and somewhat poorer later on. We expect to marry and have children at a certain age, to retire from our jobs at another. These are the common experiences of our own seven ages.

Second, and somewhat independently, there are 'accidents' of various types. They may sometimes be, literally, accidents: a fall, a car crash, an illness, which set in train a series of secondary consequences, departures from the expected course of life events. Similarly, the unexpected loss of a job, or a divorce – or a surprise promotion or a late marriage – may have consequences that fall well outside the normal run of life-course expectations. Accidents in this broad sense are from an individual point of view unexpected, and they are difficult for analysts to predict; but in the aggregate they happen with a certain regularity. A certain rate of 'accidents', and their consequences, are as much a feature of a society as are the regular transitions of the life-course. So, the particular expected events, and the unexpected ones, their incidence at particular ages and their prevalence across the population, together with their consequences for all aspects of subsequent life experiences, constitute the individual life chances in a given state of society.

Which brings us back to the grand topic of social change. The pattern of life chances may change. Particular life-course progressions, or specific sorts of accidents, may have consequences over one historical period, but somewhat different consequences at another. These trends may reflect changes in the characteristics of the population – if people are more flexibly educated, for example, they may be able to cope more effectively with a redundancy. If people have adequate savings, or private insurance and pensions arrangements, they may be more able to face retirement, or a period of unemployment, without falling into poverty. Changes in life chances also reflect not personal but institutional developments. If, for example, access to further or higher education, becomes increasingly dependent on private payments of tuition fees, if there is a decline in the range of treatments available for particular age groups in the NHS, or a reduction in the level of state pensions, then particular transitions and accidents will happen at different rates and have altered consequences. So systems of public regulation, 'regimes', may also influence life chances.

Personal dynamics may be a good way to view social statics. However, if the individual-level longitudinal data used covers a sufficiently long timespan it is possible to compare individual life-course dynamics over successive periods. From a longitudinal perspective, social trends can be viewed as a type of 'second difference'. First, individual life chances are established by examining the patterns of change in individuals' circumstances from year to year. Then social change is identified as the difference between these patterns of experience over successive periods. The seven years of the BHPS that have been examined in this book are just about enough to establish the pattern of life chances for one historical period. The comparative cross-sectional account of Chapter One provided the historical context for what followed. In another seven years, it may be possible to complement this with a comparative dynamic account of social change, a picture of how life chances may be affected (or be left unaffected) by a historical succession of public policy regimes.

However, for the moment we are left with the current patterning of life-events in Britain through the 1990s. This final chapter draws together the evidence about the streams of events in the various life-course domains that have been set out in the foregoing chapters – and then provides an initial and very preliminary illustration of a life-course account, and how it might relate to 'accidents'.

Dynamics and trends in particular life-course domains

What has the analysis of the BHPS, presented in the substantive chapters of this book, told us about the processes and trends affecting people in Britain in the 1990s?

Comparing generations

Much of Richard Berthoud's Introduction focused on the major social trends that have occurred within the lifetime of most of those who will read this book. Some of the most significant changes have been in the structure of families and the relationships between men and women. The rise in rates of cohabitation and of divorce has reduced the number of people in formal long-term marriages. Women are having their children later, and an increasing number of children are born outside marriage. A striking illustration of these trends is provided by the General Household Survey: in 1973, slightly more than two thirds of women in their late 20s were legally married and had children; in 1996, the number in that position had halved, to just less than one third. The much wider variety of family forms now available implies more choice and greater independence between men and women. On the other hand, some of the consequences do not necessarily represent an improvement in the lifestyles of the individuals concerned. Most of the growing number of one-parent families, for example, are in poverty. When the recent trends have worked their way through the life-course, it seems likely that far fewer members of the next generation of elderly people will be able to count on the support of their close family in their declining years.

There have been parallel trends in patterns of employment. It is well known that women are much more likely to remain in employment than their mothers were, although this increase has been confined to married women, especially those with young children. While one consequence has been a substantial rise in the number of couples with children both of whom have a job, another has been a rise in the number of single people, and even couples, who have no job at all. These changes show up in the social security statistics as parallel growth trends in unemployment, in the number of disabled people on benefit and in the number of one-parent families depending on the state. They show up in poverty analyses as a step increase in the number of people in poverty, from 6% of the population in 1977 to 20% in 1992. They show up in the housing market, where those in steady employment almost all now live in their own homes, while those without jobs are increasingly marginalised in unpopular council housing. Far from 'trickling down' to the poor, most of the long-term growth in employment, earnings and financial assets of which governments have been so proud has benefited the sectors of society that were already well-off in the first place. Financial and other forms of support that used to be provided as a matter of course *within* the family, now have to be provided *between* families, mediated by the tax and social security systems. Reduced dependence of women on men has been replaced by increased dependence of the poor on the state.

The theme of this book is that these and other long-term trends are outcomes that cannot be understood without studying the *processes* involved. The number of women who are now married and have children, for example, is a consequence of a series of decisions women and men have made about forming relationships, getting married and having children; and the converse of decisions about separation and divorce. These decisions may have been based not only on the personal feelings of the young people and the current set of social conventions, but also by the opportunities and constraints each of them perceived in the education system, in employment, in the housing market, and so on. An analysis of these decisions and processes will provide a much more precise picture of the underlying social and economic forces at work, a clearer indication of future trends, and a better guide for policy.

Family formation

In Chapter Two, John Ermisch and Marco Francesconi looked for explanations for two of the most important trends recorded by official

British marriage and birth statistics: the later ages at which men and women marry and have children, and the increasing number of births outside marriage. Part of the story lies in young people's pattern of leaving home. They have been moving out a little later than earlier generations did. However, the biggest change is that living as a student or independently has taken over from marriage as the primary destination when they do move out. One of the results of the fluidity of life in the 20s is that young men and women are also now more likely than before to return to live with their parents at some stage before they finally 'settle down'.

The overwhelming change in patterns of family formation is in the number of people who start by living with a partner, without (at first) marrying them. Cohabitation has become easily the most common mode of first partnership. During the early period, when cohabitation was being established as a socially acceptable way of living, it was men and women from middle class backgrounds who were most likely to live together without marrying; but the gap between social classes has been narrowed more recently. Although it might have been thought that the relative ease and informality of cohabitation might have encouraged men and women to start their live-in relationships earlier than they used to, in actual fact the age at which people start their first partnership has tended to rise slightly during this period.

Cohabitations may often be the start of a long-term, perhaps lifelong partnership, but the cohabitation itself is rarely long term. Less than one tenth of those who enter a non-marital partnership are still cohabiting 10 years later: the majority get married after a period, but up to one third split up within 10 years. The median duration of a cohabitation is only about two years. Among those who separate (without having married), many eventually cohabit with another partner, though this may not be for a few years.

It is cohabitation that explains the apparent reduction in the marriage rate. It seems that (so far) the great majority of people will marry eventually. However, marriages are being delayed: by the slight increase in the age at which men and women start their first partnership; by the period of cohabitation itself; by the fact that many cohabitations end in separation, followed by a second period of search and of cohabitation prior to possible marriage. All of these contribute to a longer time before any marriage takes place, and increase the chances that a person never marries.

Introduction of cohabitation as a life-stage (usually) prior to formal marriage is also associated with the increase in the length of time before women first have children. On the other hand, the link between marriage and parenting is much weaker than it used to be. More than one third of all births are out of wedlock; about two thirds of these children are born to cohabiting couples, the remaining third to genuinely 'single' mothers. It is the substitution of cohabitation for direct marriage in women's first partnership that accounts for most of the increase in the proportion of first births born outside marriage.

Given that the majority of live-in couples marry each other after a few years, cohabitation is often seen as a preliminary to marriage, or perhaps as a trial marriage; in that light, couples who separate are said to have tried each other out and decided against a permanent union. Many cohabitations change status quite early in their career; those who have neither married nor split up over a period of years are quite likely to carry on as they are. Marriage is more common, and separation less common, among couples where the man has a good job with high earnings. Perhaps the most surprising finding is that once a cohabiting couple has had children, they are just as likely to split up as a childless couple, and actually *less* likely to marry each other. Presumably, many of those who felt they should marry when they started a family did so before the children were born, rather than later on.

While marriages also break up, even if the couple has children, cohabitations are less stable. This is just as true of cohabiting couples with children as it is of those, without children, who might perhaps have been expected to perceive weaker ties of love or of obligation. While cohabitation is widely seen as a preliminary or an alternative to marriage, it often turns out to be a temporary relationship. For childless couples, it may be that the less formal contract between them is the advantage: less obligation, more independence, fewer tears if they decide to split up and move on. Where children are involved, though, it may be a mistake to regard cohabitation as a more modern form of joint parenting, a 'marriage without a licence'. The BHPS analysis shows that children born to cohabiting parents are *much* more likely to see their parents split up, and *much* more likely to experience a period in a one-parent family, than children born within marriage. The rise in cohabitation is implicated in the increasing prevalence of lone parenthood, and hence in the growth of child poverty discussed in Chapter Five.

Roles of partners within families

The analysis of family formation in Chapter Two was concerned with whether men and women had a partner at all. The great majority do, although a whole series of trends – later partnership formation, the introduction of cohabitation, the rise in separation and divorce – all suggest that traditional lifelong bonds are weakening. Some would say 'bondage' rather than 'bonds', on the grounds that old-fashioned marriages were based on unequal obligations. The man earned the money, the woman received a proportion of it as 'housekeeping'; the man took the decisions, the woman took the orders. In Chapter Three, Heather Laurie and Jonathan Gershuny looked for evidence about changes in the roles of husbands and wives within partnerships.

There is no doubt about the extent of change in the proportion of married women in employment – Laurie and Gershuny describe it as a 'transformation', although other writers have emphasised the continuing gap between husbands and wives in their lifetime earnings and accumulated pension rights (Joshi and Paci, 1998). The question is whether women who enter employment succeed in negotiating a more balanced share of rights and obligations within the domestic arena.

The analysis of 'housework' in Chapter Three suggested that there is a link between employment and housework which is in the expected direction, even if it is not yet equitable. Younger couples report a more equal share of the housework than older ones. Even over the short period of the 1990s, married women report a reducing amount of time on domestic work (although married men do not claim to be spending more time on this task). There are robust indications that the woman's share of the housework reduces when she takes a full-time job (and increases again when she stops working outside the home). None of these trends comes anywhere near eliminating the gendered nature of most domestic tasks, but they are at least in the expected direction.

When it comes to spending the family's money, couples where the woman earns an income of her own in the labour market are consistently more likely to report that they either share the management of their finances, or (in a minority of cases) operate independent budgets, than in couples where the woman does not go out to work. Interestingly, egalitarian money-management practices are as closely associated with the woman's and the man's *attitudes* to women's economic roles, as with the wife's actual activity. However, changes in the wife's economic activity from year to year do not have a consistent effect on changes in how the couple arrange the control of their money. Financial management practices seemed to be influenced by long-term factors such as education background and the couple's negotiated view of the appropriate balance of responsibilities. One of the factors associated with that view is the woman's decision whether to work or not. However, financial arrangements do not seem to fluctuate over time in response to the changing details of her current employment status.

Employment

In Chapter Four, the focus shifted from the family itself to the experiences faced by individual men and women in the labour market – although family factors can have an important effect on that experience.

One of Mark Taylor's themes in this chapter was the increasing 'turbulence' in the labour market. An indication of a growing sense of insecurity comes right at the start of young people's careers. Among those who left school or college in the 1960s, almost all moved straight into full-time work; by the 1990s, the majority of young people faced a potentially anxious initial period of part-time work, unemployment or economic inactivity.

Similarly, comparison of successive cohorts of workers shows substantial increases in the annual risk of leaving any particular job. Most of the rise was in the risk of what the analysts called 'layoffs' – dismissals or redundancies enforced by employers, rather than voluntary movements by workers to other jobs or different activities. These trends may be associated both with an increase in the relative importance of small rather than large firms, and increasing labour market flexibility. Historically, women tended to remain in the same job longer than men, but this difference has been reducing over time.

Turning to changes occurring while continuing to work with the same employer, the chances of promotion ranged from about 15% per year for those in their 20s to one third of that rate towards the end of people's career. The chance of being promoted is high for married men and women, those who have remained with the same employer for some time, workers in non-manual occupations, and those who put in overtime hours. People who have been promoted have a high chance of remaining with their employer for a further year, and in fact many are promoted again.

Full-time employment remains the most common single labour market status, especially for men. It is also the most stable – most full-time employees are still full-time employees the following year. However, men and women differ in their use of other forms of employment. For men, self-employment is a relatively common, and stable, alternative, especially for older workers and those with children. For women, part-time employment is often stable, and associated with family responsibilities.

Unemployment is the labour market status of greatest concern to policy makers. In particular, long-term or repeated spells of unemployment may have a serious effect on the income and social standing of an individual and his or her family. Do those who are regularly unemployed have certain characteristics (of age, education, health and so on) that reduce their chances of finding and retaining work? Following the same men from year to year shows that these underlying characteristics do play their part. Being unemployed at one point in time also has a direct effect on the probability of being unemployed on some later occasion. This implies that policies aimed at reducing short-run unemployment should have longer-term implications by reducing the overall unemployment rate.

The growing interest in polarisation between 'work-rich' and 'work-poor' families emphasises that employment may be a family issue rather than a decision taken by individuals in isolation. The employment rate of lone parents is very low, and a year-on-year analysis emphasises this: lone parents are less likely to move into work, and more likely to leave work, than non-married adults without children. There has been an increase over the years in the number of couples where both work, and in the number where neither works, leaving a decline in the number of traditional one-earner families. At a cross-sectional level, couples with children have slightly lower employment rates than those without, but a year-on-year analysis suggests that parents have rather higher rates of entry into work than members of couples who have no children.

Analysis of the probability of retiring from work confirms that retirement is a function of increasing age, with peaks at the statutory retirement ages of 65 for men and 60 for women. There is little evidence that people use part-time work as a stepping stone between full-time work and retirement. Both men and women tend to retire earlier if they experience poor health. Better-educated men retire earlier, but there is no relationship between retirement and education for women.

Poverty

The discussion of employment, unemployment and retirement leads naturally to Stephen Jenkins's analysis of the distribution of household incomes in Chapter Five. Other sources show that there was a dramatic increase in inequality and poverty during the 1980s, although the pattern stabilised during the mid- to late-1990s. Britain has a larger proportion of people in poverty (defined as being below half the national income level) than most comparable Western countries. However, until the panel survey data became available, practically nothing was known about the dynamics of poverty. It makes a great deal of difference whether a few people are poor for long periods, or many people have a brief experience of poverty.

There is a high degree of longitudinal income mobility, coexisting with cross-sectional stability in the shape of the income distribution. Only about half the population will be found in the same income band two years running. On the other hand, most income mobility is short range. Each person's income fluctuates around a fixed long-term average; they may move away from this point from one year to the next, but not too far, and they tend to rebound back towards their average over a period.

As many as one third of all individuals in the BHPS (68%) experienced poverty in at least one of the first six years of the survey. Only one in 60 (1.7%) experienced poverty in all six waves. This longer-term view shows that poverty is both more widespread, and less persistent, than might be inferred from the more commonly-quoted figure of about 17% of respondents below the poverty line in any one year (DSS, 1998). Nevertheless, inequality is almost as wide if six years' of income are averaged, as it is when a single year's income is used as the basis of measurement.

Nearly half of those starting a spell in poverty one year will have left it again the following year. After five years from the start of a spell in poverty, four out of five will have left (although many may have returned). In contrast, only 11% of people starting a spell above the poverty line will return to below it within a year; 21% will have returned to poverty within five years. Non-poverty is a more stable condition than poverty, although this varies from one group to another. For example, as many as one in six lone-parent families are estimated to be in steady poverty (defined as poor last year, this year and next year). For non-pensioners without children, the proportion in steady poverty (as just defined) is less than one in 100.

As might be expected, many moves into or out of poverty coincide with a substantial change in a member of the household's earnings – often a move into or out of work. However, work is not the whole story – a high proportion of moves across the poverty line are associated with changes in other elements in the household income, or with changes in the composition of the household (such as divorce, for example).

Housing and mobility

In Chapter Six Nick Buck argued that people's housing 'careers' are an important influence on and signal of their life chances. A house or flat is a substantial asset whose acquisition is strongly influenced by public policy, as well as by the employment and family position of its residents. Its location is an important element of people's social and economic position, which carries a substantial price and value of its own.

Private accommodation is uncommon, but there are still stages in the life-course when rented housing is an essential aid to mobility. As many as half of young adults living alone still rent privately. The income gap between owner-occupiers and social tenants is now very wide. These features of the 1990s' housing market can place immense pressures on families whose earnings are too low or too uncertain to provide the base for buying their own home. Given the degree of polarisation, exclusion from owner occupied housing means:

• the loss of opportunity to build up a substantial asset;
• the necessity to pay rent throughout your life;
• the probability of living in an area whose low status is as clear to outsiders as it is to the residents.

About 10% of the population moves every year. The rate is much higher for young adults living alone, much lower for middle-aged and elderly people. The majority of moves are over quite a short distance (within the same local authority district) and these tend to be motivated by housing and family considerations. Longer distance moves are more often associated with changes in employment or education, and with young people leaving (or returning) home.

Detailed analysis of house moves during the full panel period confirms that people are most likely to move below the age of 30, but that age effects are weak from then on. Private tenants show very high mobility; social tenants are more likely to move than owner occupiers, but this is often only over a short distance. *Within* tenures, though, it is those with higher incomes who are more likely to move, so that the tenure effect and the income effect are in potential conflict. It is low-income owner-occupiers who are least mobile.

The rigidity of tenure divisions, and the importance of the flexibility provided by private rental, are demonstrated by the fact that only about half of all house moves are associated with a change of tenure, and three quarters of those changes start or end in private rental. This is particularly important for moves that involve the break-up of former households, such as young people leaving home or separating partners. Over the medium term, owner-occupation is the most stable tenure: people are substantially more likely to enter than to exit that position. However, as would be expected, it is those with higher incomes who become owner-occupiers, while those with low incomes gravitate towards the social sector.

This conclusion is especially relevant when examining the experiences of young people at the start of their housing careers. A number of those who were living with their parents in social housing at the start of the panel had achieved owner-occupation by the time of their latest interview. However, young men and women whose parents were owner-occupiers had a much better chance of attaining that status themselves – and very few of them moved into social housing. The median income of first-time buyers was double that of the group of people below 30 who remained in the rented sector.

Desirable though it may be, owner occupation cannot provide adequate housing for all in a world of income inequality and increasing instability in family and working lives.

Longitudinal measures of health

Chapter Seven had to start further back in the methodological chain of development, because there has never been any previous attempt to develop a measure of health changes from year to year. Since it is known that the incidence and prevalence of many illnesses increases with age, it is easy to assume that ill-health is a one-way street – that people's health often deteriorates but rarely improves.

It proved possible to develop a robust measure of respondents' current health from the BHPS data. It was internally consistent, in the sense that three rather different questions from the BHPS questionnaire all gave similar answers. It was also externally logical, in the sense that those found to be in poor health made heavy use of doctors and other health services, had low employment rates and – if they were also elderly – high mortality rates. However, the measure appeared much less reliable when it came to comparisons from year to year. Differences between interviews in the answers to one of the three health questions had to be interpreted as marginal changes in the way the respondent interpreted their condition, as much as actual trends in their underlying state of health. This meant that the panel survey could not be used to track minor and short-term changes; it could only measure larger and/or longer-term trends.

It was nevertheless possible to identify those who 'fell ill' at some point during the seven years of the survey – that is, they were in good health at the first wave, but reported ill-health at one or more subsequent waves. Conversely, it was also possible to identify those who 'recovered'. Overall, three times as many respondents fell ill (21%) as recovered (7%). Nevertheless, as many as one third of those who were ill at the start did recover, so the 'one-way street' hypothesis is not strongly endorsed.

Not surprisingly, two of the most important precursors of falling ill were the person's age, and his or her starting point – those already in only moderately good health were more likely to cross the boundary to 'ill-health' than those who were in excellent health at the beginning. Women were, as expected, more likely than men to fall ill; but they were also more likely to recover, and this suggests more of an episodic character to women's illnesses.

The longitudinal analysis showed that those reporting stress at the start of the panel period had a higher than average risk of falling ill later, but the strength of this association was much weaker than it had appeared at the cross-sectional level. This implies that a large part of the high stress levels observed among those currently in poor health may have been caused by (rather than being a cause of) the illness.

One of the primary objectives of including health data in a general purpose survey such as the BHPS is to provide an opportunity to analyse the socio-economic correlates of ill-health. The panel data uniquely enables us to distinguish social characteristics that precede illness (and may help to cause physiological or mental problems) and those that follow illness (and may be a consequence of poor health). Both social class and housing tenure were associated with the risk of ill-health. A simple analysis by income seemed to suggest that poor people had a higher chance of falling ill (and a lower chance of recovering), than those with higher incomes. However, this relationship disappeared entirely when the effect of other variables such as age was controlled for. On the other hand, money problems (such as debts) continued to be associated with the risk of declining health, even after other factors had been taken into account.

This cross-analysis offers intriguing possibilities for further examination of the inter-relationships between ill-health and the other topics reviewed in this book: family structure, employment, income, housing and so on.

Political affiliations

In Chapter Eight, Malcolm Brynin showed how interweaving elements of the panel data can shed new light on a range of topics – in his case, political values. He analysed party affiliations across time, to find out how far husbands and wives seemed to influence each other in the national shift from Conservative to Labour allegiance between 1992 and 1997. Did Tory couples decide together over the breakfast table to vote Labour this time? Or, given the general instability of party-political commitment in Britain, does the family distort the individual distribution of political views, and potentially add to volatility?

An important starting point is that the apparent net flow from the Conservative to the Labour party did not consist mainly of former Tory loyalists deserting their identity. Although a significant number of people did vote first for John Major and then for Tony Blair, they mainly consisted of 'floating voters' with no strong commitments to either party. Relatively few individuals switched their identification between the two main parties at different interviews across the seven-year BHPS period.

Despite the considerable attrition of the Conservative vote between the two elections, the profile of a Tory voter remains remarkably similar – older, reading a Conservative newspaper, middle class, higher income and so on. However, those among them who stopped voting Tory tended to have the opposite of these characteristics: younger, not reading a Tory paper, working class and so on. The party lost those of its voters who were on the periphery of Conservative support in the first place.

Looking at the combined opinions of couples, more than half of husband/wife pairs report the same party identification – both Tory, both Labour or both other/none. Between one quarter and one third report split identifications, but few of these couples had polarised their views to the extent of combining a Tory and a Labour affiliation. The shift between the two main parties between 1991 and 1997 rarely took the form of both partners changing their vote from Tory to Labour. The most common switch among double Tory couples was for one of the partners to choose another party or no party. The most common source of double Labour couples was families where one partner had previously considered him or herself Labour, and the other had been in neither of the two main camps.

Nevertheless, a man or a woman was more likely to change party allegiance if his wife or her husband was also moving in the same direction during the same period. So, for example, men who voted Tory in 1992 were least likely to abandon that position in 1997 if their wives were also loyal Conservatives, and most likely to do so if their wives moved towards Labour. Those men whose wife was already a Labour voter were not especially likely to join her. So there is some evidence that a readiness to change votes is a joint characteristic of a couple.

Finally, the BHPS allows a comparison of the voting behaviour of parents and children, for those below the age of 30 who lived with their parents at the beginning of the survey. Where parents voted Conservative or Labour, about half their children followed suit. However, very few children voted Labour if their parents voted Conservative, or vice versa.

There is no doubt that family members reinforce each other's political views and behaviour. The family creates tiny knots of stability, but around these knots it also contributes to turbulence.

Life-course events – the expected and the unexpected

There is a central 'life-cycle' theme of individual and family dynamics that underlies much of the research reported here, which could usefully be made more explicit. It also provides an opportunity to bring together many of the analytical themes discussed throughout this book. Life-stage definitions have flourished in the US (reviewed in Murphy, 1987; Schaninger and Danko, 1993), but have also been applied in Britain (see, for example, O'Higgins and others, 1988; Rowlingson and others, 1999). Some writers use 'life-cycle', 'life-course' and 'life-stages' more or less interchangeably, while others distinguish between 'life-cycle' and other terms either to emphasise or to avoid the notion of a 'cyclical' (repetitive) pattern. Although many studies have allocated members of a cross-sectional sample to a sequence of stages, none has used panel data to show directly how people move from stage to stage, and what else happens when they do. Yet that should be at the very heart of the life-course approach.

The provisional set of life-stages defined here is probably the first to be applied to household panel data. This preliminary version does not use the panel element to contribute to the definition of stages, partly because of the desire to retain comparability with data from cross-sectional sources such as the General Household Survey. The categorisation is applied separately to each individual taking part in the BHPS, rather than to whole households as a unitary group (although in practice, most husbands and wives will fall into the same category). The provisional allocation of categories is shown in Table 9.1. It counts eight, rather than the classical seven, stages.

Table 9.1: Definition of life-stages

Category		Definition
Dependent child	4%	Aged less than 16, or aged up to 18 and in full-time education
Young adult	9%	No partner and no children; a student, or lives with parents
Unattached	10%	No children; not a student and lives apart from parents; aged below 40
Young family	21%	Youngest child living with subject is up to the age of 10
Older family	17%	Youngest child living with subject is aged 11 or above
Older childless	14%	No children living with subject; age 40+; not 'retired'
Retired	14%	Subject does not have a full-time job, nor children below 16; 'head of family' is retired, or long-term sick (aged 40+) or 'housewife' (aged 60+)
Old/infirm	11%	Aged above 75; or aged above 65 and suffers from ill-health

Note: Later categories supersede earlier ones. Percentages are the proportion of adults (aged 16+) in the 1996 BHPS. This means that most children (below the age of 16) are not enumerated, though they do make up the bulk of the first category

This categorisation is intended as a genuine sequence. Everyone necessarily starts as a child. Everyone hopes to reach old age, although they will hope not to become infirm. There is a very high probability that the stages will be reached in the order set down in the list, although there are some possibilities of different sequences. The main fault in the logic is that some people will miss stages altogether – most importantly, those who have no children will move straight from 'independent' to 'older-childless', without passing through the family section of the sequence.

Even at the cross-sectional level, the BHPS suggests that the life-stages move logically forward as people grow older:

- among teenagers, about half are still counted as dependent children (because they are still at school or college); most of the other half are 'young adults', having left school, but remain either at home, or in full-time education;
- by their 20s, people are divided about evenly between young adults, 'independents' and young families;
- in their 30s, most are independent or in young families;
- in their 40s, older families have begun to outnumber younger ones; by definition, the older childless group has replaced the independents;

Table 9.2: Life-stages (1973 and 1996), in row percentages

Age	Year	Young adult	Inde-pendent	Young family	Older family	Older childless	Retired
20-29	1973	27	28	46	0	0	0
	1996	31	38	31	0	0	0
30-39	1973	6	11	74	8	0	0
	1996	5	25	59	11	0	0
40-49	1973	0	0	33	40	26	1
	1996	0	0	24	45	26	5
50-59	1973	0	0	6	38	52	5
	1996	0	0	3	30	46	21
60-69	1973	0	0	1	11	38	51
	1996	0	0	0	4	22	74

Source: General Household Survey, author's analysis

- in their 50s, young families have virtually disappeared, but some individuals have already reached retirement;
- in their 60s and 70s, retirement and then old age become the dominant positions.

However, the crucial test of the idea of a sequence of stages can only be provided by the longitudinal panel data. Uniquely, it is possible to show whether members of the sample move along the expected trajectory from year to year. In fact, the great majority of those interviewed in consecutive years remained in the same life-stage in both years, and this provides evidence of stability. A total of 10% moved forwards up the list in the expected direction: 9 out of 10 of these moves were to the logical next step, only 1 out of 10 skipping one or more stages. Just 2% of the sample moved backwards, against the expected flow. These backward moves damage the life-cycle theory, but they are rare[1].

There have been some important changes in the pattern over time. The General Household Survey can be used to compare the situation in 1996 with that observed in 1973, almost exactly one generation earlier (see Table 9.2). The 1996 GHS provides figures that are encouragingly similar to those recorded by the BHPS[2]. The pattern in Table 9.2 has simplified a complex picture in two ways: teenagers and respondents aged above 70 have been omitted (there was very little change in their life-stages between the two dates); the first category is therefore irrelevant, and the last pair of categories has been combined. These abbreviations make it possible to focus on the middle stages of the cycle, where most of the change has taken place.

There have been important changes at both ends of the life-cycle. The number of younger people in the 'independent' stage – that is, living with neither their parents nor their own children, increased – from 28% to 38% of those in their 20s and from 11% to 25% of those in their 30s. The number of 'young families' decreased – a finding entirely consistent with the analysis of family formation in Chapters One and Two. As the earlier analysis would also lead us to expect, both of those stages have changed their shape. In 1973, 70% of those at the 'independent' stage were formally married, and 97% of 'young families'. By 1996, the rise in numbers living alone or cohabiting meant that only 31% and 77% of these two groups were married.

Meanwhile, the number of people at the older-childless stage of their cycle has been reduced, as a result of a rapid rise in the number who had reached the retirement stage: the latter up from 5% to 21% of those in their 50s and from 51% to 74% of those in their 60s.

These are big changes to have occurred during so short a period. On the other hand, the overall pattern of life-stages seems to remain – people may move from one stage to another more or less rapidly than they did before, but the underlying sequence seems to have been maintained. This gives further support to the idea of a life-course as an analytical framework.

As the previous chapters have shown, the panel survey provides an opportunity to measure all sorts of transitions – events in people's lives that move them from one position to another. Some events – leaving home, having a first child and so on – are directly and by definition associated with movement from one life-stage to another. On the other hand, it is a feature of its construction that transitions between different stages in the sequence are governed by different types of event. Other events may tend to occur about the same time as a move between life-stages, without being directly involved in the definition – starting work might tend to occur at the same time as leaving home, for example. Another group of events might occur more frequently in some life-stages than in others, without being associated especially with the start and finish of those stages.

There is scope here for only the briefest of illustrations of the extent to which domain transitions are associated with the sequence of life-stages. Certain types of event – especially moving house and gaining or losing children – frequently (though not exclusively) occur at a life-stage transition. Other events, such as gaining qualifications and changes in health, are hardly more common in boundary years than at other times. Some events – gaining qualifications, moving house and changes in marital status – tend quite strongly to occur at early stages, whereas others are equally frequent through most of the life-course (entering or leaving a job), or bunched towards the end (changes in health).

These findings are not unexpected: they are more reassuring than exciting. However, they do indicate the potential value of life-stages as an analytical approach, and of panel data as its raw material.

One of the earliest explicit uses of life-stages as an explanatory factor in socio-economic research was by Seebohm Rowntree (1899) in his classical study of poverty in York. He argued that:

- poverty was common in childhood;
- there would be a period of relative prosperity after a young person entered employment but before he or she started a family;
- a high risk of poverty during the period of parenthood would be followed by an easier time after children had left home;
- poverty would often return again after retirement.

Analysing the sequence of low and high incomes associated with successive stages will provide an interesting test of the life-stage categorisation proposed in this book.

In principle, we would expect people to fall into poverty when they have children following their 'independent' period, and leave poverty when their children leave home, and so on. Does the dynamic analysis offered by the panel survey confirm this expectation? It was seen in Chapter Five that year-to-year moves up and down the income scale were more common than might have been expected. For the present analysis a purely relative approach has been adopted, and rises and falls in (household equivalent) income have been defined as the largest 10% of moves in either direction. This corresponds to a fall of £80 per week or more, or a rise of £100 per week or more (at 1996 prices). Although income is calculated for a whole household, it is the individual who is followed from year to year to observe changes (which may include a move from one household to another).

At first sight Table 9.3 suggests quite a strong link between changes in income and moves through the life-cycle:

Table 9.3: Rises and falls in income, by life-stages, in row percentages (except for first column)

	Annual rate of exit from stage	Leavers		Stayers	
		Income fell	Income rose	Income fell	Income rose
Dependent child	41	22	13	9	10
Young adult	16	19	18	10	11
Independent	15	30	9	10	15
Young family	7	6	12	8	8
Older family	10	15	25	8	10
Older childless	14	33	9	13	13
Retired	14	7	12	7	9
Old	5	9	7	6	7

Note: The table should be read as follows: 41% of those who were 'dependent children' at year *t* ceased to be members of the category by year *t+1*. Among those who *left* this group, 22% experienced an increase of equivalent household income of at least £100 per week; 13% experienced a fall of at least £80. Among those who *stayed* in the group, 9% experienced a rise in income and 10% a fall in income

- 30% of those who ended their period of 'independence' (most of whom became 'young families') faced a loss of income of at least £80 per week;
- 33% of those who ceased to be 'older childless' (most of whom 'retired') experienced a similar loss of income;
- 18% of those who completed a spell as a young adult (mostly to become 'independent') enjoyed an increase in income of at least £100 per week;
- 25% of those moving out of the 'older family' category (mostly to 'older childless') also gained in this way.

Given that only 10% of all respondents moved up or down the income scale to this extent, it is clear that life-stage junctions are also points at which income tends to increase or decrease.

On the other hand, as the 'stayers' section to the right of Table 9.3 shows, there was a fair amount of movement in incomes in the middle of life-stage periods. There is also no particular stage when mid-period increases or decreases in income are especially common. Most people remain in the same life-stage most years – only 12% move on from one stage to the next in any one year. This shows that the regular ebb and flow of incomes, year in and year out, was much more important to individuals' experience than the decisive shifts that might be expected to take place at certain life-stage transitions. In fact, only:

- 15% of all falls in income (as defined) coincided with a move out of a high-income stage of the life-cycle (independent or older childless);
- 7% of all increases in income coincided with a move out of a low-income stage of the life-cycle (young adult or older family).

So the analysis of changes in income shows the limitations of the life-course perspective on its own. Regular life-stage events represent only a small proportion of the overall annual movement in incomes. 'Accidents', in the special sense outlined at the beginning of this chapter, are just as important.

Looking backwards, looking forwards

Each chapter of this book has demonstrated how a panel survey can shed new light on the processes that affect families, across a whole range of their key activities – parenthood and partnership, employment and income, housing, health and even political affiliation. The analyses have made substantial progress towards understanding what actually happens in a real world where time moves on, as opposed to the falsely static world portrayed by the 'snapshot' picture.

Some of these new dynamic perspectives have been of crucial importance. The portrait given by John Ermisch and Marco Francesconi in Chapter Two of the temporary nature of many cohabitational relationships means that such relationships should never again be considered simply as a form of marriage without the vows. They are a new and relatively unstable family structure, often extending the gap in young people's lives between leaving home on the one hand and entering long-term commitments on the other. Meanwhile, Stephen Jenkins showed how large a proportion of those recorded as poor at the time of any particular survey interview are 'just visiting': surely, then, the annual poverty statistics both understate the extent of the problem and exaggerate its severity. These two examples illustrate the relevance of the findings not only to economic and sociological scholarship, but also to policy – given the present government's flagship concerns with both lone parenthood and poverty.

The next stage of work for the ISER group is to do some 'joining up' across the various domains of life in modern Britain. In collaboration with other experts in longitudinal analysis, the focus will be to investigate, in a rather more general and comprehensive way, the determinants of life chances in Britain. The aim is to use the full range of longitudinal materials that are now available – not just the British Household Panel Survey, but also the 1946, 1958 and 1970 birth cohort studies, and the Longitudinal Survey linking Census records. Using these materials, the intention is to look at the changing pathways through life for the British population.

As always, the research reported in this book points to the need for further research, to delve deeper into the processes of change that have been identified. The analysis here has used seven waves of the panel. Running the survey itself is like painting the Forth Bridge; as soon as one wave is finished, another begins. An eighth wave is now ready for analysis; a ninth, including additional samples of low-income families, and of households in Scotland, Wales and Northern Ireland is being processed; the tenth is in the field. The BHPS now contributes to the European Community Household Panel, which so far offers three consecutive years' of data across 12 countries. This means that comparisons will be made between the patterns of social experience in different societies, to learn, for example, whether the interactions between family, employment, income and other factors are common to all countries, or depend on local traditions, national policies and the macro-economic environment. Only then will we know whether the dynamics revealed in this book are confined to Britain or have been a general feature of Western societies at the end of the 20th century.

Notes

[1] Examples include children returning to live with their parents (temporarily reversing the cycle for both generations); retired people taking work; and older people (between 65 and 74) recovering their health.

[2] The exception is that the GHS recorded fewer teenagers in full-time education. This affects both the number recorded as 'dependent child', and the number recorded as 'older family'. The GHS does not provide a measure of ill-health equivalent to that in the BHPS, so the 'old/infirm' category cannot be defined.

References

DSS (Department of Social Security) (1998) *Households below average income 1979-1996/7*, Leeds: Corporate Document Services.

Joshi, M. and Paci, P. (1998) *Unequal pay for men and women: Evidence from the British birth cohort studies*, Cambridge, MA: MIT Press.

Murphy, M. (1987) 'Measuring the family life-cycle: concepts, data and methods', in A. Bryman and others (eds) *Rethinking the life cycle*, Basingstoke: Macmillan.

O'Higgins, M., Bradshaw, J. and Walker, R. (1988) 'Income distribution over the life-cycle', in R. Walker and G. Parker (eds) *Money matters: income, wealth and financial welfare*, London: Sage Publications.

Rowlingson, K., Whyley, C. and Warren, T. (1999) *Wealth in Britain: A life-cycle perspective*, London: Policy Studies Institute.

Rowntree, B.S. (1899) *Poverty: A study of town life*, London: Macmillan.

Schaninger, C. and Danko, W. (1993) 'A conceptual and empirical comparison of alternative household life-cycle models', *Journal of Consumer Research*, no 19, pp 580-94.

Index

A

age
  of having children 5, 21, 32-3
  of marriage 3, 21, 220
  promotion rates and 84
  see also older people; young people
area deprivation 144-5

B

British Household Panel Survey 2,
  14-18

C

car ownership 12
careers
  housing 133, 136-40, 144, 147-59
  promotion 74, 83-6, 223
caring 172
Carstairs index 144-5
children
  age of having children 5, 21, 32-3
  cohabitation and 5, 33-4, 38-9, 40,
    220, 221
  employment of parents 89, 94, 95
  poverty and 11, 112, 122
  see also young people
class see social background
cohabitation 4, 24-8, 39-40, 220-1
  children and 5, 33-4, 38-9, 40, 220,
    221
  compared with marriage for first
    partnership 24-7
  decline in marriage rates and 28-32,
    220
  delay in motherhood and 32-3
  dissolution 27, 29, 30, 36-9, 221
  duration 27-8, 29, 39, 220
  employment and 10
  housing and 139
  marriage after 5, 27, 37-8, 39, 221
  money management and 49

politics and 203, 204-11, 229-30
  religious background and 35, 36
  repartnering after 28, 220
  social background and 35-6, 39, 220
consensus politics 14
Conservative Party 14, 193, 198,
  199-212, 229-30
consumer durables 11-12
council housing see social housing

D

death rates 173-4
deprivation
  areas 144-5
  see also poverty
diabetes 176
disability
  welfare benefits and 10
  see also health
dissolution of partnerships
  cohabitation partnerships 27, 29, 30,
    36-9, 221
  divorce 4-5
  housing and 138, 155
  poverty and 128
divorce 4-5
domestic work 45-6, 50-6
  division of 46-8, 69-70, 222
    changing family work patterns and
      52-6
    evidence on 50-2

E

earnings see incomes
education
  job tenure and 82
  promotion and 85
  retirement and 98, 99
  transition from education to work
    73-4, 76-9, 99, 223
  unemployment and 91

elderly people *see* older people
employment 7-10, 73-100, 219, 222-4
  data on 75-6
  domestic work and 45-6, 52-6,
    69-70, 222
  families and 74-5, 92-6, 112
  gender roles 47, 48
  health and 186
  housing and 13, 133-4
  inability to work 172
  income and 107, 111-12
  job tenure 74, 79-83, 99
  labour market transitions 86-90
  money management and 61-4, 70,
    222-3
  part-time 78, 79, 85, 86, 88-90, 223
  promotion 74, 83-6, 223
  retirement from 75, 96-9, 224
  self-employment 78, 87, 89, 90, 112,
    223
  transition from education to work
    73-4, 76-9, 99, 223
  transition from poverty and 125
  within-marriage consequences of
    change in employment structure
    45-50
  see also unemployment
ethnic minorities, poverty 112
European Community Household
  Panel survey (ECHP) 16, 111

F

family structure 3-7, 21-40, 218,
    219-21
  employment patterns and 74-5,
    92-6, 112
  health and 185-6
  income and 107
  political values and 193-213, 229-30
  young people leaving family home
    22-3, 136-7, 143, 149-50, 220
  young people returning to live with
    parents 5-6, 23-4, 150, 220
  see also cohabitation; marriage
fertility 5
finances *see* money management
future directions 236-7

G

gender roles
  domestic work 46-8, 50-6, 69-70,
    222
  employment 47, 48
  money management 49-50, 70,
    222-3
General Household Survey (GHS)
  3-13, 232
generations, comparison of 218-19
Germany 16

H

health 13-14, 161-90, 227-8
  characteristics of those with good
    and bad health 170-4
  definition of ill-health 174-5
  dynamic measures 175-80
  housing and 187, 190, 228
  incomes and 187-8, 190, 228
  index of 163-70, 189, 227-8
  older people 13-14, 162, 164, 165-6,
    180, 183, 188, 189, 228
  poverty and 187-8, 190, 228
  precursors of falling ill 180-8
    medical factors 181-5
    socio-economic factors 185-8
  retirement and ill-health 96, 98
  social background and 186-7, 190,
    228
households *see* family structure
housework *see* domestic work
housing 12-13, 93, 109, 133-59,
    226-7
  area deprivation and 144-5
  employment and 13, 133-4
  health and 187, 190, 228
  housing career 133, 136-40, 144,
    147-59, 226-7
  cumulative effects of multiple years
    of change 150-6
  establishment of 156-8
  life-course and 136-40
  mobility 144, 147-50, 226
  incomes and 133-4, 140, 153, 226
  location 144-7

older people 136, 137, 138, 140,
142, 148, 154
one parent families 136, 138, 146,
154
subjective attitudes to 146-7
tenure change 141-3
unemployment and 138, 153, 155
young people 137, 140, 143, 146,
148, 152, 157-8
see also owner-occupation; private
rented accommodation; social
housing

I

ill-health *see* health
inactivity rates 87
incomes 10-12, 93, 107-28, 224-5
accounting for transition in and out
of poverty 124-6
area deprivation and 145
changes over time in distribution of
110-12, 127
definition of income 109
employment and 107, 111-12
health and 187-8, 190, 228
housing and 133-4, 140, 153, 226
life-course and 234-6
longitudinal flux amid cross-
sectional stability 112-17
movements in and out of poverty
by family type 121-4
poverty exit and re-entry rates
117-21
promotion and 86
see also money management

J

job tenure 74, 79-83, 99
job-shopping theory 80

L

Labour Party 14, 198, 199-212,
229-30
New Deal policies 108, 127

layoffs 80, 81, 82, 223
life-course 230-6
housing career and 136-40
see also individual life stages
lone parent families *see* one parent
families

M

marriage 3-4
after cohabitation 5, 27, 37-8, 39,
221
age of 3, 21, 220
compared with cohabitation for
first partnership 24-7
decline in marriage rates 3, 28-32,
218, 220
divorce 4-5
domestic work in 45-8, 50-6, 69-70
money management in 49-50, 70,
222-3
politics and 203, 204-11, 229-30
power relationships within 45-6, 49,
57-8, 61
promotion at work and 85, 223
social background and 35-6, 197-8
within-marriage consequences of
change in employment structure
45-50
mobility
car ownership 12
housing 144, 147-50, 226
social 107-8, 117-21
money management 49-50, 57-69,
222-3
changing employment patterns and
61-4, 70
dynamics of 65-9
evidence on 57-61

N

New Deal 108, 127

O

older people 5, 8, 14

health 13-14, 162, 164, 165-6, 180,
     183, 188, 189, 228
housing 136, 137, 138, 140, 142,
     148, 154
poverty 112, 122, 123
retirement 75, 96-9, 224
one parent families 5, 40, 221
employment/unemployment and 8,
     93, 94
housing 136, 138, 146, 154
poverty 112, 122, 124, 128, 218
overtime, promotion and 85, 86
owner-occupation 12, 93, 226-7
appreciation of asset 134
area deprivation and 145
costs 135, 157-8
duration 153, 154
entry to and exit from 141-3, 155
growth in 138, 139-40
life-course and 138, 139-40

P

paid work *see* employment
Panel Survey of Income Dynamics
     (PSID) 16
parenting *see* children
part-time employment 78, 79, 85, 86,
     88-90, 223
partnerships
changing patterns 3-5
see also cohabitation; dissolution of
     partnerships; marriage
pensions 99
politics 14
families and 193-213, 229-30
cause and effect 205-11
individuals in 199-204
party identification and 204-5
voting patterns 197-9, 204-5
young people 211-12, 230
marriage/cohabitation and 203,
     204-11, 229-30
social background and 195, 203
young people and 194, 211-12, 230
poverty 10-11, 90, 107-28, 219,
     224-5, 234
children and 11, 112, 122

ethnic minorities 112
health and 187-8, 190, 228
older people 112, 122, 123
one parent families 112, 122, 124,
     128, 218
social security (welfare benefits) and
     116, 127-8
transitions in and out of 107-8,
     117-21, 225
accounting for 124-6
changes over time 110-12, 127
family type and 121-4
power relationships within marriage
     45-6, 49, 57-8, 61
private rented accommodation 12,
     134, 226, 227
decline in 137, 138, 139
duration 154
entry to and exit from 141-3
life-course and 136
preferences for moving from 146
promotion 74, 83-6, 223
prosperity 11-12

Q

quitting work 80, 81

R

religious background, cohabitation
     and 35, 36
rented accommodation *see* private
     rented accommodation; social
     housing
repartnering
cohabitation 28, 220
money management and 49
retirement 75, 96-9, 224

S

security in employment (job tenure)
     74, 79-83, 99
self-employment 78, 87, 89, 90, 112,
     223
single people 5-6

employment/unemployment and
9–10, 94
housing 146
smoking, health and 184, 190
social background
cohabitation and 35–6, 39, 220
health and 186–7, 190, 228
marriage and 35–6, 197–8
politics and 195, 203
see also social mobility
social change
dynamics of 1–19, 215–30
British Household Panel Survey 2,
14–18
changing families 1, 2–14
future directions 236–7
Social Change and Economic Life
Initiative (SCELI) survey 58
social class *see* social background
social housing 12–13, 135, 227
area deprivation and 145
decline in 138
duration 153, 154
entry to and exit from 141–3, 155–6
life-course and 136, 138–9
moving locally 152–3
preferences for moving from 147
residualisation of 93, 139, 140
social mobility 107–8, 117–21
social security 10–11, 14, 95
housing and 139
poverty and 116, 127–8
stress 185, 190
students 23
transition from education to work
73–4, 76–9, 99, 223
subsidies to mortgage payments 135

T

technological change 80, 96

U

unemployment 46, 74, 87, 90, 224
family 93, 112, 224
from full-time education 76, 77, 79,
99

housing and 138, 153, 155
persistence 90–2
social security (welfare benefits) and
10
young people 8, 24, 76, 77, 79, 99
United States of America 96, 121
Panel Survey of Income Dynamics
(PSID) 16
unpaid domestic work *see* domestic
work

V

voting *see* politics

W

wages *see* incomes
welfare benefits *see* social security
(welfare benefits)
work *see* employment

Y

young people
health 183
housing 137, 140, 143, 146, 148,
152, 157–8
leaving family home 22–3, 136–7,
143, 149–50, 220
politics and 194, 211–12, 230
returning to live with parents 5–6,
23–4, 150, 220
transition from education to work
73–4, 76–9, 99, 223
unemployment 8, 24, 76, 77, 79, 99